INTRODUCTION TO MANAGEMENT ACCOUNTING

INTRODUCTION TO
MANAGEMENT ACCOUNTING

PETER SCOTT

OXFORD
UNIVERSITY PRESS

OXFORD
UNIVERSITY PRESS

Great Clarendon Street, Oxford, OX2 6DP,
United Kingdom

Oxford University Press is a department of the University of Oxford.
It furthers the University's objective of excellence in research, scholarship,
and education by publishing worldwide. Oxford is a registered trade mark of
Oxford University Press in the UK and in certain other countries

© Peter Scott 2018

The moral rights of the author have been asserted

Impression: 1

Published in the United States of America by Oxford University Press
198 Madison Avenue, New York, NY 10016, United States of America

British Library Cataloguing in Publication Data
Data available

Library of Congress Control Number: 2018954407

ISBN 978-0-19-878738-9

Printed in Great Britain by
Ashford Colour Press Ltd, Gosport, Hampshire

BRIEF TABLE OF CONTENTS

FULL TABLE OF CONTENTS

ACKNOWLEDGEMENTS

Thanks are due to many individuals. Firstly, to all of the staff at Oxford University Press who have been involved with this project: to Amber Stone-Galilee, Commissioning Editor, who first proposed this book in June 2015 and who provided help and encouragement throughout the writing process; to Nicola Hartley who was initially entrusted with the development process; Livy Watson, Development Editor, who then took up the development role and who has been a model of enthusiasm, patience and quiet encouragement throughout; and to Fiona Burbage who was responsible for turning my ideas and outlines into the online resource material. Secondly, a big thank you to the many reviewers who took the time to work through the draft chapters to put together positive and constructive comments that have informed the development of this book and its online workbook. Thirdly, thanks must go to the hundreds if not thousands of students who have, over many years, been the testing ground for the material presented here: their ability to grasp concepts, ideas and techniques served up in various different formats has helped guide me in the formulation of my ideas on the most effective approach to providing the solid foundations upon which later studies in accountancy are built. Fourthly, thanks go to all my former colleagues at De Montfort University for their constant interest, encouragement and enthusiasm for the project. Finally, the deepest debt of gratitude must go to my family, and above all to my wife, Christine, for their forbearance, patience and encouragement during the time it took to develop and write this book.

Peter Scott, June 2018

The author and publisher would like to sincerely thank all those people who gave their time and expertise to review draft chapters throughout the writing process. Your help was invaluable.

Thanks are also extended to those who wished to remain anonymous.

Dr Sandar Win, University of Bedfordshire
Dr Brian Gibbs, University of Bolton
Dr Octavian Ionescu, University of East Anglia
Dr Alaa Alhaj Ismail, Coventry University
David Gilding, University of Leeds
Barry McCarthy, University College London
Dave Knight, Leeds Beckett University
Nicola Horner, University of the West of England
David Kyle, York St John University
Dr Emer Gallagher, Liverpool John Moores University
Samuel O Idowu, London Metropolitan University
Terry Harris, Durham University
Dr Anwar Halari, The Open University
Gayle Waddell, University of Liverpool
Dr Mariannunziata Liguori, Queen's University Belfast
Dr Pik Kun Liew, University of Essex

Christopher Kelsall, University of Central Lancashire
Ian Andrews, University of Exeter
Wondimu Mekonnen, University of Buckingham
Dr Androniki Triantafylli, Queen Mary University of London
Elizabeth Vokes, University of Northampton
Michael Barker, Coventry University
Kevin Burrows, University of Plymouth
Acheampong Charles Afriyie, University of Gloucestershire
Dr ChunLei Yang, University of Manchester
Dr Naser Makarem, University of Aberdeen
Daniel Johnson, Coventry University
Dr Sayjda Talib, Lancaster University
Susan Lane, University of Bradford
Samuel Hinds, University of Surrey
Dr Akrum Helfaya, Keele University, UK & Damanhour University, Egypt

PREFACE

Accounting: building a solid foundation

Welcome to your study of management accounting. This first year of your studies is extremely important as the understanding you develop during it and the techniques you learn will provide the foundation upon which both your future studies and your professional career will be built. Everything you study in the next nine months will continue to be relevant in the next two years of degree studies and throughout your time in a professional role. At this initial stage of your studies, the approach to the subject adopted in this package is completely practical: accounting is a 'doing' subject and the best way to learn how it works and what it does is to practice the various techniques and approaches as frequently as possible. You are provided with careful, step-by-step guidance showing you how management accounting techniques are applied to practical problems and how to interpret and evaluate the resulting accounting information. You are then given numerous further opportunities to apply what you have learnt with a view to enhancing your understanding and ability to produce and interpret management accounting information. Only once you have mastered the techniques and practice of management accounting can you move forward to look at the more theoretical aspects of the subject and question why things are done as they are.

The integrated online workbook: how this package works

This textbook is published with a free online workbook containing a large bank of examples and exercises that relate to, and are thoroughly integrated with, the material in each chapter. (For details on how to access this, please refer to the 'Guided tour of the online workbook'.)

The integration of these online resources with the textbook provides the supportive learning environment necessary to allow you to develop the specialist practical skills required in management accounting. Clear signposts in the chapters offer you numerous opportunities to reinforce, revisit, and revise your understanding of the subject, prompting you to apply your knowledge as you work through each topic. Your understanding of the material will strengthen as approaches and techniques are frequently recapped, including through the use of running examples throughout the book.

The textbook

This book deals with cost and management accounting and the ways in which accounting can be used in decision making and in controlling a business's future development through planning and forecasting. The key techniques of costing, budgeting and capital investment appraisal are covered in the requisite depth and detail to provide you with a ready guide to the production and presentation of meaningful information for use both in the running of a business and in the evaluation of its performance. Users of financial statements require reassurance about the accuracy and integrity of the information they are presented with and, in addition, they want to be confident that companies are good corporate citizens who always do the right thing. Therefore, the final chapter provides an introduction to the corporate governance rules, corporate social responsibility reporting and sustainability, topics that you will go on to consider in much greater depth in both your degree and professional studies.

A note on terminology

Business is increasingly international in its focus. As a result, the accounting terminology adopted throughout this book is that of international accounting standards rather than that of UK standards. Where different terms for the same statements are in common usage, these are noted throughout the book as they arise and summarised in the terminology converter at the back of the book.

GUIDED TOUR OF THE BOOK

Identifying and defining

Learning outcomes

Clear, concise learning outcomes begin each chapter and help to contextualise the chapter's main objectives. This feature can help you plan your revision to ensure you identify and cover all the key concepts.

LEARNING OUTCOMES

Once you have read this chapter and worked through the questions and examples in both this chapter and the online workbook, you should be able to:

- Define cost accounting and explain its role in organisations
- Define management accounting and explain its role in organisations
- Explain the differences between financial accounting and cost and management accounting

Key terms and glossary

Key terms are highlighted where they first appear in the chapter and are also collated into a glossary at the end of the book. This provides an easy and practical way for you to revise and check your understanding of definitions.

Welcome to your study of cost and management accounting. You are now taki the road to building your career in one or more of the varied roles which business and the wider economy. In order to help you fulfil your ambition duce you to the key techniques and practical applications of cost and ma to provide you with a very strong foundation on which to build your furt professional studies.

Accountability Managers provide an account of how they have managed resources placed in their care. In this way, those appointing managers can assess how well their managers have looked after the resources entrusted to them.

Accounting The summarising of numerical data relating to past events and presenting this data as information to managers and other interested parties as a basis for both

more than on break-even po the contributi

Budget The e a prediction c inflows and ca

Budgetary c

Understanding accounting principles

Illustrations

Illustrations display accounting statements and documents and serve to set out the numbers discussed in the text in an easily readable format. This enables you to follow the explanations closely and to become familiar with the layout of such documents.

Illustration 7.10 Accounting for the sale of abnormal losses from a process

Process 1 account					
	Litres	£		Litres	£
Materials	5,000	25,000	Transfer to process 2	4,700	58,582
Labour		20,000	Normal loss scrap value	200	192
Overhead		15,000	Abnormal loss account	100	1,248
	5,000	**60,000**		**5,000**	**60,000**

Abnormal loss account

In-text examples

Regular hypothetical examples are presented throughout each chapter to illustrate how accounting material is used in a variety of different business contexts. The diversity in cases demonstrates how accounting information can be interpreted in different ways to achieve different ends according to business needs.

EXAMPLE 3.2

Anna is a self-employed carpenter working at home producing handmade wooden the month of June, she produced 30 chairs. What price should she sell her chairs for? invoices showing the costs of the materials she used in June:

	£
Wood	540
Glue	18
Screws	30
Sandpaper	12

Totalling up the costs above, Anna has spent £600 on making 30 chairs. Dividing th chairs made gives a cost of £20 per chair.

Accounting in practice

'Give me an example' boxes

Topical examples taken from the *Financial Times*, the BBC and other news outlets and numerous references to real companies will help your understanding of how the theory being discussed in the chapter plays out in business practice.

'Why is this relevant to me?' boxes

These short and frequent explanations clarify exactly how the accounting material under discussion will be important and relevant to accounting professionals. They are an important reminder of how important even theoretical accounting knowledge will be in enabling you to succeed in your future career, whether it be as an accountant or as a business professional working with accounting information.

Testing and applying understanding

End-of-chapter questions

There is a set of questions at the end of every chapter designed to test your knowledge of the key concepts that have been discussed. They are divided into two tiers according to difficulty, allowing you to track your progress, and for many chapters there are further questions available online. Use them during your course to ensure you fully understand the accounting principles before moving on, or when revising to make sure you can confidently tackle the more difficult questions. The solutions are supplied within the **online workbook**, in an easily printable format.

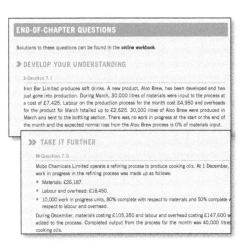

Chapter summary

Each chapter concludes with a bulleted list linking to the learning outcomes, outlining the key points you should take away from the chapter. This provides another useful method of checking that you have covered the key points when you come to revise each topic.

GUIDED TOUR OF THE ONLINE WORKBOOK

Access the interactive online workbook by visiting www.oup.com/uk/scott_management/.

Resources in the online workbook have been specifically designed to support you throughout your management accounting studies. References within the textbook indicate the relevant resource accompanying that section or topic, thereby allowing you to reinforce your learning as you progress through the book and ensuring that you take full advantage of this fantastic package.

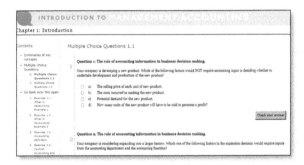

Summaries of key concepts

Key glossary terms are provided in interactive flashcard format.

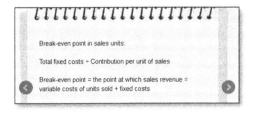

Multiple-choice questions

Interactive multiple-choice questions for every chapter give you instant feedback as well as page references to help you focus on the areas that need further study.

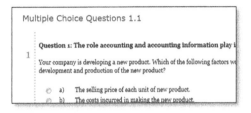

Numerical exercises

These exercises, often based in Excel, give you the opportunity to calculate management accounting information from given sets of data, thereby practising what is discussed and illustrated in the book.

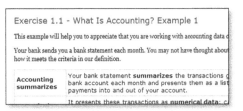

Go back over this again

Containing a mixture of further examples, written exercises, true or false questions and annotated accounting information, this section provides the perfect opportunity for you to revise and revisit any concepts you might be unsure of.

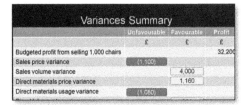

Show me how to do it

Video presentations, accompanied by a voice-over, allow you to watch practical demonstrations of how more complex management accounting tasks are dealt with by the author.

Web links

Arranged by chapter, these web links will take you directly to the websites of the companies and organisations covered in the book, as well as websites of more general accounting interest. Follow the links to learn more about how accounting plays out in the real world of business.

Further reading

Arranged by chapter, this section provides you with a list of additional resources you may wish to consult if you'd like to take your learning further, or simply consider a topic from a different perspective.

GUIDE TO THE LECTURER RESOURCES

Test bank

A wealth of additional multiple-choice questions that can be customised to meet your specific teaching needs.

Lecturer examples and solutions

Additional exercises that can be used alongside the PowerPoint slides in lectures or seminars.

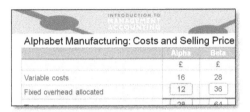

Group tutorial exercises

A range of more detailed, workshop-based activities that students can complete prior to and during tutorials.

Lecturer examination questions and answers

Additional problem solving and suggested essay-based exam questions with accompanying answers.

PowerPoint slides

Illustrated PowerPoint slides for each chapter that can be used in lectures or printed as handouts, and can be easily adapted to suit your teaching style.

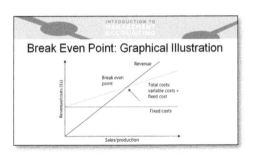

DASHBOARD

Dashboard is a cloud-based online assessment and revision tool. It comes pre-loaded with the resources listed in the 'Guide to the lecturer resources', as well as additional questions to use for assessment and functionality to track your students' progress.

Visit www.oxfordtextbooks.co.uk/dashboard/ for more information.

Simple: With a highly intuitive design, it will take you less than 15 minutes to learn and master the system.

Informative: Assignment and assessment results are automatically graded, giving you a clear view of the class' understanding of the course content.

Mobile: You can access Dashboard from every major platform and device connected to the Internet, whether that's a computer, tablet or smartphone.

Gradebook

Dashboard's Gradebook functionality automatically marks the assignments that you set for your students. The Gradebook also provides heat maps that allow you to view your students' progress and quickly identify areas of the course where your students may need more practice or support, as well as the areas in which they are most confident. This feature helps you focus your teaching time on

the areas that matter. The Gradebook also allows you to administer grading schemes, manage checklists, and administer learning objectives and competencies.

INTRODUCTION

INTRODUCTION

Welcome to your study of cost and management accounting. You are now taking your first steps on the road to building your career in one or more of the varied roles which accountants fulfil in business and the wider economy. In order to help you fulfil your ambition, this book will introduce you to the key techniques and practical applications of cost and management accounting to provide you with a very strong foundation on which to build your further degree and future professional studies.

WHAT SKILLS DO I NEED?

Many students find the thought of accounting worrying as they do not feel they have the necessary mathematical ability to be able to understand or apply the subject in practice. However, do be assured that accounting needs no particular mathematical strengths, just some basic applications of arithmetic and an ability to reason. As long as you can add up, subtract, multiply and divide figures you have all the arithmetical skills you will need to undertake the calculations and apply this subject. The ability to reason is a skill that you will need in every subject of study and it will be fundamental to the success of any career, not just to a career in accounting.

Once you have learnt how to apply the basic techniques, accounting is much more about understanding what the figures are telling you and about interpreting the data in front of you—this requires you to think in a logical fashion and to investigate the meaning beneath the surface. Therefore, it is much more accurate to say that accounting requires the ability to communicate and express your ideas in words rather than being dependent upon mathematical skills.

WHY IS THIS RELEVANT TO ME?   Skills needed to study accounting

- To reassure you that the study of accounting requires no further special skills than those you already possess
- To enable you to appreciate that the study of accounting will further develop the skills you have already acquired in reaching your current level of education

---

WHAT IS ACCOUNTING?

Let's start with a definition.

Accounting summarises numerical data relating to past events and presents this data as information to managers and other interested parties as a basis for both decision making and control purposes as presented in Figure 1.1.

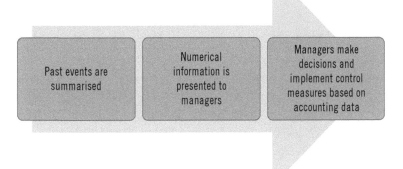

Figure 1.1 What is accounting?

This is quite a lot to take in, so let's unpick the various strands of this definition.

1. Numerical data: accounting information is mostly, but not always, presented in money terms. It could just as easily be a league table of football teams with details of games won, games lost and games drawn, goals for and goals against and points gained, all of which is numerical information. Or it could be a list of schools in a particular area with percentages of pupils gaining five GCSEs grades 1–9 and average A level points at each school. In a business, it could be the number of units of product produced rather than just their cost, or the number of units sold in a given period of time. The critical point here is that accounting data is presented in the form of numbers.

2. Relating to past events: accounting systems gather data and then summarise these data to present details of what has happened. A league table is a summary of past results. Similarly, a total of sales for the month will be a summary of all the individual sales made on each day of that month and relating to that past period of time.

3. Information presented to managers: managers have the power and authority to use accounting information to take action now to maintain or improve future outcomes. In the same way, if a team is in the middle of the league table but aspires to a higher position, the team manager can take steps to hire better coaches, buy in the contracts of players with higher skill levels and sell the contractual rights of underperforming players. If a school wants to improve their examination results, they will take steps to determine what is preventing better performance and try to correct these deficiencies.

4. As a basis for decision making: accounting information is used to determine what went well and which events did not turn out quite as anticipated. For example, demand for a business's product over the past month might not have reached the levels expected. If this is the case, managers can take steps to determine whether the selling price is too high and should be reduced, whether there are defects in the products that require rectification or whether the product is just out of date and no longer valued by con-

1

sumers. On the other hand, if demand for a product is outstripping supply, then managers can take the decision to divert business resources to increase production to meet that higher demand.

5. Control purposes: businesses, as we shall see in Chapter 6, prepare budgets prior to the start of an accounting period (usually 12 months) which set out what they aim to achieve in terms of sales, profits and cash flows. A comparison of actual outcomes with the budget will enable managers to decide where the budget was met, where the budget was exceeded and where the budget failed to reach expectations. Then the causes of the last two outcomes can be investigated and action taken to address the reasons behind the underperformance or to take advantage of better than expected results. The future is uncertain, but businesses will still plan by predicting to the best of their ability what they expect to occur in the following months and then compare actual outcomes with what they expected to happen as a means of controlling operations.

WHY IS THIS RELEVANT TO ME?   Accounting definition

To enable you as an accounting professional to:

• Understand what accounting is

• Appreciate that the production of accounting information is not an end in itself but is a tool to enable you to understand, direct and control business, investment, lending or other activities

SUMMARY OF KEY CONCEPTS   How clearly have you remembered the definition of accounting? Go to the **online workbook** to revise this definition with Summary of key concepts 1.1.

GO BACK OVER THIS AGAIN!   If this all still seems very complicated, visit the **online workbook** Exercises 1.1 and 1.2 to enable you to appreciate that you are already working with accounting data on a daily basis.

GO BACK OVER THIS AGAIN!   Are you certain you can define accounting? Go to the **online workbook** Exercises 1.3 to make sure you can say what accounting is and what role it performs in a business context.

CONTROL, ACCOUNTING AND ACCOUNTABILITY

The function of accounting information as a mechanism through which to control outcomes and activities can be illustrated further. Representatives are accountable for their actions to those people who have placed them in positions of power or trust. Accounting information is thus provided so that individuals and organisations can render an account of what they have done with the resources placed in their care. Example 1.1 provides an everyday illustration of these ideas.

Your employer pays your salary into your bank account while various payments are made out of your account to pay your bills and other outgoings. Your bank then provides you with a statement (either online or in paper copy) on a regular basis so that you can check whether they have accounted for your money correctly or not.

In the same way, company directors present financial accounts to shareholders and other interested parties on an annual basis to give an account of how they have looked after the money and other resources entrusted to them and how they have used that money to invest and generate income for shareholders. Local and national governments regularly publish information on the taxes collected and how those taxes have been spent. This information enables politicians to render an account of how taxes collected have been used to provide goods and services to citizens.

Where power and resources are entrusted to others, it is important that they are accountable for what they have done with that power and those resources. If your bank makes mistakes in the management of your account or charges you too much for managing your account, then you can change banks. If shareholders are unhappy with their directors' performance, they will not reappoint them as directors of their company. Instead, they will elect other directors to replace them in the expectation that these new directors will manage their investment much more carefully and profitably. Alternatively, they can sell their shares and invest their money in companies that do provide them with higher profits and higher dividends. If voters are unhappy with how their local and national politicians have taxed them or how they have spent their taxes, they will vote for different representatives with different policies more to their liking.

Persons entrusted by others with resources are in the position of stewards, looking after those resources for the benefit of other parties. Providing an account of their stewardship of those resources helps those other parties control the actions of their stewards. At the same time, accounts enable these other parties to make decisions on whether to continue with their current stewards or to replace them with others who will perform more effectively and provide them with a more efficient and profitable service. These relationships are summarised in Figure 1.2.

WHY IS THIS RELEVANT TO ME?   Control, accounting and accountability

To enable you as an accounting professional to:

- Appreciate that accounting functions as a control on the actions of others
- Understand how you will be entrusted with a business's resources and that you will be accountable for your stewardship of those resources

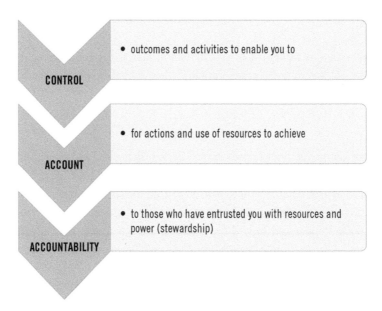

Figure 1.2 Control, accounting and accountability

GO BACK OVER THIS AGAIN!   Are you quite sure you understand how accounting helps with control and accountability? Go to the **online workbook** Exercises 1.4 to make sure you understand the links between accounting, accountability and control.

THE ROLE OF ACCOUNTING INFORMATION IN BUSINESS DECISION MAKING

Businesses are run to make a profit. Businesses that do not make a profit fail and are closed down. In order to achieve this profit aim, businesses need to make and implement decisions on a daily basis. Such decisions might comprise, among others, some or all of the following:

- What products should we produce?
- What services should we provide?
- How much do our products cost to make?
- How much do our services cost to provide?
- What price should we charge for our products or services?
- Should we be taking on more employees?
- How much will the additional employees cost?
- Will the cost of the new employees be lower than the income they will generate?
- Should we be expanding into bigger premises?
- Will the costs of the bigger premises be outweighed by the increase in income?

- How will we finance our expansion?
- Should we take out a bank loan or ask the shareholders to buy more shares?

All of these decisions will require accounting input:

- The marketing department can use reports from sales personnel and consumer evaluations to tell us what the demand for a product is, but it will be up to the accounting staff to tell us what the product costs to make and what the selling price should be in order to generate a profit on each sale.

- The personnel department can tell us about hiring new staff and the legal obligations incurred in doing so, the training required and the market rates for such workers, but it will be the accounting staff who can tell us what level of productivity the new employees will have to achieve in order to generate additional profit for the business.

- The strategy department can tell us what sort of premises we should be looking for, how these new premises should be designed and what image they should present, but it will be the accounting staff who can tell us how many products we will have to make and sell for the new premises to cover their additional costs and the best way in which to finance this expansion.

Accounting is thus at the heart of every decision and every activity that a business undertakes, as shown in Figure 1.3.

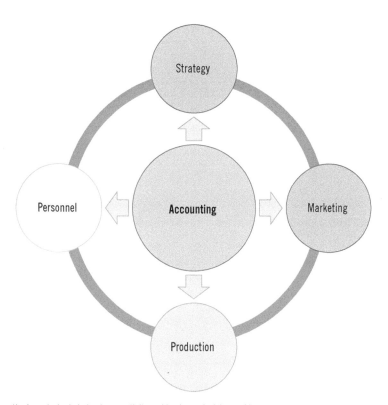

Figure 1.3 Accounting's central role in business activity and business decision making

1

At this early stage of your studies, it is easy to think of each department in a business just sticking to its own specialist field of expertise, operating in isolation from all the others, concentrating on their own aims and goals. You might reply that you would never think of a business as just a loose grouping of separate departments all doing their own thing with no thought for the bigger picture. But pause for a moment and ask yourself whether you treat all your current year study modules as interlinked or as totally separate subjects? You should see them as interlinked and look to see how all the subjects interact, but it is too easy to adopt a blinkered approach and compartmentalise each different aspect of your studies.

As the previous decisions and discussion illustrate, all business decisions require input from different departments and information from one department has to be integrated with information from other departments before an overall coordinated plan of action is put into operation. Businesses operate as cohesive entities, with all departments pulling in the same direction rather than each following their own individual pathway. Management make decisions and implement strategies, but underpinning all these decisions and strategies is accounting information.

This central role for accountants and accounting information puts accounting staff under pressure to perform their roles effectively and efficiently. After all, if the information presented by the accounting staff is defective in any way, the wrong decision could be made and losses rather than profits might result. Therefore, accountants have to ensure that the information they provide is as accurate and as up to date as possible to enable management to make the most effective decisions. Ideally, accounting staff will always be striving to improve the information they provide to management as better information will result in more informed and more effective decisions.

To illustrate the importance of the accounting function, take a moment to think what would happen if we did not have accounting information. Businesses would be lost without the vital information provided by accounting. If accounting did not exist, there would be no information relating to costs, no indication of what had been achieved in the past as a point of comparison for what is being achieved now, no figures on which to base taxation assessments, no proof that results are as companies claim they are. In short, if accounting did not exist, someone would have to invent it.

WHY IS THIS RELEVANT TO ME?   The role of accounting information in business decision making

To enable you as an accounting professional to:

- Appreciate that business decisions depend upon input from different departments and that decisions are not made in isolation by one department acting on its own
- Appreciate the importance of accounting information in business decision making
- Understand that accounting is not a stand-alone department but an integral part of all organisations

---

MULTIPLE CHOICE QUESTIONS   Are you convinced that you understand what role accounting plays in business decision making? Go to the **online workbook** Multiple choice questions 1.1 to make sure you can suggest how accounting and accounting information would be used in the context of a business decision.

WHAT QUALITIES SHOULD ACCOUNTING INFORMATION POSSESS?

Given the pivotal role of accounting information in business decision making, what sort of qualities should such information possess for it to be useful in making these decisions? Helpfully, the International Accounting Standards Board (IASB) in its *Conceptual Framework for Financial Reporting* provides guidance in this area. While the IASB is concerned with the qualities of information presented in external financial reports, the qualitative characteristics of financial information are applicable, as we shall see (Chapter 2, Financial accounting information v cost and management accounting information), to varying degrees to cost and management accounting information. The IASB states that financial information should possess the following two fundamental qualitative characteristics:

- Relevance
- Faithful representation

In addition, the IASB's *Conceptual Framework* identifies the following qualitative characteristics that enhance the usefulness of information that is relevant and faithfully represented:

- Comparability
- Verifiability
- Timeliness
- Understandability

This hierarchy of qualitative characteristics is shown in Figure 1.4.

What does each of the above qualitative characteristics represent? Table 1.1 considers the characteristics of each of the two fundamental and four enhancing qualities of financial information.

Let's think about how the qualities considered above apply to accounting information. Taking the bank statement (Example 1.1) considered under control, accounting and accountability earlier in this chapter, our thoughts might be as shown in Table 1.2.

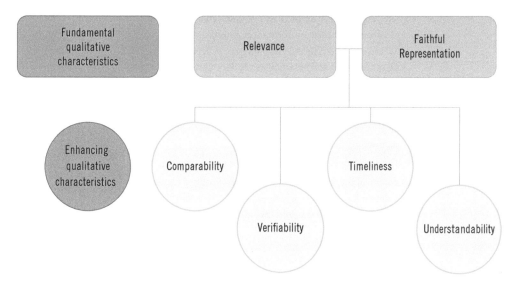

Figure 1.4 The qualitative characteristics of financial information

Table 1.1 The qualities of accounting information

Qualitative characteristic	Considerations
Relevance	• To be relevant, information must be capable of making a difference in the decisions made by users. • Relevant information may be predictive and assist users in making predictions about the future or it may be confirmatory by assisting users to assess the accuracy of past predictions. • Relevant information can be both predictive and confirmatory.
Faithful representation	• Financial information must not only represent relevant economic phenomena (transactions and events), but it must also faithfully represent the phenomena that it purports to represent. • Perfectly faithful representation of economic phenomena in words and numbers requires that the information presented must have three characteristics: it must be complete, neutral and free from error. • Do note that free from error does not mean that information must be perfectly accurate. Much accounting information, as you will see throughout your studies, relies on best estimates or the most likely outcomes. The IASB *Conceptual Framework* makes it clear that 'free from error means there are no errors or omissions in the description of the phenomenon, and the process used to produce the reported information has been selected and applied with no errors in the process' (IASB *Conceptual Framework for Financial Reporting* paragraph 2.18).
Comparability	• Information should be comparable over time. • The usefulness of information is enhanced if it can be compared with similar information about other entities for the same reporting period and with similar information about the same entity for other reporting periods. • Where information is comparable, similarities and differences are readily apparent. • Comparability does not mean consistency. However, consistency of presentation and measurement of the same items in the same way from year to year will help to achieve comparability. • Similarly, comparability does not mean that economic phenomena must be presented uniformly. Information about the same phenomena will be presented in similar but not in the same ways by different entities. The differences in the presentation of such phenomena will not be so great as to prevent comparability.
Verifiability	• Verifiability provides users with assurance that information is faithfully presented and reports the economic phenomena it purports to represent. • To ensure verifiability, it should be possible to prove the information presented is accurate in all major respects. • The accuracy of information can be verified by observation or recalculation. • Financial information will often be subject to independent audit and the independent auditors will use various techniques and approaches to verify the financial information presented.

Qualitative characteristic	Considerations
Timeliness	• The decision usefulness of information is enhanced if it is available to users in time for it to be capable of influencing their decisions. • The decision usefulness of information generally declines with time although information used in identifying trends continues to be timely in the future.
Understandability	• This characteristic should not be confused with simplicity. • As you will see in your future studies, accounting can involve very complex calculations, details and disclosures. Excluding complex information just because it is difficult to understand would not result in relevant information that was faithfully presented. Reports that excluded such information would be incomplete and would thus mislead users. • Readers of financial reports are assumed to have a reasonable knowledge of business and economic activities in order to make sense of what they are presented with. When they are unable to understand the information presented, then the IASB recommends using an adviser. • To help users understand information presented, that information should be classified, characterised and presented clearly.

Table 1.2 How your bank statement fulfils the qualities of accounting information

Relevant?	• Your bank statement is capable of making a difference to the decisions you make. Depending on your current level of cash, you are able to decide to spend less, increase the income into your bank account or decide to invest surplus funds in high interest accounts. • Looking at your current income and expenditure, you can predict what is likely to happen in the future in your bank account. Where you have made predictions about what cash you would have left at the end of each month, you can then confirm how accurate or inaccurate those predictions were and make future predictions about how much you will have left at the end of the next month to decide what you should do with these surplus funds. • Accurate predictions in the past will enable you to be confident that your future predictions will be accurate too.
Faithful representation?	• Your bank statement is presented by your bank, so this should be a faithful representation of your income and expenditure (economic phenomena, transactions and events) over a given period of time. • It is in your bank's interest to ensure that the information presented in your bank statement is complete, neutral (the statement just presents the facts of your income and expenditure) and free from error. Any errors you do pick up can be notified to your bank for correction.

→

Comparable?	• Presentation of your bank statement does not differ over time and is presented in the same format every month so this information is comparable over different periods of time.
	• This consistency of presentation and measurement of income and expenditure in the same way from month to month and year to year will help to achieve the required comparability.
Verifiable?	• The accuracy of your statement can be verified by reference to your list of standing orders, direct debits, debit card transactions, cheques written and income from payslips and other sources.
	• You can add up your bank statement to make sure the balance at the end of each month is correct (recalculation).
	• You are thus the auditor of your own bank account, checking and verifying that the information presented is accurate and free from error to ensure that your statement is faithfully presented and reports the economic phenomena it purports to represent.
Timely?	• Your bank statement is received each month (or you can access it instantly online), so it is presented in time for it to be capable of influencing your decisions. If your bank statement were to be sent annually, this would be much less relevant information as it would be seriously out of date by the time you received it and much less capable of making a difference to the decisions you make.
	• However, past bank statements are still timely when comparing trends of income and expenditure across different periods of time.
Understandable?	• You can certainly understand your bank statement as it shows you the money going into and out of your account.
	• You have a reasonable knowledge of your finances so you can make sense of what your bank statement presents you with. If you are unable to understand the information presented, then you can always contact your bank for advice.
	• To help you understand the information presented, transactions are classified, characterised and presented clearly in your bank statement.

GO BACK OVER THIS AGAIN!   Are you sure that you can define relevance, faithful representation, comparability, verifiability, timeliness and understandability? Go to the **online workbook** Exercises 1.5 to make sure you can define these qualities of financial information accurately.

SUMMARY OF KEY CONCEPTS   Can you state and define the two fundamental and four enhancing qualities of financial information? Go to the **online workbook** to check your grasp of these qualities with Summary of key concepts 1.2–1.7.

MATERIALITY

A further requirement of financial information for decision making purposes is that it should not be overloaded with unnecessary detail. This leads us on to the concept of materiality. The IASB defines materiality as follows:

Information is material if omitting it or misstating it could influence decisions that … users … make on the basis of financial information about a specific reporting entity. In other words, materiality is an entity-specific aspect of relevance based on the nature or magnitude, or both, of the items to which the information relates in the context of an individual entity's financial report.

Source: IASB *Conceptual Framework for Financial Reporting,* paragraph 2.11

How is materiality applied in practice? Example 1.2 provides instances of the circumstances in which an item might be defined as material.

EXAMPLE 1.2

An item could be material by size ('magnitude' in the above definition). If a shop makes £2m of sales a year, then the sale of a 50p carton of milk missed out of those sales will not be material. However, in a steel fabrications business making £2m of sales a year, the omission of a £250,000 sale of a steel frame for a building would be material as it makes up 12.5 per cent of the sales for the year.

As well as size, items can be material by nature. The theft of £5 from the till by a member of staff would be unlikely to be material. However, the theft of £5 from the till by the managing director would be: if you are an investor in the business, this tells you that your investment might not be very safe if the managing director is willing to steal from the business.

MULTIPLE CHOICE QUESTIONS   Are you confident that you can decide whether a piece of information is material or not? Go to the **online workbook** Multiple choice questions 1.2 to make sure you can determine whether information is material or not.

SUMMARY OF KEY CONCEPTS   Can you recall the definition of materiality? Go to the **online workbook** to check your grasp of this definition in Summary of key concepts 1.8.

COST V. BENEFIT

The IASB recognises that there is a cost in collecting, processing, verifying and disseminating financial information (IASB *Conceptual Framework for Financial Reporting,* paragraphs 2.39–2.43). Therefore, information should only be presented if the benefits of providing that information outweigh the costs of obtaining it. Example 1.3 suggests how you might weigh up the costs and benefits in a practical but non-accounting situation.

EXAMPLE 1.3

You know that there is a wonderful quote in a book that you have read that would really enhance your essay and provide you with a brilliant conclusion. However, you have forgotten where to find this quote and you have not written down the name of the book or the page reference. Your essay must be handed in by 4.00 p.m. today and it is already 3.40 p.m. You still have to print off your essay before handing it in. If your essay is handed in after 4.00 p.m. you will be awarded a mark of 0 per cent and so fail the assignment.

The costs of searching for the quote outweigh the benefits of finding it as you will not receive any marks if your essay is late so you print off your essay and hand it in on time and, when it is returned, you have scored 65 per cent and gained a pass on this piece of coursework.

WHY IS THIS RELEVANT TO ME?   The qualities of accounting information

To enable you as an accounting professional to:

• Understand what qualities useful accounting information should possess

• Appreciate the constraints imposed upon the provision of useful accounting information by the materiality concept and the cost/benefit consideration

• Understand the standards against which to measure financial information presented by you

GO BACK OVER THIS AGAIN!   Are you quite certain that you understand how cost v. benefit works? Visit the **online workbook** Exercises 1.6 to reinforce your understanding.

SUMMARY OF KEY CONCEPTS   Do you think you can remember how to define cost v. benefit? Go to the **online workbook** to check your grasp of this definition in Summary of key concepts 1.9.

THE USERS OF ACCOUNTING INFORMATION

As we have seen, accounting is all about providing information to interested parties so that they can make decisions on the basis of that information. But who are the users of this accounting information and what decisions do they make as a result of receiving that information?

Accounting is made up of two branches. The first of these branches provides information to external users and the other provides information to internal users. The information needs of both these user groups differ in important ways as we shall see.

Accounting branch 1: financial accounting

Financial accounting is the reporting of past information to users outside the organisation. This information is presented in the annual report and accounts that all companies are obliged to produce by law, publish on their websites and lodge with the Registrar of Companies at Companies House. Directors of companies produce these annual reports and accounts for issue to shareholders to provide an account of how they have used the resources entrusted to them to generate profits, dividends and value for the shareholders. Even if a business entity is not a company and there is no legal obligation to produce accounts, it will still produce financial statements to provide evidence of what it has achieved over the past year. These accounts will also be used as a basis for enabling the business's managers or owners and its lenders and advisers to make decisions based upon them as well as being used by the taxation authorities to determine the tax due on the profits for the year.

What is the aim of these financial accounts and reports and what do they provide? The International Accounting Standards Board states that the objective of financial reporting (not just financial statements) is as follows.

> The objective of general purpose financial reporting is to provide financial information about the reporting entity that is useful to existing and potential investors, lenders and other creditors in making decisions relating to providing resources to the entity. Those decisions involve decisions about:
>
> a) buying, selling or holding equity and debt instruments;

b) providing or settling loans and other forms of credit; or

c) exercising rights to vote on, or otherwise influence, management's actions that affect the use of the entity's economic resources.

Source: IASB *Conceptual Framework for Financial Reporting,* paragraph 1.2

While the IASB focuses on the financial information needs of existing and potential investors, lenders and other creditors, it does envisage that other users might find general purpose financial reports useful:

> Other parties, such as regulators and members of the public other than investors, lenders and other creditors, may also find general purpose financial reports useful. However, those reports are not primarily directed to these other groups.

Source: IASB *Conceptual Framework for Financial Reporting,* paragraph 1.10

Financial information is reported to users external to the organisation through three key statements: the statement of financial position, the statement of profit or loss and the statement of cash flows. You will study or will have studied in a financial accounting or financial reporting module these three statements, how they are put together and what information they provide to users.

As well as the three primary user groups noted by the IASB, other parties who might find general purpose financial statements useful include the following:

- Employees and their representative groups
- Customers
- Governments and their agencies
- The public

What information would each of the identified user groups expect to find in external financial reports that would enable them to make economic decisions? Table 1.3 provides examples of some of the questions that the seven categories of user will ask when looking at financial statements: can you think of additional questions that each user group will ask?

Many questions that users of financial reports ask will be common to all categories of user. For example, investors might ask questions about the ethical and environmental record of the company and whether this is the kind of organisation they would want to be involved with and be seen to be involved with. But ethically and environmentally concerned employees might also ask the same questions and lenders, concerned about their reputation and being seen to do business with unethical organisations, might be looking for the same information. Suppliers and customers will have similar concerns as their image and reputation will be shaped by those they do business with.

Similarly, all user groups will want to know about the availability of cash with which to pay dividends (investors), salaries (employees), loan interest and loan repayments (lenders), goods supplied on credit (suppliers) and taxes due (governments). Even customers and the public will be concerned about the availability of cash, as, without sufficient inflows of cash from trading, companies will collapse.

1

Table 1.3 The external users of financial statements

User group	Examples of questions asked by each user group
Existing and potential investors (this group would include investment advisers)	• What profit has the company made for me in my position as a shareholder/investor? • What financial gains am I making from this company? • Would it be worthwhile for me to invest more money in the shares of this company? • If the company has not done well this year, should I sell my shares or hold onto them? • Does my company comply with all the relevant company and stock market regulations? • Is my company run effectively and efficiently?
Lenders	• Will this company be able to repay what has been lent? • Will this company be able to pay loan instalments and interest as they fall due? • Is this company in danger of insolvency? • What cash resources and cash generating ability does this company have?
Other creditors (this group will include suppliers of goods and services to the entity)	• Will I be paid for goods or services I have supplied? • Will I be paid on time so that I can pay my suppliers? • Will my customer expand so that I can expand, too?
Employees and their representative groups	• How stable is the company I work for? • Is the company I work for making profits? • If the company is making losses, will it survive for the foreseeable future? • What about the continuity of my employment? • Should I be looking for employment elsewhere? • If the company I work for is profitable, will I be awarded a pay rise or a bonus? • What retirement benefit scheme does my company offer to employees? • Is my employer investing in the future prosperity of the business?
Customers	• Will the entity survive in the long term so that it can continue to provide me with goods and services?
Governments and their agencies	• What taxation does this entity pay? • What contribution does this entity make to the economy? • Does this entity export goods to other countries?
The public	• What contribution does this entity make to society? • Does this entity make donations to charity? • If this entity is a major local employer, will they survive into the future to ensure the health of the local economy?

While users of external financial statements might legitimately ask the questions mentioned, the extent to which such reports provide this information varies. Some financial reports are very detailed in their coverage, others less so.

WHY IS THIS RELEVANT TO ME?   The users of accounting information

To enable you as an accounting professional to understand:

- Who the target audience is for the reports that you will produce
- Which external parties are interested in the financial information provided by business entities
- The kinds of answers users of external financial reports expect from the information provided

---

GO BACK OVER THIS AGAIN!   Are you convinced that you understand what information particular user groups are looking for in published financial reports? Go to the **online workbook** Exercises 1.7 to check your understanding in this area.

SUMMARY OF KEY CONCEPTS   Can you recall the seven user groups of financial accounting information? Go to the **online workbook** to check your knowledge of these user groups with Summary of key concepts 1.10.

SUMMARY OF KEY CONCEPTS   Are you confident that you can state the objective of financial statements? Go to the **online workbook** to check your knowledge of this objective with Summary of key concepts 1.11.

Accounting branch 2: cost and management accounting

Cost and management accounting is concerned with reporting accounting and cost information to users within an organisation. As the name suggests, management accounting information is used to help managers manage the business and its activities. Cost and management accountants are first concerned with the costs that go into producing products and services to determine a selling price for those products and services that will generate a profit for the business. Management accounting information is then used to plan levels of production and activity in the future as well as deciding what products to produce and sell to maximise profits for the business. As well as planning what the business is going to do, management accounting produces reports to evaluate the results of past plans to see whether they achieved their aims and the ways in which improvements could be made.

While financial accounting reports what has happened in the past, management accounting is very much concerned with both the present and the future and how accounting information can be used for short-term decision making and longer-term planning. Chapter 2 (Management accounting: a definition) will consider the ways in which the topics covered in this book fulfill these roles.

WHY IS THIS RELEVANT TO ME?   The two branches of accounting

To enable you as an accounting professional to:

- Appreciate the wide range of internal and external users of accounting information
- Distinguish quickly between financial and management accounting

THE STRUCTURE AND REGULATION OF THE ACCOUNTING PROFESSION

Professional accounting bodies have been set up in many countries around the world. These professional accounting bodies are responsible for admitting individuals to membership and for regulation and oversight of their conduct as professional people once they have been accepted as members. Admission to the professional bodies is achieved through a combination of examinations and practical experience. The main professional accounting bodies in the United Kingdom and Ireland are:

- The Association of Chartered Certified Accountants (ACCA)
- The Chartered Institute of Management Accountants (CIMA)
- The Chartered Institute of Public Finance and Accountancy (CIPFA)
- The Institute of Chartered Accountants in England and Wales (ICAEW)
- The Institute of Chartered Accountants in Ireland (ICAI)
- The Institute of Chartered Accountants in Scotland (ICAS).

Qualified accountants undertake the preparation of financial statements and reports, the audit of financial statements and the provision of taxation and business advice to individuals and organisations. As professionals, qualified accountants are expected to adhere to high standards of conduct to maintain the standing of the profession and to provide a professional service to their clients and the public. Accountants are expected to behave with integrity, being honest in all their professional and business relationships. They are also expected to be objective, to carry out their duties with due care and competence, to maintain the confidentiality of information acquired in the course of fulfilling their duties and to comply at all times with relevant laws and regulations. Where accountants breach these ethical rules of conduct, their professional bodies will take action to discipline them with warnings, fines and, in the most serious cases, exclusion from membership.

As well as adhering to the professional bodies' expected standards of behaviour and ethical conduct, qualified accountants are expected to ensure that accepted accounting standards have been applied correctly in the presentation of financial information. In the European Union and in the UK accounting standards are set by the International Accounting Standards Board (IASB) for companies listed on a Stock Exchange and by the UK Financial Reporting Council (FRC) for smaller unlisted and non-public interest companies. Failure to apply these accounting standards correctly will also result in an accountant's professional body taking disciplinary action against a member.

Poor management and dishonest behaviour on the part of directors in the past led to investors losing a lot of money. Governments and stock exchanges around the world responded by setting up various committees to report on the state of corporate governance, the way in which large companies were run and to make recommendations for improvement. As a result of these recommendations, corporate governance codes were formulated to enshrine best practice and to ensure that large companies were run in an open and honest manner to safeguard shareholders' and the general public's interests in those companies. Professional accountants are expected to adhere to and apply these corporate governance codes in businesses in which they work to ensure the transparency of information presented by these companies. Further consideration of corporate governance will be presented in Chapter 9 and this introduction to the topic will form the basis of your future studies in this area.

WHY IS THIS RELEVANT TO ME?   Structure and regulation of the accounting profession

To provide you as an accounting professional with:

- A quick overview of the accounting profession and the ways in which it is regulated
- An indication of the standards of behaviour to be expected from professional accountants and other persons holding positions of responsibility in companies

THE INTERNATIONAL ACCOUNTING STANDARDS BOARD (IASB)

As noted earlier (this chapter, The structure and regulation of the accounting profession), the IASB is responsible for developing and issuing accounting standards. These accounting standards must be adhered to by companies when producing and presenting their annual financial statements. The development process for an accounting standard follows the process outlined in Figure 1.5.

The first step in developing a new standard is the identification of a reporting problem. There may be a variety of different approaches to presenting information about a particular item in financial statements. Such variety will lead to a lack of relevant information due to the lack of comparability between the financial statements of different entities. The IASB then develops a

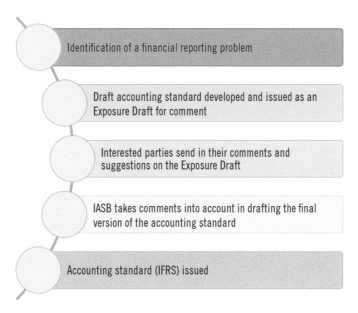

Identification of a financial reporting problem

Draft accounting standard developed and issued as an Exposure Draft for comment

Interested parties send in their comments and suggestions on the Exposure Draft

IASB takes comments into account in drafting the final version of the accounting standard

Accounting standard (IFRS) issued

Figure 1.5 The accounting standard development process

1

draft accounting standard called an Exposure Draft. This Exposure Draft will propose a single approach to the reporting of the particular item in the financial statements to ensure that reporting differences are eliminated. Interested parties then comment on the proposals in the Exposure Draft, supporting or disagreeing with the proposed approach. Once the comment period is complete, the IASB takes all the comments into account when developing the final accounting standard. The standard developed and issued is known as an International Financial Reporting Standard, abbreviated to IFRS. Prior to the establishment of the IASB under its current constitution in 2001, its predecessor body the International Accounting Standards Committee issued statements called International Accounting Standards, abbreviated to IAS. As each IAS is revised in line with current accounting and reporting practice, it is reissued as an IFRS.

WHY IS THIS RELEVANT TO ME?   The International Accounting Standards Board

To enable you as an accounting professional to:

- Appreciate the process of developing and issuing accounting standards
- Understand the role of the IASB in the accounting standard development process

---

THE LIMITATIONS OF ACCOUNTING INFORMATION

We have seen that accounting information plays an anchor role in decision making for businesses and other users. However, there are various aspects of business performance that accounting does not cover. While it is important to know what accounting is and what it does, it is just as important to be aware of what accounting does not do.

First, accounting does not provide you with measures of the quality of an organisation's performance. The quality of what an entity produces or provides is measured by its customers and their level of satisfaction with goods and services delivered, their willingness to recommend an organisation's products and the number of times they return to buy more goods or use more services. While measures can be devised to assess recommendations and repeat business, this is not a function that accounting would normally fulfil.

Similarly, a business entity may make a profit, but accounting does not tell us the time, effort and thought that went into delivering the products and services to generate that profit. In the same way, your team may win, draw or lose, but the bare result does not tell you about the quality of entertainment on offer, whether your team played badly but still managed to scrape a vital goal or whether they played brilliantly and were just unlucky.

Second, accounting does not tell you about the pollution and environmental or social damage an entity has caused. Organisations will report redundancies as an internal cost-saving opportunity for the business while ignoring the wider external effects of their actions. Thus, businesses do not report the destruction of communities built around an organisation's operations and all the burdens that this imposes upon families, social services, the National Health Service and the state. Similarly, while companies use air, water and other natural resources in their production processes,

1

there is no formal, legal requirement that they should report on the damage they cause to these resources. Despite the lack of regulation in this last area, we shall look in more detail in Chapter 9 at the current debate surrounding accounting for the environment and sustainability accounting.

Finally, accounting does not provide any valuation or measure of the skills base and knowledge of organisations. Boards of directors will thank their staff for all their hard work and efforts during the previous financial year, but the monetary value of the employees to the business does not feature in financial statements. This is attributable to the fact that valuing staff is exceptionally complex due to the subjective nature of such valuations and the fact that employees do not meet the IASB's asset definition and recognition criteria. While employees, their skills, knowledge and abilities are the most valuable resources in a business, these resources cannot be measured in money or any other numerical terms and so do not appear in the financial statements. As accounting is about measuring items in financial statements, you might find this omission rather odd given the significance of employees to the success or failure of a business. However, it is important to remember that Albert Einstein's famous dictum is just as applicable to accounting as it is to many other disciplines: 'Not everything that can be counted counts. Not everything that counts can be counted.'

WHY IS THIS RELEVANT TO ME?   The limitations of accounting information

To enable you as an accounting professional to:

- Gain an awareness of the aspects of business performance that accounting does not cover
- Appreciate the limitations of accounting and accounting information
- Understand that accounting and accounting information will not necessarily provide you with all the information you need to make decisions or evaluate an organisation's performance

SUMMARY OF KEY CONCEPTS   Are you confident that you can state the limitations of accounting and accounting information? Go to the **online workbook** to check your knowledge of these limitations with Summary of key concepts 1.12.

CHAPTER SUMMARY

You should now have learnt that:

- Accounting summarises numerical data relating to past events and presents this data as information to managers and other interested parties as a basis for both decision making and control purposes
- Accounting information is the bedrock upon which all business decisions are based
- Financial information should possess the two fundamental characteristics of relevance and faithful representation

- The qualitative characteristics of comparability, verifiability, timeliness and understandability will enhance the usefulness of information that is relevant and faithfully represented
- Financial accounting generates reports for users external to the business
- Financial accounting information is primarily aimed at existing and potential investors, lenders and other creditors who will find this information useful in making decisions about providing resources to the reporting entity
- Other user groups such as employees, customers, governments and the public may also find financial reporting information useful in making decisions and evaluating the performance of organisations
- Management accounting is prepared for internal users in a business to help them manage the business's activities
- Accounting does not measure, among other things, quality, pollution, social and environmental damage, human resources and the skills and knowledge base of organisations

QUICK REVISION   Test your knowledge with the online flashcards in Summary of key concepts and attempt the Multiple choice questions, all found in the **online workbook**.

END-OF-CHAPTER QUESTIONS

Solutions to these questions can be found in the **online workbook**.

›Question 1.1

What accounting and other information would the managers of the following organisations require in order to assess their performance and financial position?

- A charity
- A secondary school
- A university
- A manufacturing business

›Question 1.2

A premier league football club has received an offer for its star striker from Real Madrid. The star striker is eager to leave and join the Spanish team and the board of directors has reluctantly agreed to let him go for the transfer fee offered. The team now needs a new striker and the manager has been put in charge of identifying potential new centre forwards that the club could bid for. You have been asked by the manager to draw up a chart listing the numerical information about potential targets that the manager should take into account when evaluating possible replacements.

COST AND MANAGEMENT ACCOUNTING IN CONTEXT

2

LEARNING OUTCOMES

Once you have read this chapter and worked through the questions and examples in both this chapter and the online workbook, you should be able to:

- Define cost accounting and explain its role in organisations

- Define management accounting and explain its role in organisations

- Explain the differences between financial accounting and cost and management accounting

- Describe the overlaps between financial accounting and cost and management accounting information

- Understand how cost and management accounting is both internally and externally focused

- Describe the qualities that cost and management accounting information possesses

- Understand that all organisations use cost and management accounting information to make decisions, to plan and to control their operations

2

INTRODUCTION

As we saw in Chapter 1, financial accounting records and reports economic outcomes to users external to the business. Behind these economic outcomes lie a host of internal organisational processes and decisions that go into shaping and determining the results achieved. Decisions are made about the products to make or the services to provide and organisations have to calculate the prices they will charge for the various products and services offered. How is the cost of each product or service determined? Do organisations just produce products and provide services and hope for the best or is there an underlying logic and plan to what they do? What role does accounting play in making these decisions and in costing and pricing these products? How is accounting information used to monitor and review outcomes as they happen? How do decisions made at the micro level impact upon the macro level strategy and aims of organisations? We briefly touched on the roles and functions of cost and management accounting in Chapter 1 (Accounting branch 2: cost and management accounting). It is now time to look in much greater detail at the ways in which cost and management accounting is used to inform all business decisions, both strategic and operational, to present the ways in which product and service costs are calculated with a view to determining a selling price which will fulfil an organisation's objectives and to show how cost and management accounting is used in the fundamental business cycle of decision making, planning and controlling activities (Figure 2.1).

Figure 2.1 The roles of cost and management accounting

COST ACCOUNTING AND COST OBJECTS: DEFINITIONS

What do we mean by costing and how is this term defined? Let's look at the definitions of cost accounting and cost objects provided by the Chartered Institute of Management Accountants (CIMA) in that body's *Official Terminology*:

> [The] gathering of cost information and its attachment to cost objects (for example a product, service, centre, activity, customer or distribution channel in relation to which costs are ascertained), the establishment of budgets, standard costs and actual costs of operations, processes, activities or products; and the analysis of variances, profitability or the social use of funds.
>
> Source: *CIMA Official Terminology, The Chartered Institute of Management Accountants, 2005*

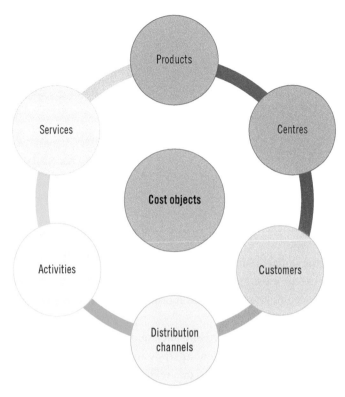

Figure 2.2 Examples of cost objects

From the definitions, it is clear that cost accounting embraces a very wide set of different approaches to gathering and allocating costs. Cost accounting revolves around the determination of the cost of cost objects as shown in Figure 2.2. These examples of cost objects are not exhaustive and costs can be accumulated for any clearly defined activity or event. The different levels of expenditure on module materials might be one example from your own experience or the varying costs of different social or sporting activities.

WHY IS THIS RELEVANT TO ME?   Cost accounting and cost objects: definitions

To enable you as an accounting professional to understand:

- The wide range of activities encompassed by cost accounting
- That organisations adopt the most appropriate and meaningful methods of gathering and allocating costs to cost objects

SUMMARY OF KEY CONCEPTS   Are you totally sure you can remember the definitions of cost accounting and cost objects? Go to the **online workbook** to check your recollection with Summary of key concepts 2.1 and 2.2.

GO BACK OVER THIS AGAIN!   Quite certain you appreciate what cost accounting involves and how it works? Go to the **online workbook** and have a look at Exercises 2.1 and 2.2 to clarify your understanding of cost accounting and how you are working with cost accounting data on a daily basis.

2

Figure 2.3 Steps in the cost allocation process

Costs can be allocated to cost objects in any way required, so organisations must first determine the most effective or most appropriate way in which they wish to gather costs and then decide how they will accumulate these costs in order to allocate them to cost objects as shown in Figure 2.3.

Once the costs have been accumulated and allocated, then this financial information can be distributed to interested parties for review, analysis and interpretation. Decisions will then be taken and plans will be made based upon this review, analysis and interpretation. Plans will be turned into budgets, the monetary expression of expected outcomes, which will be used to compare actual results to ensure that the plan is on track; where plans are not on track, corrective action can be proposed or the plans revised in the light of changed circumstances. Costing information can also be used to improve organisational efficiency and effectiveness through eliminating unnecessary costs or streamlining processes to improve profitability. Taking these decisions and making these plans is the role of management who use the management accounting information gathered and presented to make decisions, to plan and to control operations.

MANAGEMENT ACCOUNTING: A DEFINITION

But what is management accounting and how does it differ from cost accounting? Cost accounting gathers costs and summarises them. These costs form the basic building blocks upon which management build and monitor their strategic and operational plans for an organisation. Costs are the foundation for the decisions that management take in running an entity and in planning its future direction with a view to fulfilling its objectives in the short, medium and long term. The Chartered Institute of Management Accountants defines management accounting as follows:

> Management accounting is the application of the principles of accounting and financial management to create, protect, preserve and increase value for the stakeholders of for-profit and not-for-profit enterprises in the public and private sectors. Management accounting is an integral part of

management. It requires the identification, generation, presentation, interpretation and use of relevant information to:

- Inform strategic decisions and formulate business strategy
- Plan long, medium and short-run operations
- Determine capital structure and fund that structure
- Design reward strategies for executives and shareholders
- Inform operational decisions
- Control operations and ensure the efficient use of resources
- Measure and report financial and non-financial performance to management and other stakeholders
- Safeguard tangible and intangible assets
- Implement corporate governance procedures, risk management and internal controls

Source: *CIMA Official Terminology, The Chartered Institute of Management Accountants, 2005*

The role of management accounting and management accountants is thus very widely drawn, but it is clear that accounting lies at the heart of the strategic and operational decision-making process whose aim is to create, preserve and improve value for stakeholders. Give me an example 2.1 illustrates the ways in which management use accounting information and techniques to make long-term business decisions.

In the following chapters we shall present a detailed review of the short-term operational planning and decision-making aspects of cost and management accounting together with the ways in which

GIVE ME AN EXAMPLE 2.1   The role of cost and management accounting in the strategic management of businesses

Rio Tinto plc is a mining company which is split into divisions mining and trading in iron ore, aluminium, copper and diamonds and energy and minerals. The group's strategic report for 2016 describes the ways in which accounting information is used to manage the operations and the strategy of the business.

'Current business planning processes within Rio Tinto require the preparation of detailed financial plans over a three-year time horizon. The Group's strategy is developed, and capital investment decisions are made, based on an assessment of cash flows over a multi-decade horizon, with financial investment capacity regularly tested to ensure capital commitments can be funded in line with the Group's capital allocation model. This multi-year planning approach reflects our business model of investing in, and operating, long-life mining assets, whose outputs we sell into commodity markets over which we have limited influence.

The planning process requires modelling under a series of macroeconomic scenarios and assumptions of both internal and external parameters. Key assumptions include: projections of economic growth, and thus commodity demand in major markets, primarily China; commodity prices and exchange rates, often correlated; cost and supply parameters for major inputs such as labour and fuel; and a series of assumptions around the schedule and cost of implementation of organic and inorganic growth programmes.'

Source: *Rio Tinto plc Strategic report 2016* http://www.riotinto.com

cost and management accounting information is used to control operations. Thus in Chapters 3 and 7, the accumulation and allocation of costs to products, activities and processes will assist in the calculation of a selling price that will enable an organisation to make a profit. The role of marginal costing in short-term management decisions will be considered in Chapter 4 while the measure of control exercised through standard costs, variance analysis and budgets will be considered in Chapters 5 and 6. Chapter 8 will review the various techniques used to evaluate investments in long-term projects before Chapter 9 presents an overview of corporate governance and the ways in which control over the whole organisation and its operations is exercised. All of these practices and techniques will form the foundation of your later studies in both management accounting and strategy so careful and active consideration of these practices and techniques now will give you a very solid grounding upon which to build your second and final year studies.

WHY IS THIS RELEVANT TO ME?   Management accounting: a definition

As an accounting professional you should appreciate:

• The critical role that cost and management accounting plays in the planning and evaluation of business activities

• That no matter what your particular business specialism, a knowledge of the techniques and practice of management accounting will be crucial to your success in that specialist role

---

SUMMARY OF KEY CONCEPTS   Can you recall the CIMA definition of management accounting? Go to the **online workbook** to have a look at Summary of key concepts 2.3 to test your recollection.

GO BACK OVER THIS AGAIN!   Are you quite sure you appreciate how the definition of management accounting applies in practice? Have a look at Exercises 2.3 in the **online workbook** for a practical application of this definition.

COST AND MANAGEMENT ACCOUNTING V. FINANCIAL ACCOUNTING

As we have seen, financial accounting reports summarise accounting data, usually on an annual basis, for presentation to interested external parties. It is important to appreciate the historical aspect of these financial accounting statements, that they report on what has happened not on what might or is expected to happen in the future. They are thus not specifically designed to be used for planning purposes although users of these financial accounts might use them as a basis for making investment decisions, to buy, hold or sell shares in an entity. Financial accounts are prepared for parties outside the business and summarise all the transactions that have taken place, together with information relevant to a specific accounting period. The content of these financial statements is highly regulated by law and accounting standards. Annual financial statements are subject to audit to ensure that a true and fair view of the results, cash flows and financial position of the entity is presented. The rigidly specified content means that financial

2

accounting reports tend to be inflexible and are general in nature rather than being shaped to the specific needs of individual users.

By contrast, cost and management accounting reports are produced as frequently as required by management: reports are most commonly provided on a monthly basis but weekly or even daily information can be generated in critical situations which require very careful and constant monitoring. There is no prescribed content or format and reports can be presented in the way that is most helpful in highlighting the required information in order for effective decisions to be made. Cost and management accounting reports often set out data that relates to past performance, but this past performance information is used to inform present decisions with a view to improving future outcomes to fulfil short- and long-term goals. These reports are thus forward rather than backward looking and the focus is very much on internal not external users. Instead of a summary of transactions, there is a detailed analysis of costs, selling prices and any other decision relevant financial and non-financial information. All of this cost and management accounting information is reported with a view to making decisions, planning for the future and guiding and controlling outcomes in the most effective and efficient way. Such careful attention to detail enables entities to work towards achieving their short- and long-term objectives. Without planning and decision making, no one, whether an individual or a business, will achieve anything. Without monitoring actual outcomes against the plan entities will be unable to determine whether their plans are reaching fulfilment or not. Figure 2.4 compares and contrasts the characteristics of both financial accounting and cost and management accounting.

Financial accounting reports	Cost and management accounting reports
Reports produced infrequently, usually annually	Reports produced as frequently as required for the effective management of the organisation
Decision usefulness is limited	Decision usefulness is very high
Backward looking	Forward looking
Reports on the past	Reports on the past and present to inform the future
External user focus	Internal user focus
Summary of transactions	Detailed analysis of costs, selling prices and any other information required for the management of the entity
Usually financial information only	Both financial and non-financial information
Content and presentation highly regulated	No regulation of content and presentation. Complete freedom to present information in the most decision-useful and effective way
High degree of comparability with current and previous reports for the same organisation	High degree of comparability with current and previous reports for the same organisation
High degree of comparability with present and past reports of other organisations	No comparability with reports of other organisations
Results are presented in a rigid format	Information is presented in a fluid format so that, for example, sensitivity analysis can be applied to forecast information

Figure 2.4 A comparison of financial accounting and cost and management accounting

WHY IS THIS RELEVANT TO ME?   Cost and management accounting v. financial accounting

To enable you as an accounting professional to appreciate:

- The differences between financial accounting and cost and management accounting
- The different purposes served by financial accounting and cost and management accounting
- The different audiences for financial and cost and management accounting information

GO BACK OVER THIS AGAIN!   Have you fully understood the differences between financial and cost and management accounting? Go to the **online workbook** and complete Exercises 2.4 to make sure you understand the distinctions.

SUMMARY OF KEY CONCEPTS   Are you quite sure you understand the differences between financial accounting and cost and management accounting? Go to the **online workbook** to take a look at Summary of key concepts 2.4 and 2.5 to reinforce your understanding.

FINANCIAL ACCOUNTING INFORMATION V. COST AND MANAGEMENT ACCOUNTING INFORMATION: A COMPARISON

What sources of information does cost and management accounting information use? Given that financial and cost and management accounting reports have such different functions, it might be expected that they would both derive their financial information from completely different sources. However, both financial accounting and cost and management accounting reports derive their numerical input from the same internal sources. In the financial accounting system, a purchase of raw materials on credit is debited to the raw materials account and credited to the trade payables control account. In the cost and management accounting system, after the initial debit to the raw materials account and the initial credit to the trade payables account, the value of the raw materials is reallocated to each of the cost objects (jobs) using those raw materials as shown in Illustration 2.1. The double-entry system can thus also be used in the management accounting system to take the total figures for the costs of materials, labour, overheads and other expenses and break these total costs down further to allocate them to the cost objects that consume those resources as required by cost accounting. A total for each resource is debited to the master account for that resource and as costs are consumed by cost objects, the master resource account is credited and each cost object account is debited with the costs reallocated. In this way it can be seen that the financial and cost and management accounting systems both rely on the same cost information for their reports: while financial accounting uses the total figures, cost and management accounting breaks those total figures down into their relevant sub-headings.

Illustration 2.1 Double entry for raw materials purchased on credit in both the financial and cost and management accounting systems

Financial and cost and management accounting systems

Raw materials					Trade payables			
Dr	£	Cr	£		Dr	£	Cr	£
Trade payables	24,000						Raw materials	24,000

Cost and management accounting system

Raw materials					Job 3620			
Dr	£	Cr	£		Dr	£	Cr	£
Trade payables	24,000	Job 3620	7,500		Raw materials	7,500		
		Job 3627	4,800					
		Job 3629	6,000					

Job 3627					Job 3629			
Dr	£	Cr	£		Dr	£	Cr	£
Raw materials	4,800				Raw materials	6,000		

While the same base internal financial figures are used to allocate costs to cost objects, management accounting also makes use of other external financial and non-financial information in the decision making, planning and controlling process. For example when deciding on a selling price for a product or service, that selling price cannot be set by reference to the internal financial costs alone. Attention must also be paid to the prices charged by other providers of the same or similar products and services so that the entity's own products and services remain competitive within the overall market. There is a very great deal of external financial and non-financial information that can be used by organisations in their decision-making and planning processes and cost and management accounting will make full use of this information to reach economically valid conclusions. Figure 2.5 illustrates the sources of information used in generating both financial accounting reports and cost and management accounting reports. Cost and management accounting reports have both an internal and an external focus whereas financial accounting reports present internal information to external parties.

In Chapter 1 (What qualities should accounting information possess?) we considered the distinct qualities of useful financial information. These characteristics are also applicable to cost and management accounting information. To be useful, cost and management accounting information must be relevant, timely, comparable and understandable. However, unlike financial accounting information, management accounting information does not have to be verifiable and does not have to faithfully represent what it purports to represent. As long as management are confident that the accounting system is generating accurate information, there is no further need for verification of the details produced. Faithful representation is a quality of accounting information that is only required when reporting to third parties, individuals and organisations with no connection to the reporting entity: management accounting information is reported within

2

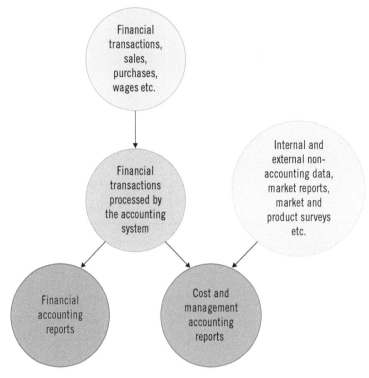

Figure 2.5 Sources of information used in financial accounting and cost and management accounting reports

organisations for internal purposes only and does not purport to represent anything further to outside parties. Useful management accounting information is also subject to the cost-benefit rule: the cost of obtaining the information should always be lower than the benefit gained from that information. Where this is not the case, time and effort should not be wasted on acquiring the information. Likewise, immaterial information should not be included in management accounting reports as this will only distract attention away from the critical details.

WHY IS THIS RELEVANT TO ME?   Financial accounting information v. cost and management accounting information: a comparison

To enable you as an accounting professional to appreciate:

- The ways in which financial accounting and cost and management accounting reports depend upon the same data

- That cost and management accounting reports increase their relevance and effectiveness by incorporating both internal and external data

- That the data in management accounting reports should be relevant, timely, comparable and understandable but does not have to be verifiable or faithfully represent what it purports to represent

SUMMARY OF KEY CONCEPTS   How well do you remember the qualities of useful financial information? Go to the **online workbook** to check your recollection by referring to Summary of key concepts 1.2–1.7.

GO BACK OVER THIS AGAIN!   Are you quite certain you can remember the definitions of relevance, comparability, timeliness and understandability? Go to the **online workbook** Exercises 2.5 to make sure you can define these qualities of financial information accurately.

CHAPTER SUMMARY

You should now have learnt that:

- Cost accounting embraces a wide range of activities and includes the costing of products and services, the setting of budgets and standard costs, determining the actual costs of operations, processes and activities and the analysis of variances from expected outcomes

- Management accounting creates, preserves and increases value for stakeholders through the application of the principles of accounting and financial management to strategic and operational decision making, planning and control

- Financial accounting reports are backward looking summaries of past results produced annually and are presented to external users as a basis for assessing past performance

- Cost and management accounting reports are detailed, forward looking and presented as frequently as required to internal users as a basis for making decisions to improve present and future outcomes

- Financial accounting and cost and management accounting reports are based upon the same financial data which is presented in the most appropriate format to suit the purposes of each type of report

- Cost and management accounting reports are prepared using both internally focused and externally focused financial and non-financial data whereas financial accounting reports are based on just internal financial data

- Management accounting information possesses the qualitative characteristics of relevance, timeliness, comparability and understandability, but does not have to be faithfully represented or verifiable

- Both financial and management accounting information is subject to the same cost-benefit and materiality constraints

QUICK REVISION   Test your knowledge with the online flashcards in Summary of key concepts and attempt the Multiple choice questions in the **online workbook**.

2

END-OF-CHAPTER QUESTIONS

Solutions to these questions can be found in the **online workbook**.

❯ DEVELOP YOUR UNDERSTANDING

❯Question 2.1

Your friend is an experienced cake maker who has worked for several baking companies in the past but he is now keen to branch out on his own and to open his own cake shop in his local town. He will bake all the cakes himself and offer a selection of regular cakes each day as well as making cakes to order for specific events such as birthdays, weddings and other special occasions. Your friend has applied to the local bank to open a business bank account. However, the bank has asked him to produce a business plan and present this to the bank for consideration before opening a business bank account can be considered. Your friend has identified a suitable shop and has asked for your help in putting his business plan together. List the information you will require to enable you to assist your friend in writing and completing his business plan.

❯Question 2.2

Your friend runs a packaging business which makes flat-pack cardboard boxes in standard sizes. The boxes are sold to numerous online retailers who use the boxes to package up customers' orders, which are then delivered by parcel couriers. Your friend's business operates from a rented factory. The business now has more orders for flat-pack cardboard boxes than can be fulfilled from the current factory and your friend is considering expansion to a larger factory with a much larger capacity in a different part of town. There are several local factory units to choose from with various different levels of rent. What factors would you advise your friend to take into account when making her decision about which factory to rent for her expanded business?

PRODUCT COSTING: ABSORPTION COSTING

3

LEARNING OUTCOMES

Once you have read this chapter and worked through the questions and examples in both this chapter and the online workbook, you should be able to:

- Understand the importance of costing to business organisations in making pricing decisions
- Explain what is meant by the terms direct costs and indirect costs
- Explain the distinction between fixed costs and variable costs
- Construct simple costing statements to determine the total cost of products on an absorption (full) costing basis
- Draw simple graphs to illustrate fixed, variable and total cost behaviour in a business context
- Outline the limitations of absorption costing approaches in allocating overheads to products
- Apply activity-based costing to overhead allocation problems
- Discuss the assumptions on which costing is based

3

INTRODUCTION

In Chapter 2 we considered the role of cost and management accounting in organisations. Managers make decisions, they plan and they control their organisations' operations. The first aspect of a business that managers must understand is the costs of products and services produced. Without knowing the costs of an organisation and how these are incurred, managers will not be able to make decisions about selling prices or to know what they are controlling and they will not be able to plan for the future. But how are the costs of a product or service made up? What costs are incurred by a business and how can these costs all be allocated to the products and services provided by a business in order to determine a selling price? This chapter will look in detail at the different categories of costs incurred by organisations and consider the ways in which the cost of products and services can be determined.

WHY IS IT IMPORTANT TO KNOW ABOUT COSTS?

Businesses exist to make a profit. Without knowing what costs a business will incur in producing goods for sale or in providing a service, it will not be possible for that business to set a selling price higher than the costs incurred. When selling price exceeds the costs, a profit is made. Should selling price be lower than the costs, then a loss will be made and the business will soon be in financial trouble. Revenue (income, sales) − costs = profit. All businesses will be seeking to increase their profits over time 'to create, protect, preserve and increase value for the stakeholders of for-profit and not-for-profit enterprises in the public and private sectors' (*CIMA Official Terminology, The Chartered Institute of Management Accountants, 2005*). There are two paths an entity can take when it wishes to increase profits: either revenue has to increase or costs must decrease. Let's prove this in Example 3.1.

EXAMPLE 3.1

Henry buys T-shirts for £5 and sells them for £10 each. Currently he sells 1,000 T-shirts a year on his market stall. He wishes to increase his profits.

Given his current level of sales, Henry now has a profit of:

	£
Sales 1,000 × £10	10,000
Cost of sales 1,000 × £5	5,000
Profit	**5,000**

If Henry could buy 1,000 T-shirts for £4 while still selling them for £10 his profit would be:

	£
Sales 1,000 × £10	10,000
Cost of sales 1,000 × £4	4,000
Profit	**6,000**

Henry has reduced the cost of the goods he sells without reducing his selling price and so his profit has increased from £5,000 to £6,000.

However, by increasing his sales to 2,000 T-shirts, while still buying them at £5 each, his profit will be:

	£
Sales 2,000 × £10	20,000
Cost of sales 2,000 × £5	10,000
Profit	**10,000**

Reducing costs or increasing sales are thus the two ways in which businesses can increase their profits.

WHY IS THIS RELEVANT TO ME?   Costs and pricing

- No matter what field of commercial or not-for-profit activity you are engaged in, as an accounting professional you must know about costs and income
- Knowing about your costs will enable you to determine a selling price to cover those costs and to generate a profit/surplus for your organisation
- Knowledge of an activity's costs will enable you as an accounting professional to devise strategies by which to increase profit, whether by reducing costs, increasing income or both

GO BACK OVER THIS AGAIN!   Are you quite sure that you understand the relationship between selling price, costs and profit? Go to the **online workbook** Exercises 3.1 to make sure you understand these relationships.

Give me an example 3.1 shows how cost reductions increase profits.

GIVE ME AN EXAMPLE 3.1   **EasyJet on path to profit after fuel price fall**

A lower fuel bill has set easyJet on a course to record an interim pre-tax profit for the first time in 13 years, Europe's second largest low-cost airline by revenue said yesterday. Carolyn McCall, easyJet chief executive, said yesterday the company expected its fuel bill to be £35m less in the six months to the end of March compared with the same period a year earlier—highlighting how airlines are benefiting from the 50 per cent plunge in oil prices since last summer.

Source: Jane Wild, 2015, *EasyJet set for first-half profit on lower fuel bill*, the Financial Times, 26 March. Used under licence from the Financial Times. All Rights Reserved.

COSTS AND COSTING

We have seen that costs are important to businesses, but what costs will a business consider in making its decisions? The type and number of costs will depend upon the complexity of each business. Very simple businesses will have very simple costing systems and very few costs, while more complex businesses will have many costs and very complex costing systems to inform management decisions. Consider Example 3.2.

Anna is a self-employed carpenter working at home producing handmade wooden dining chairs. During the month of June, she produced 30 chairs. What price should she sell her chairs for? She provides you with invoices showing the costs of the materials she used in June:

	£
Wood	540
Glue	18
Screws	30
Sandpaper	12

Totalling up the costs above, Anna has spent £600 on making 30 chairs. Dividing the total costs by the 30 chairs made gives a cost of £20 per chair.

Setting a selling price

As long as Anna sells her chairs for more than £20 each, then she will make a profit on each sale. However, what other considerations should she bear in mind when setting her selling price? First, she will think about what a reasonable profit on each chair sold would be. If each chair takes her an hour to make, she would probably consider a profit of £30 to be a reasonable reward for the time and effort she has put into making each chair. The selling price for each chair would then be £50: £20 costs plus £30 profit. If each chair takes Anna five hours to make, then she would want significantly more profit and a significantly higher selling price to reflect the time spent on producing each chair.

While considering her own internal perspective, the profit she would like to make based on her time spent on making chairs, she will also need to consider the external market. She will thus take into account the prices her competitors are charging for the same type of chair; if she charges more than her competitors, she will not have many sales as buyers in the market like to buy goods as cheaply as possible. Alternatively, if she sets her selling price lower than her competitors, then she will expect to have a lot of orders from her customers, all of whom will want to buy her chairs at her lower price. However, can she fulfil all those orders? Does she have the time to produce as many chairs as her customers will demand?

Setting a selling price is thus a complex decision that needs to factor in many considerations. While cost is only one of those considerations it is now time to look in more detail at the types of cost that organisations incur in their operations.

DIRECT COSTS, VARIABLE COSTS AND MARGINAL COSTS

In our example, each one of Anna's costs can be attributed directly to each chair she produces. If she were to produce 31 chairs, we would expect her to incur costs of £600 ÷ 30 chairs × 31 chairs = £620. That is, for each additional chair she produces she will incur an additional £20 of materials cost. These costs are called the direct costs of production, the costs that are directly attributable to each unit of output. In Anna's case, these direct costs vary directly in line with each unit of output that is produced and are therefore her variable costs of production. Variable costs reflect the additional costs that are incurred by a business in producing one more unit of a product or service. Borrowing a term from economics, these variable costs are also known as the marginal cost of production, the costs that are incurred in producing one more unit of a product or service. However, as we shall see, not all direct costs of production are variable costs.

SUMMARY OF KEY CONCEPTS   Are you quite sure you understand what direct cost, variable cost and marginal cost mean? Go to the **online workbook** Summary of key concepts 3.1 to 3.3 to check your understanding.

Direct costs can be of three types. The first direct cost is materials. In Example 3.2 the wood, glue, screws and sandpaper are all materials used in the production of each chair. The second direct cost is labour, the amount paid to workers for making products. Direct labour may be paid to workers on the basis of an agreed amount for each unit of product produced so that the more the work-force produces, the more they are paid. In this case, direct labour is a variable cost of production. Where production workers are paid a fixed salary that does not depend upon the number of goods produced, this is still a direct cost of production. However, it is not a variable cost as salary costs do not rise or fall in line with production. The final type of direct cost is direct expense, costs other than material and labour that can be traced directly to the production of each unit of product. An example of a direct expense would be the electricity required to power machinery to produce one unit of production: the total amount of electricity used by a piece of machinery can be measured precisely and the total cost of electricity divided by the number of units of production to determine a per unit expense for electricity. Example 3.3 presents examples of direct costs.

EXAMPLE 3.3

To illustrate the three types of direct cost, material, labour and expense, let us consider the costs incurred in the bread making section of a bakery. Think about each cost and decide whether it is an example of direct material, direct labour or direct expense.

Cost:

- Flour
- Gas used to heat the ovens
- Bakers' wages paid on the basis of the number of loaves of bread produced
- Ingredient mixing costs

- Equipment cleaning costs after each batch of loaves is produced
- Yeast
- Bakers' productivity bonus
- Olive oil
- Packaging for loaves
- Water

Which of these costs are direct material, direct labour and direct expense? We can allocate these costs to each heading as shown in Table 3.1.

Table 3.1 Cost allocation

Cost	Direct material	Direct labour	Direct expense
Flour	✓		
Gas used to heat the ovens			✓
Bakers' wages paid on the basis of the number of loaves of bread produced		✓	
Ingredient mixing costs			✓
Equipment cleaning costs after each batch of loaves is produced			✓
Yeast	✓		
Bakers' productivity bonus		✓	
Olive oil	✓		
Packaging for loaves	✓		
Water	✓		

Flour, yeast, olive oil, water and packaging are clearly materials used in each loaf, while the bakers' wages and productivity bonus are labour costs. The gas used to heat the ovens is a direct expense used in production of each loaf as, without the gas to heat the ovens to bake the loaves, there would be no product to sell. The gas is not a material as it is not part of the finished loaf. Similarly, the ingredient mixing costs (by machine rather than by hand) are expenses: the cost of mixing ingredients together is essential to the production of the loaves but is neither direct labour nor direct material. Cleaning the equipment after each batch of loaves is produced is another expense that has to be incurred in the production of bread. Each time a batch of loaves is produced, more cleaning costs are incurred so the cleaning costs are the direct result of production.

GO BACK OVER THIS AGAIN! Are you confident you can distinguish between direct materials, direct labour and direct expenses? Go to the **online workbook** Exercises 3.2 to make sure you understand what types of cost fall into each category.

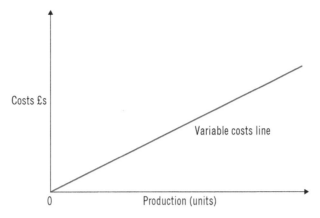

Figure 3.1 Graph showing the effect of production on variable costs

Variable cost behaviour: graphical presentation

In costing, the variable costs of production are assumed to behave in a linear fashion. This mathematical term just means that the variable costs of production rise precisely in line with the number of units produced. For each additional unit of production, the additional cost of producing that additional unit (the marginal cost) will be exactly the same as for all the previous units of production. In Example 3.2, the additional cost of producing one more chair is £20, which is exactly the same cost as all the other chairs Anna has produced.

The relationship between the variable costs of production and the number of units produced can be illustrated graphically as shown in Figure 3.1.

As production increases, variable costs rise in line with that production. Production of one chair costs Anna £20 in materials. Production of two chairs costs her £40 and so on. As each chair costs exactly the same to produce as the previous one, the total variable costs of production on the graph will rise in a straight line. If Anna produces no chairs, she will incur no variable costs and so the variable costs line starts at zero.

FIXED COSTS

However, not all costs incurred by a business are variable, marginal costs. There are also costs that are fixed, which do not vary in line with production. These costs are called fixed costs because, for a given period of time, they are assumed to remain the same whether zero units, 10 units or 1,000 units of product are produced. Fixed costs can be direct costs of production (such as the fixed salaries of production workers) or they may be general overheads incurred in the running of the business, costs that cannot be directly attributed to specific products or services. Fixed costs come in many forms, but let us start with the following simple example, Example 3.4.

EXAMPLE 3.4

Anna is so successful in her chair-making enterprise at home that she decides to expand and set up a workshop from which to produce her chairs. She starts renting a small workshop at an annual rental cost of £6,000. Business rates on the workshop amount to £1,000 per annum and the workshop heating

3

and lighting bills amount to £800 for the year. In addition, she takes on two employees who are paid £25 for each chair that they make. Anna now concentrates on running the business rather than crafting chairs herself. How would you classify these additional costs? Which of these new costs do not vary directly in line with production and which will rise or fall precisely in line with the number of chairs produced?

Rent and business rates on the workshop are totally fixed as Anna has to pay these costs whether the employees make no chairs in the year or whether they make 10,000. Thus, her workshop can produce as few or as many chairs as she likes without incurring any additional rent or business rate costs. The rent and business rates are thus both fixed costs. They are also the indirect costs of production: the workshop is essential to the production of the chairs, but the rent and business rates cannot in any way be attributed directly to each chair produced.

By contrast, the employees are a direct cost of production as each additional chair that is made by each employee incurs a further cost of £25, this cost varying directly in line with production. Thus, £25 is a completely variable cost of production, the marginal labour cost of producing one more chair. This £25 will be added to the £20 material costs to give the total direct cost of one chair of £45.

The heating and lighting bills are a little trickier to classify. How much is paid for lighting will depend on how many days the workshop is open. If the workshop is closed, then the lights will not be turned on and no cost will be incurred. Similarly, if no one works in the workshop for the whole year, there will be no need to turn on the lights or the heating and the heating and lighting costs will be £Nil. However, even if the workshop is open and the lights are turned on, there is no guarantee that a consistent level of production will be achieved each day. The two employees might be able to produce eight chairs in a day between them, but if either of them is unwell and absent from work, then only four chairs will be produced, assuming that they each make four chairs a day. However, the lighting cost would still be the same for four chairs as it was for eight chairs. If the weather is hot, then the employees will work more slowly and only six chairs a day might be produced. In the same way, more lighting will be used in winter than in summer and this variability is also true of the heating costs: a very cold winter will mean a higher heating bill than when the winter weather is milder. Given this difficulty in allocating the costs of heating and lighting to individual units of production, it is safer to treat these costs as a fixed cost for the year.

Can we illustrate the relationship between fixed costs and production as we did for variable costs in Figure 3.1? Yes we can and this relationship is shown in Figure 3.2.

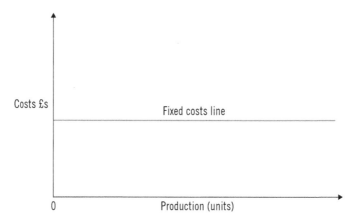

Figure 3.2 Graph showing the effect of production on fixed costs

The fixed costs line is a straight line just like the variable costs line. However, the fixed cost line shows that fixed costs are the same for all levels of production over a given period of time. As we noted earlier, the fixed costs are the same whether no chairs or 10,000 chairs are produced. Thus, the fixed cost line does not pass through zero but starts at the level of the fixed costs on the cost axis and continues as a straight line across the graph as there is no variation in the level of fixed costs. Even when no chairs are produced, the fixed costs are still incurred and have to be paid.

3

WHY IS THIS RELEVANT TO ME?   Direct costs and indirect costs

In your role as an accounting professional you will be expected to be able to:

- Identify those costs that are directly attributable to units of production or to services provided
- Identify those costs that vary in line with increased or decreased business activity
- Identify those costs that do not vary in line with increased or decreased business activity
- Possess the knowledge required to identify costs that are relevant in decision making (discussed further in Chapter 4)

GO BACK OVER THIS AGAIN!   Are you sure that you appreciate the difference between fixed and variable costs? Go to the **online workbook** Exercises 3.3 to make sure you understand this distinction.

VARIABLE COSTS, FIXED COSTS AND TOTAL COSTS

Total costs for an accounting period are the total variable costs incurred in producing goods or services plus the total fixed costs incurred in that same time period. This is illustrated graphically in Figure 3.3.

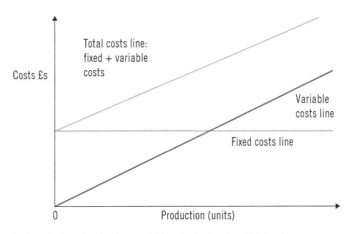

Figure 3.3 Graph showing the behaviour of production on variable costs, fixed costs and total costs

The variable cost and fixed cost lines are drawn on the graph as before in exactly the same positions. The total cost line adds together the variable and fixed costs for a period to give the total costs incurred by an organisation. At a zero level of production, variable costs are zero, so total costs are the same as fixed costs. However, as production takes place, variable costs are incurred and the total costs line rises as these variable costs are added to fixed costs. As production increases, the average total cost of each product produced will fall as the fixed costs are spread across more units of production. To prove that this is the case, consider Example 3.5.

EXAMPLE 3.5

Using the facts from Examples 3.2 and 3.4, let's work out the average cost per unit for levels of production of Anna's chairs at 100 units, 200 units, 300 units and 400 units. Remember that variable costs are materials (£20) + labour (£25) = £45 per chair while the fixed costs of the workshop are £6,000 (rent) + £1,000 (business rates) + £800 (heating and lighting) = £7,800.

As Table 3.2 shows, the average total cost per chair falls as production increases and the fixed costs are gradually spread over an increasing number of chairs.

Table 3.2 Anna's average cost per chair at different levels of production

(a) Units of production	(b) Variable cost per unit	(c) = (a) × (b) Total variable costs	(d) Fixed costs	(e) = (c) + (d) Total costs	(f) = (e) ÷ (a) Average total cost per chair
100	45	4,500	7,800	12,300	123.00
200	45	9,000	7,800	16,800	84.00
300	45	13,500	7,800	21,300	71.00
400	45	18,000	7,800	25,800	64.50

NUMERICAL EXERCISES   How well have you appreciated that higher levels of production mean a smaller average total cost for each product produced? Go to the **online workbook** and complete Numerical exercises 3.1 to prove to yourself that this is still true for higher levels of production in Anna's workshop.

ALLOCATING FIXED OVERHEAD COSTS TO PRODUCTS: ABSORPTION COSTING

We noted earlier in this chapter that organisations need to know the total cost of their products or services so that they can calculate a suitable selling price to enable them to make a profit on their activities. As we have seen, the costs involved are the direct and indirect costs of production and organisations will take both of these types of cost into account when setting their selling prices. Typically, a cost card will be drawn up for each product that shows the direct costs for one unit of production. Anna's cost card for one chair is shown in Example 3.6.

However, how should the indirect costs of production be allocated to products? Organisations have to take into account their indirect costs when setting a selling price for a product otherwise they might set the selling price too low and fail to cover their indirect as well as their direct costs. But different levels of production will result in different allocations of indirect costs to products and in different total costs for products. Anna has indirect costs of £7,800 for her rent, rates, heating and lighting. As we saw in Table 3.2, at different levels of production the average total cost for each product rises or falls depending on how many or how few products are produced. How can Anna set a selling price for her chairs if actual numbers of chairs produced are not known?

The answer to this problem is that entities will estimate the normal, expected level of production achievable within an accounting period and use this normal level of production as the basis for allocating indirect costs to products. Thus, an allocation of indirect costs is made to each unit of production on the basis of this expected production level so that the indirect costs are recovered with each unit of production sold. This technique is called absorption costing: indirect costs are absorbed into (allocated to) each unit of production to give a total cost for each product. At the same time, the indirect costs are recovered (essentially, paid for by the customer) as each unit of production is sold. Let us see how this will work in the case of Anna's chairs in Example 3.6.

EXAMPLE 3.6

Anna decides that her workshop will be capable of producing 1,000 chairs in the next year. She now needs to calculate the total cost for one chair based on the figures given in Examples 3.2 and 3.4 so that she can decide upon her selling price. Her cost card for one dining chair is shown here.

Cost card: wooden dining chair	£
Direct production costs	
Wood £540 ÷ 30 (Example 3.2)	18.00
Glue £18 ÷ 30 (Example 3.2)	0.60
Screws £30 ÷ 30 (Example 3.2)	1.00
Sandpaper £12 ÷ 30 (Example 3.2)	0.40
Direct labour (Example 3.4)	25.00
Prime cost (total direct cost of production	45.00
of one chair:	
direct material + direct labour + direct expenses)	
Indirect production costs (overheads)	
Rent £6,000 ÷ 1,000 (Example 3.4)	6.00
Business rates £1,000 ÷ 1,000 (Example 3.4)	1.00
Heating and lighting £800 ÷ 1,000 (Example 3.4)	0.80
Total production cost of one chair	**52.80**

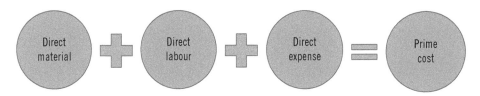

Figure 3.4 The components of prime cost

Figure 3.5 The total production cost of one unit of production

Direct costs of production are split into their component parts (direct material, direct labour and direct expense). The total direct production cost is called prime cost (Figure 3.4), the direct cost of producing one dining chair. Indirect (overhead) costs are then allocated to each item of production on the basis of what production is expected to be, the normal level of production. Thus, each element of indirect costs is divided by the total expected production of 1,000 units to give the overhead cost that should be allocated to each unit of production. Adding the indirect (overhead) costs per unit of production to the total direct cost (prime cost) gives the total production cost of one chair (Figure 3.5).

SUMMARY OF KEY CONCEPTS   Can you define prime cost and production cost? Go to the **online workbook** Summary of key concepts 3.4 to reinforce your understanding.

WHY IS THIS RELEVANT TO ME?   Prime cost and production cost

As an accounting professional you should understand that:

• Setting a selling price to achieve a profit requires knowledge of all the costs incurred in the production of a good or service

• Indirect overhead costs as well as direct costs of production have to be taken into account when setting a selling price

• A suitable method of allocation of indirect overhead costs to products has to be found in order to build the indirect costs incurred into the cost of each product produced and sold

NUMERICAL EXERCISES   Are you convinced you can allocate direct and indirect costs to a product or service? Go to the **online workbook** and complete Numerical exercises 3.2 to make sure you can apply this technique.

SETTING THE SELLING PRICE

As management accounting is about informing operational decisions as well as costing, Anna will now consider (in Example 3.7) what selling price she ought to charge for each chair and how much profit she will make on the basis of her decision.

EXAMPLE 3.7

Given that each chair is expected to incur a total production (absorption) cost of £52.80, Anna decides that a selling price of £85 is reasonable and will meet market expectations. How much profit will she make if she sells all of the 1,000 chairs produced? The detailed profit calculation is shown below.

	£	£
Sales 1,000 × £85		85,000
Direct costs		
Wood 1,000 × £18	18,000	
Glue 1,000 × £0.60	600	
Screws 1,000 × £1	1,000	
Sandpaper 1,000 × £0.40	400	
Direct labour 1,000 × £25	25,000	
Prime cost (total direct cost for 1,000 chairs)		45,000
Rent 1,000 × £6	6,000	
Business rates 1,000 × £1	1,000	
Heating and lighting 1,000 × £0.80	800	
Indirect production costs		7,800
Total expected profit for the year		**32,200**

Rather than drawing up the detailed costing statement shown above, you might have taken a short cut to determine Anna's expected profit for next year. You could have taken the selling price of one chair of £85 and deducted the total production cost of one chair of £52.80 to give you a profit per chair of £32.20 (£85.00 − £52.80). Multiplying this profit per chair of £32.20 by 1,000 chairs produced and sold would give you the same answer of £32,200.

> **NUMERICAL EXERCISES**   How well have you understood the calculation of profit from a given set of costing data? Go to the **online workbook** Numerical exercises 3.3 to make sure you can apply this technique.

ABSORPTION COSTING AND INVENTORY VALUATION

At the end of each accounting period, most organisations will hold unsold items of production. The question that arises is how such inventory should be valued. Retail businesses value their inventory at the cost to the business, the costs charged by suppliers for goods sold to the business.

This is an acceptable method of inventory valuation in a retail trading business as this is the cost of the inventory to the business. However, international accounting standards (IAS 2) require organisations to value their inventory on an absorption costing basis, the direct production costs of a product plus a proportion of the indirect production overheads incurred in each product's manufacture. Therefore, it is important for organisations to be able to calculate the costs associated with each item of production both in terms of its direct costs and the proportion of indirect production overhead costs attributable to each unit of product.

In Anna's case, any unsold chairs at the end of the accounting period would be valued at £52.80 each, the direct costs of £45 per chair plus the attributable overheads of £7.80 allocated to each chair. These costs would be carried forward under the accruals basis of accounting to match against sales made in the following accounting period.

Give me an example 3.2 reproduces Rolls Royce Holdings plc's accounting policy on inventory valuation: note how direct materials, direct labour and overheads are included in the valuation of inventory.

GIVE ME AN EXAMPLE 3.2   Overheads included in inventory valuation

Inventories

Inventories and work in progress are valued at the lower of cost and net realisable value on a first-in, first-out basis. Cost comprises direct materials and, where applicable, direct labour costs and those overheads, including depreciation of property, plant and equipment, that have been incurred in bringing the inventories to their present location and condition.

Source: www.rolls-royce.com

NUMERICAL EXERCISES   Are you happy that you know how to calculate the value of inventory at the end of an accounting period? Go to the **online workbook** Numerical exercises 3.4 to make sure you can calculate an inventory valuation.

WHY IS THIS RELEVANT TO ME?   Inventory valuation

As an accounting professional you should understand that:

- Not all production will be sold by the end of an accounting period
- This inventory has to be valued to determine the profit for the accounting period and to match costs to products actually sold
- To comply with IAS 2 inventory should be valued at direct cost plus a proportion of the indirect production overheads incurred

Anna's business is simple, with just three indirect overhead costs to allocate to production units of one product. How would these indirect overhead costs be allocated in a more complex organisation in which more than one product is produced?

ABSORPTION COSTING: OVERHEAD ALLOCATION

In reality, manufacturing and service organisations have many indirect production overhead costs and many different products and services. Entities will seek to allocate these overheads to departments and then to products on the most appropriate basis. This will enable organisations to absorb these overheads into products or services on the way to determining a selling price for each product or service. Commonly, each overhead is determined in total and it is then apportioned to departments. The overhead total for each department is then divided up into an hourly rate on the basis of the number of labour hours or the number of machine hours used in each department (Figure 3.6).

Where labour is the key input to a production process, overheads will be allocated on the basis of the number of labour hours worked in a year. Service industries such as car maintenance, delivery services or catering will allocate overheads on the basis of labour hours as the provision

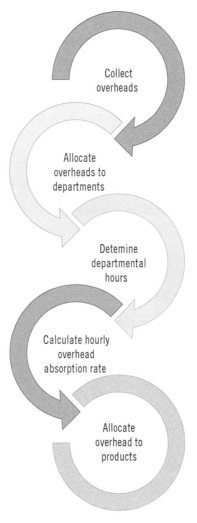

Figure 3.6 The overhead allocation process

3

of the service is based on employees rather than on machines. Where a production process is highly mechanised, as is the case in most manufacturing industries, then machine hours will be used as the basis for overhead allocation.

How will the number of hours of labour or machine time be calculated? Businesses will first determine their operating capacity, the number of hours that production employees work or the number of hours that production machinery operates during a year. Once capacity has been determined, then overheads will be totalled up and divided by the number of hours of capacity to give an hourly overhead absorption rate.

As an example of this technique, suppose that a car maintenance operation has 10 employees who each work a 40-hour week for 48 weeks of the year (allowing for four weeks of holidays for each employee). The labour hour capacity of the business in one week is 10 employees × 40 hours = 400 hours. The labour hour capacity of the business for the year is then 400 hours in one week × 48 working weeks = 19,200 hours. Annual overheads incurred in the car maintenance operation will be totalled up and this total divided by the 19,200 available hours in the year to determine an overhead recovery rate for each job that the operation quotes for. If the total overheads of the business come to £288,000, then the hourly allocation rate will be £288,000 ÷ 19,200 labour hours = £15 per hour. If a job is expected to take five hours, then an overhead cost of £15 × 5 hours = £75 will be added to the direct cost estimate for that job when the customer is quoted a price. Remember that direct costs plus overhead costs give the total cost of providing a service and will be used as a basis on which to determine a selling price that will give a profit on each job.

The car maintenance operation is a simple example. In more complex situations, the stages in overhead allocation will be to:

1. Determine each overhead cost from invoices and payments.
2. Allocate overhead costs to departments on the most appropriate basis.
3. Total up overhead costs for each department.
4. Determine a labour hour or machine hour absorption rate for departmental overheads.
5. Allocate overheads to products or services on the basis of labour or machine hours used in the production of each product or provision of each service.

Think about how steps 1–5 are applied in Example 3.8.

Information relating to the overheads (indirect costs) of the Picture Frame Company is presented in Table 3.3. You have been asked to allocate the costs to two departments, machining and finishing. The directors of the Picture Frame Company want to absorb overheads in each department into products on the basis of machine hours used in each department, as they consider that this basis will best reflect the way in which departmental overheads are incurred. The Picture Frame Company sells its products at absorption cost plus 20 per cent.

Table 3.3 The Picture Frame Company's annual overhead costs and machine hours

Annual Costs	Total £	Machining	Finishing
Rent	100,000	Floor area: 1,800 square metres	Floor area: 1,200 square metres
Business rates	25,000		
Depreciation	40,000	Machinery value: £160,000	Machinery value: £240,000
Heating	15,000	Departmental volume: 10,000 cubic metres	Departmental volume: 5,000 cubic metres
Directors' salaries	80,000	Percentage of directors' time spent in department: 37.5%	Percentage of directors' time spent in department: 62.5%
Machining department manager	29,000		
Finishing department manager	34,000		
Employee salaries	270,000	Number of employees in department: 9	Numbers of employees in department: 6
Repairs: machining	19,000		
Repairs: finishing	35,000		
Water rates	20,000	Departmental water usage: 1,800,000 litres	Departmental water usage: 1,200,000 litres
Lighting	18,000	Number of lights in department: 3,600	Number of lights in department: 1,800
Service department	50,000	Departmental usage: 20% of service department	Departmental usage: 80% of service department
Total hours	**Total hours**	**Machining**	**Finishing**
Machine hours	195,000	75,000	120,000

This mass of information might look daunting, but the application of common sense to how these overheads should be allocated to machining and finishing should enable you to determine the total overheads for each department. When allocating overheads, you should use any systematic basis that will result in a fair and equitable allocation of overheads to each department. Taking rent as an example in Table 3.3, the total floor area for the two departments is 3,000 square metres, 1,800 square metres in machining + 1,200 square metres in finishing. The total rent cost is £100,000 so £100,000 × 1,800/3,000 = £60,000 allocated to machining and 1,200/3,000 × £100,000 = £40,000 allocated to finishing.

Using the additional information on departmental usage of each particular production overhead cost and department specific details on particular production costs, overheads can be allocated to the machining and finishing departments as shown in Table 3.4.

Table 3.4 The Picture Frame Company's annual costs allocated to machining and finishing

Annual costs	Total £	Machining £	Finishing £	Notes
Rent	100,000	60,000	40,000	Total floor area: 3,000 sq metres, split both rent and rate costs 1,800:1,200
Business rates	25,000	15,000	10,000	Split on the basis of total floor area 1,800:1,200
Depreciation	40,000	16,000	24,000	Split according to machinery value, 160,000:240,000
Heating	15,000	10,000	5,000	Split according to volume heated, 10,000:5,000
Directors' salaries	80,000	30,000	50,000	£80,000 split according to usage, 37.5%:62.5%
Machining department manager	29,000	29,000	—	Actual departmental cost
Finishing department manager	34,000	—	34,000	Actual departmental cost
Employee salaries	270,000	162,000	108,000	£270,000 split 9:6 on the basis of the number of employees in each department
Repairs: machining	19,000	19,000	—	Actual departmental cost
Repairs: finishing	35,000	—	35,000	Actual departmental cost
Water rates	20,000	12,000	8,000	Split according to water usage, 1,800:1,200
Lighting	18,000	12,000	6,000	Split according to number of lights, 3,600:1,800
Service department	50,000	10,000	40,000	Split according to usage, 20%:80%
Totals	735,000	375,000	360,000	

SHOW ME HOW TO DO IT   Are you quite sure you understand how these allocations were calculated? View Video presentation 3.1 in the **online workbook** to see a practical demonstration to reinforce your understanding of how this overhead allocation between departments was carried out.

Now that overheads have been allocated to each department, we can work out an overhead absorption rate, the amount to be charged per hour of resource consumed within the department. As noted in Example 3.8, the directors have chosen to allocate overheads to products on the basis of machine hours as the most appropriate method of overhead allocation and absorption.

In the machining department, £5 of overhead will be allocated to products per machine hour (£375,000 ÷ 75,000 hours), while in finishing, products will absorb £3 of overhead per machine hour (£360,000 ÷ 120,000 hours).

Let us assume that the 50 × 60 centimetre gilt edged frame has a direct material, direct labour and direct expense cost of £56 and requires four hours of machining department time and eight hours of finishing department time. The total absorption cost for 50 × 60 centimetre gilt edged frames is then as follows:

	£
Direct material, direct labour and direct expense cost (prime cost)	56
Machining department overhead absorbed: 4 hours at £5/hour	20
Finishing department overhead absorbed: 8 hours at £3/hour	24
50 × 60 centimetre gilt edged frame total absorption cost	**100**

Selling price for 50 × 60 centimetre gilt edged frames will be £100 absorption cost × 120 per cent (100 per cent cost + 20 per cent of the absorption cost) = £120.

WHY IS THIS RELEVANT TO ME?   Overhead allocation, overhead allocation rates

As an accounting professional you will be expected to be able to:

- Allocate total overheads between different operating departments with a view to determining overhead allocation rates for each department

- Use overhead allocation rates to determine the overhead absorbed by particular products or services

- Recommend a selling price on the basis of the total absorption cost of a product or service

---

NUMERICAL EXERCISES   Are you convinced you could carry out this kind of overhead allocation exercise for yourself? Go to the **online workbook** Numerical exercises 3.5 to practise this technique.

Give me an example 3.3 illustrates the level of overhead allocation practices in businesses across the world.

GIVE ME AN EXAMPLE 3.3   The use of overhead allocation in business

The July 2009 CIMA report, *Management accounting tools for today and tomorrow*, surveyed the current and intended usage by business of more than 100 management accounting and related tools based on a questionnaire completed by 439 respondents from across the globe. The 7th most commonly used technique in practice was overhead allocation. When used as an operational tool, overhead allocation was undertaken by 66 per cent of respondents, the second most popular operational tool in use behind variance analysis on 73 per cent. The survey discovered that the larger the organisation, the more likely it was that overhead allocation would be in use in determining product cost.

Source: www.cimaglobal.com

3

ALLOCATING SERVICE DEPARTMENT OVERHEADS

Service departments do not produce products or make sales of services to outside parties, but they are an essential support activity in many business operations. Service department costs are allocated to production departments on the basis of each department's usage of each service department. In this way, service department costs are allocated to products and thus built into product selling prices to enable all costs incurred to be recovered through sales of products and services. In the example of the Picture Frame Company, the service department's overheads were allocated on the basis of usage by the two departments, machining and finishing. But what happens in cases where one service department provides services to another service department? In situations such as this, costs are apportioned between production departments and service departments until all the overheads have been allocated. Consider how this approach works in Example 3.9.

Alpha Manufacturing has three production departments, welding, sanding and painting, and three service departments, parts, set up and repairs. The costs and overheads of the six departments together with the usage made of each of the service departments by the production and service departments are given in Table 3.5.

Table 3.5 Alpha Manufacturing's production and service department costs and overheads and service department usage percentages

	Production departments			Service departments		
	Welding	Sanding	Painting	Parts	Set up	Repairs
Costs and overheads	£94,200	£86,200	£124,200	£40,000	£24,000	£26,400
Percentage usage of parts	25%	30%	25%		20%	
Percentage usage of set up	20%	40%	10%			30%
Percentage usage of repairs	40%	25%	35%			

You are required to reallocate the overheads for the three service departments to the welding, sanding and painting departments to determine the total costs and overheads for each of the three production departments.

Method

The parts department's overheads of £40,000 will be allocated to each of the three production departments in the proportions indicated in Table 3.5 (25 per cent to welding, 30 per cent to sanding and 25 per cent to painting) and then 20 per cent of the £40,000 overheads will be allocated to the set up department. This will now give overheads in the set up department of £24,000 + (£40,000 × 20 per cent) = £32,000. The set up department's new overheads of £32,000 will now be allocated in the proportions given in the question to the production departments (20 per cent to welding, 40 per cent to sanding and 10 per cent to painting) while

30 per cent of the set up department's overheads will be allocated to the repairs department. The repairs department now has overheads of £26,400 + (£32,000 × 30 per cent) = £36,000 to allocate to each of the three production departments in the proportions 40 per cent to welding, 25 per cent to sanding and 35 per cent to painting.

These calculations are shown in Table 3.6.

All the service department costs and overheads have now been reallocated to production departments. The overhead recovery rates can be determined on the basis of labour or machine hours in those production departments and overheads allocated to products produced in the welding, sanding and painting departments.

Table 3.6 Alpha Manufacturing's service department overheads reallocated to production departments

| | Production departments | | | Service departments | | |
| | Welding | Sanding | Painting | Parts | Set up | Repairs |
	£	£	£	£	£	£
Costs and overheads	94,200	86,200	124,200	40,000	24,000	26,400
Parts costs reallocated	10,000	12,000	10,000	(40,000)	8,000	—
Set up costs reallocated	6,400	12,800	3,200	—	(32,000)	9,600
Repairs costs reallocated	14,400	9,000	12,600	—	—	(36,000)
Total costs and overheads	125,000	120,000	150,000	—	—	—

SHOW ME HOW TO DO IT   Are you sure that you understand how service department overheads are reallocated to production departments? View Video presentation 3.2 in the **online workbook** to see a practical demonstration of how this reallocation between service and production departments is carried out.

WHY IS THIS RELEVANT TO ME? ABSORPTION COSTING: overhead allocation, allocating service department overheads

As an accounting professional you will be expected to:

• Understand how costs relating to non-production service departments are allocated to production departments

• Appreciate that this reallocation process is necessary to ensure that all production overhead costs are absorbed into products and services to provide a solid basis on which to determine selling prices

NUMERICAL EXERCISES   Are you confident you could carry out this kind of overhead reallocation exercise for yourself? Go to the **online workbook** Numerical exercises 3.6 to practise this technique.

3

ADMINISTRATION OVERHEADS, MARKETING OVERHEADS AND FINANCE OVERHEADS: PERIOD COSTS

So far, we have considered the costs of production, direct and indirect, fixed and variable. However, all business entities incur overhead costs through administration activities, marketing activities and the costs of financing their operations.

It is possible that marketing activities will incur certain costs that vary in line with sales: such costs might be the commission paid to sales representatives to reward them for the sales they generate, as higher sales would incur higher commission. However, most marketing costs such as advertising, brochures, product catalogues, the salaries of marketing staff, the costs of running delivery vehicles and of running sales representatives' cars will all count as fixed costs.

Administration, marketing and financing fixed costs are known as period costs and they relate only to the period in which they are incurred. Therefore, while these costs are not taken into account in the valuation of inventory, it is still important to set the production levels and selling prices of products and services in order to cover these costs. Thus, these additional period costs will be built into the cost price of products in the same way as indirect production costs are allocated to products.

GO BACK OVER THIS AGAIN!   An example of a cost card for a product that includes all costs and the determination of a selling price is presented in Exercises 3.4 in the **online workbook**.

PROBLEMS WITH ABSORPTION COSTING

Absorption costing seems like an easy and effective way in which to build costs into products to determine first the total cost of the product and then its selling price. However, absorption costing has come in for criticism in recent years. The technique was originally developed as a way to cost products during the early part of the twentieth century. Each factory would turn out products that were all alike for undiscerning customers. Production runs were long and it was easy to spread fixed overheads over many products using the traditional absorption costing technique.

But times have changed. Modern manufacturers are no longer suppliers of goods to a passive market that accepts mass produced products lacking any individual distinction. Today's producers work assiduously to meet and fulfil customer demands and expectations. Production runs are now very short and products are individualised and tailored to each customer's specific requirements. Markets are not easily satisfied: customers have very specific requirements and, if their regular supplier is unable to meet those requirements, there are plenty of other businesses that will. Costs are thus no longer incurred in a steady, easy to allocate way. Lots of different organisational activities give rise to costs as businesses seek to fulfil each order's very specific requirements. As a result, the simplistic allocation of costs to particular products on an absorption costing basis may no longer be the most appropriate method in which to determine a product's total costs. A different approach has to be found to allocate overheads to products so that a more accurate cost and a more competitive selling price for each product can be determined.

Commentators have criticised absorption costing on the following grounds:

- The allocation of costs to products on either a labour or machine hour basis is too simplistic and does not reflect the actual costs incurred in the provision of specific goods and services.
- Traditional absorption costing fails to recognise the demands made by particular products on an entity's resources.
- Overheads arise not in proportion to direct labour and machine hours but as a result of the range and complexity of products and services offered.
- Selling prices calculated on the basis of absorption costs may be wrong in one of two ways:
  - overhead is either underallocated to products that consume more activities resulting in underpricing of these products, or
  - overhead is overallocated to products consuming lower levels of activity and so overprices these products.
- As a result of these misallocations, some products are subsidised by others rather than making a profit in their own right.

WHY IS THIS RELEVANT TO ME?   Problems with absorption costing

To enable you as an accounting professional to appreciate that traditional absorption costing:

- Is not the only way in which costs can be allocated to products
- May not provide accurate product or selling prices
- May not be particularly well suited to allocating overhead costs to products in modern manufacturing environments

GO BACK OVER THIS AGAIN!   Are you confident that you understand the limitations of traditional absorption costing? Go to the **online workbook** Exercises 3.5 to make sure you appreciate these shortcomings.

SUMMARY OF KEY CONCEPTS   Are you quite sure that you can state the limitations of traditional absorption costing? Go to the **online workbook** to take a look at Summary of key concepts 3.5 to reinforce your knowledge.

OVERHEAD ALLOCATION: ACTIVITY-BASED COSTING

As we have seen, the aim of costing is to allocate costs to products and services to enable businesses to determine selling prices for those goods and services so that entities generate profits. Absorption costing works well in the case of mass produced, indistinguishable products, but modern manufacturing approaches require a more sophisticated cost allocation mechanism. Activity-based costing has been put forward as a way of providing this more sophisticated, more precise method of costing products and services to enable businesses to produce more accurate costs and hence more realistic selling prices.

3

How does activity-based costing work?

Traditional absorption costing adds together all the indirect production overheads incurred by a business and then allocates them across products on the basis of the labour or machine hours. Activity-based costing recognises that activities cause costs: the more activity that is undertaken, the higher the cost incurred. Under activity-based costing, costs are allocated to products on the basis of activities consumed: the more activities that are associated with a particular product, the more overhead is allocated to that product and so the higher its cost and selling price will be.

Activity-based costing allocates overheads to products using the following two-step approach.

Step 1: establish cost pools

- Rather than lumping all indirect production overheads into cost centres (departments), activity-based costs are allocated to cost pools.
- Cost pools reflect different activities incurred in the production of goods and services.
- Examples of cost pools might be design costs, set up costs, quality control costs, material ordering costs and production monitoring costs.
- The number of cost pools will depend upon the complexity or simplicity of an entity's operations: the more complex the operations, the more cost pools there will be.

Step 2: allocate costs to products and services

- Once cost pools have been established, a systematic basis on which to allocate those costs to products and services has to be found.
- The most logical method of allocating costs is on the basis of cost drivers: cost drivers reflect the level of activity associated with each cost pool.
- For example, if there were 50 machine set ups in a year, then the total cost in the machine set ups cost pool would be divided by 50 to give the cost per machine set up.
- Costs in the cost pools are then allocated to products on the basis of the activities consumed by those products. In our set up costs example, if a product used five machine set ups in the year, then the cost for five machine set ups would be allocated to that product.
- Where product costs turn out to be very high, management can take steps to reduce the activities consumed by those products as a way to lower costs and improve price competitiveness.

It is important to remember that activity-based costing is used to allocate overhead costs to products. Direct costs are still allocated to products in the usual way. Any costs directly linked to a product are still allocated to and form part of the prime cost of that product.

WHY IS THIS RELEVANT TO ME?   Activity-based costing

To enable you as an accounting professional to:

- Understand how activity-based costing works
- Appreciate the terminology used in activity-based costing and what each term means

GO BACK OVER THIS AGAIN! Are you sure that you understand the differences between traditional absorption costing and activity-based costing? Go to the **online workbook** Exercises 3.6 to make sure you can distinguish between these two methods of overhead allocation.

SUMMARY OF KEY CONCEPTS Do you think you can state the steps involved in activity-based costing? Go to the **online workbook** to take a look at Summary of key concepts 3.6 to reinforce your knowledge of these steps.

3

Having dealt with the theory and logic behind activity-based costing, let's look now at Example 3.10 to see how overheads allocated under both the traditional absorption costing and activity-based costing methods produce different results.

EXAMPLE 3.10

Cookers Limited assembles microwave ovens and traditional electric cookers from parts produced by various suppliers. The following information relates to the costs and production of the two products:

	Microwave ovens	Electric cookers
Direct materials	£30	£52
Direct labour	£24	£48
Direct labour hours	3	7
Annual production in units	5,000	15,000
Annual number of set ups	15	30
Number of parts suppliers	14	6

Overheads	£
Output related overheads	160,000
Quality control	60,000
Set up related overheads	90,000
Supplier related overheads	50,000
Total overheads	**360,000**

The directors of Cookers Limited have traditionally allocated overhead costs to the two products on an absorption costing basis based on total labour hours. They have heard of activity-based costing and are wondering whether this would make a difference to the costing of their products. Selling prices for the company's two products are set at cost plus 25 per cent, rounded to the nearest whole £.

Absorption costing

On an absorption costing basis, the first task will be to determine the total labour hours as the basis on which to allocate overheads: 5,000 microwaves each take three hours while 15,000 cookers each take seven hours of labour time to produce. Total labour hours are thus $3 \times 5,000 + 7 \times 15,000 = 120,000$ hours. The overhead absorption cost per labour hour is thus £360,000 ÷ 120,000 labour hours = £3 per labour hour.

Using this absorption cost rate gives us the following product costs on a traditional overhead absorption basis:

	Microwave ovens £	Electric cookers £
Direct materials	30	52
Direct labour	24	48
Production overhead: 3 × £3/7 × £3	9	21
Total cost	63	121
Selling price (cost + 25%, rounded)	**79**	**151**

Activity-based costing

In this question, our overhead costs have already been allocated to cost pools for output, quality control, set up and supplier related overheads. In order to allocate the costs in these cost pools to products, we now need to determine the cost drivers of each particular overhead cost pool.

Output related and quality control overhead costs will most logically be driven by the number of production units. The more of a particular product that is produced, the more that product drives those particular categories of overhead costs as more output is achieved and more quality control inspections take place.

Production units total up to 20,000 units (5,000 microwaves + 15,000 electric cookers) so the output related overhead per unit of production is £8 (£160,000 ÷ 20,000 units of production). Here, 15,000 × £8 = £120,000 output related overhead will be allocated to electric cookers and 5,000 × £8 = £40,000 will be allocated to microwaves.

Similarly, quality control costs are allocated over 20,000 units of production. The quality control overhead per unit of production is £3 (£60,000 ÷ 20,000 units of production). In this case £45,000 of quality control costs will be allocated to electric cookers (15,000 × £3) and £15,000 to microwaves (5,000 × £3).

The unit cost for set up overheads will be based upon the number of set ups consumed by each product. Microwaves have 15 set ups in the year and electric cookers have 30, so the total set up related overhead of £90,000 is divided by 45 (15 + 30) set ups to determine the cost per set up of £2,000. Thus, 15 × £2,000 = £30,000 set up related costs are allocated to microwaves and 30 × £2,000 = £60,000 set up costs are allocated to electric cookers.

In the same way, supplier related overheads will be driven by the number of suppliers for each product. The more suppliers of parts there are for a particular product, the more overhead cost will be incurred in ordering, handling and processing those parts from the different suppliers. There are 14 parts suppliers for microwaves and six for electric cookers, a total of 20 suppliers. The total supplier related overhead of £50,000 is divided by 20 to determine the cost per supplier of £2,500 and then 14 × £2,500 = £35,000 of supplier related costs allocated to microwaves and 6 × £2,500 = £15,000 supplier related costs allocated to electric cookers.

Summarising the above calculations, the total overhead cost allocated to each product is as follows:

Overhead	Allocation basis	Unit cost	Microwave ovens	Electric cookers
		£	£	£
Output related	Production	8	40,000	120,000
Quality control	Production	3	15,000	45,000
Set up related	Set ups	2,000	30,000	60,000
Supplier related	Number of parts suppliers	2,500	35,000	15,000
			120,000	240,000

These total overhead costs are now divided by the number of units of production and allocated to product costs to determine the total cost price of each product. The 5,000 microwaves drive £120,000 of related costs, so £24 is added to the cost of each microwave (£120,000 ÷ 5,000); £240,000 of overhead cost is driven by electric cookers, so £240,000 ÷ 15,000 = £16 is added as the unit overhead to the cost of electric cookers. These overhead allocation rates now give the following costs and selling prices.

	Microwave ovens £	Electric cookers £
Direct materials	30	52
Direct labour	24	48
Production overhead	24	16
Total cost	78	116
Selling price (cost + 25%, rounded)	**98**	**145**

As the above calculations demonstrate, overheads have been underallocated to microwaves and overallocated to electric cookers under the traditional absorption costing approach. Under activity-based costing, microwaves carry a much greater load of overhead cost compared with electric cookers and should sell for a much higher price. Once management are aware of this overhead cost burden attaching to microwaves, they can begin to think about reducing these costs. Most obviously, they should start by sourcing parts for microwaves from fewer suppliers to reduce the supplier related overheads allocated to this product and so lower the cost and selling price.

WHY IS THIS RELEVANT TO ME?   Traditional absorption costing v. activity-based costing overhead allocation

To enable you as an accounting professional to:

• Allocate overheads to products using both absorption costing and activity-based costing

• Make recommendations for ways in which product costs could be lowered to improve profitability and make product pricing more competitive

> **SHOW ME HOW TO DO IT**   Did you follow the overhead allocation process using the activity-based costing methodology? View Video presentation 3.3 in the **online workbook** to see a practical demonstration of how this allocation of overheads was carried out.

> **NUMERICAL EXERCISES**   Do you think you can allocate overheads using the activity-based costing methodology? Go to the **online workbook** and complete Numerical exercises 3.7 to test out your ability to apply your knowledge to activity-based costing problems.

What advantages does activity-based costing bring in practice? Give me an example 3.4 provides a summary of a case study that illustrates the benefits of adopting an activity-based costing approach to product costing.

> **GIVE ME AN EXAMPLE 3.4   The practical benefits of implementing activity-based costing**
>
> Dr Lana Yan Jun Liu of the University of Newcastle in the UK and Professor Fei Pan of the Shanghai University of Finance and Economics in China studied the implementation of activity-based costing (ABC) at Xu Ji Electric Co. Ltd, a large Chinese manufacturing company (*Activity Based Costing in China: Research executive summary series*, vol. 7(13), 2011, CIMA). An ABC pilot was implemented in one of the main production divisions in December 2001, with two further attempts to expand the use of ABC in a subsidiary and in its sales functions in 2005 and 2008. The subsidiary ran trials with the system in 2009 and then in 2010 reported a record an-
>
> nual sales increase of 50 per cent over 2009 together with a net profit margin increase of 13 per cent. Following the introduction and roll out of the ABC system, management expressed confidence in the accuracy of the company's product costs while the marketing department was able to compete more quickly and more effectively in its market as quotes could now be given instantly. The cost information presented by the new system made staff much more aware of cost savings and the ways in which to achieve them while top management were able to use the ABC information to exercise informed control over sales expenses.
>
> Source: www.cimaglobal.com

THE LIMITATIONS AND ASSUMPTIONS OF COSTING

So far, we have taken it for granted in this chapter that fixed and variable costs are easily identifiable and that they behave in exactly the way we have described. Thus, it has been stated that variable costs vary directly in line with production and that fixed costs for a period (usually one year) are fixed and do not vary at all in that period. However, as we shall see, these assumptions should be challenged and it is important to understand the limitations of costing analysis when you are considering what price to charge for a product or service.

Assumption 1: fixed costs are fixed

In all of our examples so far we have assumed that fixed costs will remain at the same level for all levels of production over that period. However, this might not be the case. Once a certain level of

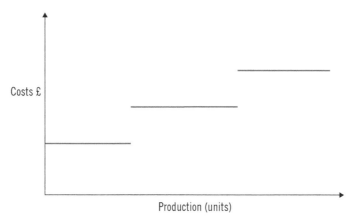

Figure 3.7 Stepped fixed costs behaviour

production is reached, additional fixed costs might have to be incurred to cope with the increase in capacity. Thus, once Anna's production reaches, say, 2,000 chairs in a year, she might have to rent additional workshop space in which to increase production to more than 2,000 chairs. This would entail more rent, more business rates and more heating and lighting costs causing her fixed costs to jump when production reaches 2,001 units. This increased level of fixed costs would stay the same until production reached 4,000 chairs, at which point Anna would need to rent even more workshop space to produce 4,001 chairs or more. Fixed costs thus rise in steps, staying the same up to a certain level of production and then rising to a new level once the limit of production capacity is reached.

Fixed costs might thus behave in a stepped fashion as shown in Figure 3.7. In this figure, costs remain fixed for a given range of production and then they rise to a new level once the original range of production is exceeded, remaining steady over the next range of production. Once this increased range of production is exceeded, the fixed costs rise again. Thus, it might not be true to say that fixed costs remain fixed for a given period of time; they might only be fixed for a given range of production.

GO BACK OVER THIS AGAIN!   Are you certain you understand how fixed costs might rise in steps? Visit the **online workbook** and work through Exercises 3.7 to see how fixed costs will rise in steps as production increases.

Assumption 2: variable costs remain the same for all units of production

Our analysis in this chapter has been based on the assumption that variable costs remain the same for all units of production. A moment's thought should enable you to see that this assumption will probably not be true in the real world. Increased purchases of materials from suppliers will earn quantity or bulk discounts from those suppliers. The higher the level of direct material purchases, the bigger the discounts and so the lower the average price of those materials will become.

Similarly, we have assumed that the unit cost of labour for each item produced will remain constant. However, this assumption, too, will not hold in the real world as increased productivity will earn productivity bonuses for employees, thereby pushing up the average cost of each unit of production.

GO BACK OVER THIS AGAIN!   Are you sure you understand how bulk discounts and productivity bonuses might affect the variable cost of materials and labour per unit of production? Try Exercises 3.8 in the **online workbook** to see how variable costs can change at different levels of production.

In situations in which production facilities use materials that fluctuate in price, such as metals and oil, the price of these direct materials can rise and fall during an accounting period. This makes forecasting very difficult but, again, it illustrates our point that variable costs will not necessarily remain the same for all units of production during an accounting period.

It is thus quite likely that the variable costs of production will not behave in the truly linear fashion we have assumed and that variable costs will not be represented by a sloping line of a perfectly even gradient as shown in Figures 3.1 and 3.3.

Assumption 3: costs can be determined with the required precision

An underlying assumption of all the discussions thus far has been that the costs of products and of activities in making those products can be determined with the necessary degree of accuracy in order to produce accurate selling prices. This is highly unlikely in practice as there are often under or over estimations of the time it will take to complete a given task, of the cost of materials used in the production of goods and of the amount of direct expenses used to make products. Material costs will vary in line with market prices or become cheaper or more expensive depending on the current supply of those materials to the market. Labour may become more expensive if the required skills are in short supply and so push up the direct labour cost of production.

In the same way, your estimate of how quickly you expected to work through this chapter and the online workbook may have proved completely wrong. Whatever your original estimate, it is likely to have been rather different from the actual time taken. Similarly, you may over or under estimate how much you will spend on a night out with your friends; again, though you have been out with them many times before, your expectations of what each evening out will cost will be very different from the costs in reality.

Cost accountants in industry may not achieve complete accuracy in their calculations and they may under or over estimate the cost of direct materials, the time that it will take direct labour to produce each unit of production and the overheads that will be incurred in a given period. Absolute accuracy is not going to be achieved and the best that can be done is a reasonably close estimate. As we shall see in Chapter 5, standard costing makes assumptions about what the costs of production should be and then uses variance analysis to explain the differences between what costs and income were expected to be and what they turned out to be.

WHY IS THIS RELEVANT TO ME?   The limitations and assumptions of costing

As an accounting professional you should:

- Appreciate that product costing is not an exact science
- Understand the bases of product costing and how these give rise to its limitations
- Be equipped with the tools to critique solutions that are produced by product costing analysis in a real world context

CHAPTER SUMMARY

You should now have learnt that:

- Direct costs are those costs directly attributable to products or services
- Direct costs of production may be variable or fixed
- Variable costs are assumed to vary directly in line with levels of activity
- Fixed costs are assumed to be fixed for a given period of time
- Product and service costing is used by business organisations in making pricing decisions
- A cost card for a product is drawn up by splitting product costs into direct and indirect production costs
- Indirect production costs (overheads) are apportioned to departments to determine total overhead costs for each production department
- Overhead recovery rates for products are calculated on the basis of total departmental overheads and expected levels of production
- Service department overheads are reapportioned to production departments as part of each production department's total overheads
- Simple graphs can be drawn up to illustrate fixed, variable and total cost behaviour in a business context
- Using traditional absorption costing to allocate overhead costs to products may no longer be relevant in modern manufacturing environments and may result in the mispricing of products
- Activity-based costing allocates overhead costs to products on the basis of resources consumed by each product
- Costing is based on the assumptions that:
    - Fixed costs are and remain fixed for a given period of time or range of production
    - Variable costs remain the same for all units of production
    - Costs can be determined with the required precision

QUICK REVISION   Test your knowledge with the online flashcards in Summary of key concepts and attempt the Multiple choice questions, all in the **online workbook**.

END-OF-CHAPTER QUESTIONS

Solutions to these questions can be found in the **online workbook**.

❯ DEVELOP YOUR UNDERSTANDING

❯Question 3.1

Mantinea Limited manufactures various kitchenware products. The following direct costs are incurred in producing a batch of 2,000 food processors.

	£
Materials	22,500
Direct labour	16,500
Direct expenses	13,000

The factory overheads for the year are £3,000,000. Total machine hours for the year are 750,000 and each processor takes 4.5 hours of machine time to produce. The selling price of food processors is total absorption cost plus 50 per cent.

Required

Calculate the total absorption cost of one food processor together with the selling price for each food processor produced by Mantinea Limited.

❯Question 3.2

Printers Limited has been asked by the local university press to quote for the printing of a new book. The print run will be for 2,000 books of 400 pages each. The costing records of Printers Limited contain the following information:

- Paper is bought from a local supplier. The local supplier provides paper at a price of 2,500 sheets for £9.
- Printing ink costs £57.50 per gallon, which is sufficient to print 20,000 pages.
- Covers for each book will be bought in at a cost of 66 pence for each book.
- Finishing costs per book are 50 pence.
- Production workers are paid an hourly rate of £12.50. The costing records show that a print run of 2,000 books would require 200 hours of production labour time.
- Printers' total production overheads for the year are £500,000 and the normal production level of the business is 50 million pages per annum.
- Printers Limited's pricing policy is to set selling price at total absorption cost plus 25 per cent.

Required

Calculate the price that Printers Limited should charge the local university press for the print run of 2,000 books.

>> TAKE IT FURTHER

>> Question 3.3

Applokia Limited is a manufacturer of smart phones. The company has the following costs for the month of September:

	£000
Factory rent	100
Factory manager's salary	38
Administration salaries	85
Marketing costs*	50
Plastic smart phone covers	250
Quality control staff salaries	75
Production line workers' salaries*	500
Chip assemblies for smart phones produced	1,498
Administration office rent	25
Marketing office rent	20
Factory rates	47
Power for production machinery	50
Factory lighting and heating	43
Administration lighting and heating	5
Marketing lighting and heating	4
Marketing department salaries	51
Batteries	242
Production machinery depreciation*	37

*These costs remain the same no matter how many or how few smart phones are produced and sold in the month.

Required

(a) For the above costs, state whether they are:
- Fixed or variable.
- Direct production costs, production overheads or period costs.

(b) Draw up a table that summarises the above costs into prime cost, production cost and total cost.

(c) If Applokia produces 130,000 smart phones in a month and selling price is total cost + 25 per cent, calculate the selling price for each smart phone produced in September.

(d) If rival companies are selling similar products for £27, what margin will Applokia make on its costs per smart phone if it sells its smart phones at the same price as its rivals?

>> Question 3.4

Folly Limited produces novelty products. The products are produced on machines in the manufacturing department and they are then hand painted and finished in the finishing department. Folly Limited has forecast the following indirect production overheads for the year ended 31 January 2020:

	£000
Machinery maintenance staff salaries (manufacturing department)	100
Employees' salaries (painting and finishing department)	300
Employers' national insurance contributions for both departments	40
Rent and rates	60
Heating (the manufacturing department is not heated)	25
Lighting	25
Machinery depreciation	75
Canteen expenses*	56
Electricity for machinery	50
Insurance: machinery	25

*The canteen is in a separate building. The canteen rent, rates, heating, lighting, insurance and staff costs are all included in the figure for canteen expenses.

The manufacturing department has a capacity of 96,000 machine hours and 2,000 labour hours. The painting and finishing department has a capacity of 4,000 machine hours and 80,000 labour hours.

Additional information:

Recovery/absorption bases	Manufacturing	Painting and finishing
Area (square metres)	4,800	1,200
Value of machinery	£360,000	£15,000
Number of employees	5	15

Required

(a) Using the information provided, calculate the total production overheads to be allocated to the manufacturing and painting and finishing departments.

(b) Calculate the most appropriate overhead recovery/absorption rate for the manufacturing and painting and finishing departments and justify your choice of machine or labour hours as an absorption basis for the two departments.

(c) Using the rates you have calculated in (b), calculate the cost of the following job:

Novelty Christmas pixies: 5,000 units	
Direct materials and packaging	£10,000
Direct labour	£1,000
Machine time: manufacturing department	500 hours
Labour time: manufacturing department	5 hours
Machine time: painting and finishing department	10 hours
Labour time: painting and finishing department	1,000 hours

>> Question 3.5

Metal Bashers Limited produces steel fabrications for the construction industry. Steel girders and supports are cut to size and welded in the welding department and then painted in the paint shop before proceeding to the finishing department. Details of the overheads incurred by the three production departments are given below along with information on the two additional departments, the canteen and the service department. The canteen is used by all the employees of Metal Bashers Limited but the canteen staff are too busy to make use of the canteen facilities themselves. The service department repairs and cleans the machinery used in the three production departments. External catering equipment maintenance contractors service the canteen equipment.

	Welding	Painting	Finishing	Canteen	Service
Overheads	£100,000	£75,000	£43,000	£60,000	£42,000
Number of employees	15	5	6	2	4
Percentage usage of service department	40%	30%	30%		
Department labour hours	30,000	12,500	10,000		

Metal Bashers Limited is currently quoting for Job No 12359 which will require £1,500 of direct material, £2,000 of direct labour and £500 of direct expenses. It is estimated that job 12359 will use 120 hours of labour in the welding department, 50 hours in the painting department and 25 hours in the finishing department. Overheads are absorbed into jobs on the basis of direct labour hours in each department. The selling price for jobs is the total production cost of each job plus 40 per cent of cost.

Required

(a) Calculate overhead recovery rates for the welding, painting and finishing departments.

(b) Calculate the production cost and selling price of job 12359.

>> Question 3.6

Playthings Limited produces two dolls houses, the standard and the deluxe. The direct costs and overhead information relating to these two dolls houses are listed below.

	Standard	Deluxe
Direct materials	£50	£76
Direct labour	£30	£42
Labour hours	5	7
Annual production	2,500	1,000
Direct materials orders	400	600
Employees	5	10
Machine hours	10,000	5,000
Annual number of set ups	15	35

Overheads

	£
Machining	45,000
Factory supervisor	30,000
Set up related overheads	50,000
Purchasing department costs	25,000
Total overheads	**150,000**

3

Playthings currently absorb their total overheads into their dolls houses on the basis of machine hours. The selling price of dolls houses is total production cost plus 50 per cent. The directors are concerned about a build-up in the warehouse of standard dolls houses. Deluxe models are still selling well and the current price charged by Playthings is the most competitive in the market: their nearest rivals are selling the same type of dolls house for £300. Investigations have shown that competitors are selling comparable standard dolls houses for £165. You have been asked for your advice on the current costing system at Playthings and whether you can suggest a better way in which to allocate overheads to products together with any other suggestions you are able to provide.

Required

(a) Calculate the current total absorption cost and selling price for standard and deluxe dolls houses based on the absorption of total overheads on a machine hour basis.

(b) Determine suitable cost drivers for the four overhead cost pools.

(c) Calculate the activity-based cost of standard and deluxe dolls houses and determine the selling price of each based on activity-based cost plus 50 per cent.

(d) Given your results in (a), advise the directors on how they might reduce the cost of deluxe dolls houses in order to compete more effectively in the market.

RELEVANT COSTS, MARGINAL COSTING AND SHORT-TERM DECISION MAKING

4

LEARNING OUTCOMES

Once you have read this chapter and worked through the questions and examples in both this chapter and the online workbook, you should be able to:

- Define contribution

- Use the distinction between fixed and variable costs to determine the costs that are relevant and those that are irrelevant in making short-term decisions

- Understand how analysis of contribution is used to make short-term decisions

- Undertake break-even analysis and determine the margin of safety

- Use marginal costing and contribution analysis to make a range of decisions aimed at maximising short-term profitability

- Understand the assumptions upon which marginal costing analysis is based

INTRODUCTION

The previous chapter discussed the various types of costs that organisations incur in their activities. These costs can be variable or fixed and can be categorised as direct costs of production, indirect costs of production and period costs. We also saw how fixed production overheads are absorbed into products to enable organisations to make pricing decisions to set the selling price at the right level so that an overall profit is generated from operations.

> **SUMMARY OF KEY CONCEPTS**   Are you a little unsure about the terminology here? Go to the **online workbook** to revisit Summary of key concepts 3.1, 3.2 and 3.3 to revise direct, variable and marginal costs.

In this chapter, we will expand the analysis of costs to enable us to use this costing information in making decisions that will be valid in the short term (a period of one year or less). This analysis will be used to show which costs are relevant in short-term decision-making situations and which costs are not. In making these decisions, the profitability of the organisation will always be uppermost in our minds and we will be seeking to maximise the profits that can be made.

DECISION MAKING: NOT JUST SELLING PRICE

Our focus in Chapter 3 was on determining a product's costs to make just one decision: what our selling price should be to enable us to cover all our expenses and make a profit. However, there are other decisions that entities need to make. For example:

- What minimum level of production and sales is required to ensure that all costs are covered and that losses are not incurred?
- What level of production would be required to make a certain target profit?
- How profitable will our business be if the economy takes a downturn and sales and profits fall?
- If we lowered our selling price as a marketing strategy, would we make more or less profit?
- Will orders from new customers be profitable if these customers are looking to buy our products at a price lower than our usual selling price?
- Is it more profitable to make components for our products ourselves or to buy those components in the open market?
- If there are several products that could be made, but there are only sufficient resources to make some of them, which product(s) should be made in order to maximise the short-term profits of the organisation?

The first step on the road to using costing to help us make these additional decisions is to look at the calculation and definition of contribution, the surplus that arises from the production and sale of one unit of product or service. As we shall see, contribution is a highly relevant consideration in the decision-making process and is a crucial step in determining those costs that are relevant and those costs that are irrelevant in a short-term decision-making context.

CONTRIBUTION

Figure 4.1 The calculation of contribution per unit

We noted in the last chapter that fixed costs are assumed to be fixed over a given period of time and that variable costs vary with production or service delivery. Variable costs thus rise and fall directly in line with rises and falls in production as more or fewer goods or services are produced. However, no matter what the level of production is, fixed costs remain the same. Contribution for one unit of production and sales is the selling price less the variable costs of production (Figure 4.1). Our first practical example in this chapter is presented in Example 4.1.

EXAMPLE 4.1

Taking the example of Anna from Chapter 3 (Example 3.6), the contribution from selling one dining chair is given as follows:

	£	£
Selling price for one dining chair		85.00
Materials (wood, glue, screws and sandpaper) for one chair	20.00	
Direct labour cost to produce one chair	25.00	
Total variable cost for one chair		45.00
Selling price per unit − variable costs per unit = contribution per unit		**40.00**

So, with a selling price of £85 and a total variable cost of £45, Anna is making £40 contribution from each dining chair that she sells. Contribution is very similar to gross profit, the selling price less the directly attributable costs of making each sale.

WHY IS THIS RELEVANT TO ME?   Contribution

- To provide you as an accounting professional with knowledge of the basic building blocks used in marginal cost decision making
- As an accounting professional, you will need to appreciate that contribution = selling price − the variable costs of production/service provision

SUMMARY OF KEY CONCEPTS   Go to the **online workbook** to use Summary of key concepts 4.1 to remind yourself of how contribution is calculated throughout your reading of this chapter.

MARGINAL V. ABSORPTION COSTING

But hold on, you might say. In Chapter 3, we used absorption costing and a production level of 1,000 dining chairs per annum to work out the total cost of one chair at £52.80, which would give a profit per chair of £85 − £52.80 = £32.20. This is different from the analysis undertaken above. Why is this?

The answer to this question lies in the distinction between fixed and variable costs. The variable costs rise and fall directly in line with production whereas the fixed costs do not. Remember that Anna set her production level at 1,000 chairs per annum and absorbed her fixed costs into each chair on this basis to enable her to set a selling price. However, the rate at which Anna absorbed her fixed costs into her production was based on a purely arbitrary assumption that production would be 1,000 chairs in a year. To illustrate the effect that this decision has had on the absorption cost of one chair, consider the following alternative scenarios in Example 4.2.

EXAMPLE 4.2

Anna's total fixed cost of £7,800 means that each of the 1,000 chairs was allocated a fixed cost element of £7,800 ÷ 1,000 chairs = £7.80. Anna could just as easily have set her production level at 2,000 dining chairs per annum and she would then have absorbed her fixed costs into production at the rate of £7,800 ÷ 2,000 chairs = £3.90 per chair. Alternatively, Anna might have been less optimistic about the level of production her workshop could achieve and set her expected production level at 500 chairs. In this case, her fixed costs would have been absorbed into production at the rate of £7,800 ÷ 500 chairs = £15.60 per chair.

The total fixed costs do not change, but the rate at which they are absorbed into the cost of products changes depending on the assumptions made about the normal level of production. The absorption rate adopted is a decision for management, a decision that is a matter of judgement completely dependent upon management's expectations of what represents a normal level of production over a given period of time.

Have a look now at Example 4.3. What are the differences between the two production and sales scenarios in this example? The fixed costs have not changed, but have remained the same for both the original and the increased levels of production and sales. Sales, however, have increased by the selling price of one additional dining chair (£85) and variable costs have increased by the cost of materials (£20) and the cost of direct labour (£25) for one additional dining chair. This has had the effect of both increasing contribution by £40 (selling price of £85 − materials cost of £20 − direct labour cost of £25) and increasing profit for the year by £40. Fixed costs have already been more than covered by the contribution generated by sales of 1,000 chairs per annum, so every additional unit of production and sales will add all of the contribution to the profit for the year.

EXAMPLE 4.3

While fixed costs in total are fixed, sales, variable costs and profits all change with each additional unit of production and sales. To prove that this is true, consider what the profit would be if Anna produced 1,001 chairs rather than 1,000 chairs in a year.

	Selling 1,000 chairs in a year		Selling 1,001 chairs in a year	
	£	£	£	£
Sales: 1,000 × £85/1,001 × £85		85,000		85,085
Materials 1,000 × £20/1,001 × £20	20,000		20,020	
Direct labour 1,000 × £25/1,001 × £25	25,000		25,025	
Total variable costs		45,000		45,045
Selling price − variable costs = contribution		40,000		40,040
Fixed costs (rent, rates, heating and lighting)		7,800		7,800
Profit for the year		**32,200**		**32,240**

4

This approach, as we saw in Chapter 3 (Direct costs, variable costs and marginal costs), is called marginal costing: the costs and revenues of producing and selling one more or one fewer unit of product or service and the contribution that results from this increased or decreased activity at the margin. The contribution from each unit of production and sales contributes towards meeting the fixed costs of the organisation. The higher the sales, the higher the contribution and the more easily a business can generate a net profit (sales less all fixed and variable costs) by covering its fixed costs and providing a profit on top.

WHY IS THIS RELEVANT TO ME?   Marginal v. absorption costing

As an accounting professional you need to be aware:

- That a product's absorption cost depends upon the production level used to absorb fixed costs into products or services
- That fixed costs do not change in line with production and sales over a given period of time
- That variable costs and contribution vary directly in line with production and sales
- Of the distinction between contribution and the absorption cost profit per unit of production and sales
- That, once fixed costs are covered, the contribution from every additional unit of production and sales is pure profit

GO BACK OVER THIS AGAIN!   Are you confident that you can distinguish between fixed and variable costs? Go to the **online workbook** and complete Exercises 4.1 to make sure you understand the distinction.

SUMMARY OF KEY CONCEPTS   Have you fully grasped the ideas of contribution and marginal cost? Go to the **online workbook** to take a look at Summary of key concepts 4.1 and 4.2 to reinforce your understanding.

4

RELEVANT COSTS AND SUNK COSTS

Contribution and marginal costing analysis helps us to consider the short-term costs that are relevant and those that are irrelevant when a choice between two alternatives has to be made. Relevant costs are those costs that we will incur if we decide to follow a certain course of action. Relevant costs are the costs that influence our decision making.

Costs already incurred cannot influence future decision making as this money has already been spent and nothing you subsequently do will change those costs. Costs that have already been incurred and that do not influence future decisions are known as sunk costs. Sunk costs are past costs and have no further influence on decisions to be made for the future. To illustrate this idea of sunk costs, consider Example 4.4.

EXAMPLE 4.4

You are on holiday for a week in a seaside town. Your train fare has been paid and cost you £70 for a return ticket. Your hotel bill for the week is £500, which you have paid in advance. Now you have arrived you are free to decide what you want to do during your week. You have the option of going to the beach, going walking in the hills, visiting the local historical sites or travelling to another local town that is staging a sporting event you are keen to attend. You have £300 spending money for the week. What are the relevant costs and the sunk costs in this situation?

Your train fare and your hotel bill are now sunk costs, costs that have been paid and that have no further bearing on how you will spend your week. The only costs you will take into account now are the different costs of the four options in front of you and how much of your spending money each of these activities will use up. Going to the beach and going walking in the hills are likely to be less expensive alternatives compared with visiting the historical sites or attending the sporting event: both of the latter two options will require the purchase of entrance tickets whereas the former two options will not.

The past sunk costs will have no influence on your decisions about how to spend your time and money and so are disregarded when you consider your future options and actions. What counts now and what will influence your decisions are the costs and benefits that will be incurred enjoying any one of the four options available to you and the relative costs of each.

In the same way, costs that an entity incurs, whether any activity takes place or not, are irrelevant to its short-term decision making. Costs relevant in short-term decision making are those costs that will be incurred as a result of making decisions and implementing a particular course of action. In Anna's case, the relevant costs are the variable costs of producing a larger or smaller number of dining chairs. The rent, rates and heating and lighting costs are all fixed and will be incurred regardless of the number of chairs produced and sold. All Anna has to do is to decide what level of production she needs to achieve in order to cover her fixed costs and what additional revenue she will generate and what additional costs she will incur in doing so.

WHY IS THIS RELEVANT TO ME?   Relevant costs and sunk costs

As an accounting professional, knowledge of relevant and sunk costs will enable you to:

- Distinguish between those costs that are relevant and irrelevant in a decision-making context
- Appreciate that costs that do not change as a result of a decision have no bearing on that decision
- Understand that fixed costs are irrelevant in short-term decision making

GO BACK OVER THIS AGAIN!   Do you think you can identify sunk costs and costs relevant to a decision? Go to the **online workbook** and complete Exercises 4.2 to reinforce your understanding of this distinction.

SUMMARY OF KEY CONCEPTS   Are you confident that you understand what relevant costs and sunk costs represent? Go to the **online workbook** to take a look at Summary of key concepts 4.3 and 4.4 to reinforce your understanding.

RELEVANT COSTS: OPPORTUNITY COST

4

Another relevant cost that has to be taken into account is opportunity cost. This is the loss that is incurred by choosing one alternative course of action over another. Opportunity cost only applies when resources are limited: when there is no shortage of a resource, then there is no opportunity cost. This might seem like an academic exercise, but a moment's reflection will enable you to see that opportunity cost is involved in many everyday choices. See how the idea of opportunity cost works in Examples 4.5 and 4.6.

EXAMPLE 4.5

Before you started your university course, you were faced with a choice. You could spend three years gaining your degree or you could start work immediately and earn money straight away. Choosing to study for your degree involves the loss of income from employment for three years and the loss of being able to spend that money on whatever you wanted. However, by deciding to start work immediately, you faced the loss of three years studying a subject you enjoy and the improved personal and career prospects that such study would have brought to you. Time is limited and you can only make one of the two choices, so making either choice for your time involves an opportunity cost.

EXAMPLE 4.6

In a decision-making context in business, opportunity cost will be the next best alternative use for a resource. In a manufacturing business, raw materials can either be used for one project or another. That piece of steel that cost £100 could be used to produce a new steel fabrication to sell to a customer for £5,000 or it could be scrapped for £20. The opportunity cost of using the steel in the new fabrication is the next best alternative to using it, which is scrapping it. Therefore, the opportunity cost of using the steel in the fabrication is £20. The £100 purchase cost is irrelevant as this is a past cost, a sunk cost and a cost that has no further bearing on your decision. Your choice lies in using the steel in the fabrication to sell to a customer or scrapping it and receiving £20.

WHY IS THIS RELEVANT TO ME?   Relevant costs: opportunity costs

As an accounting professional:

- You should appreciate that the opportunity cost of a decision is the next best alternative use for the resource used in that decision
- You need to be able to identify the opportunity cost of a resource as a relevant cost in a decision-making context

4

GO BACK OVER THIS AGAIN!   Opportunity cost sounds like a difficult concept. Go to the **online workbook** and complete Exercises 4.3 to see if you can decide what the opportunity costs of various decisions are.

SUMMARY OF KEY CONCEPTS   Are you sure that you understand what opportunity cost represents? Go to the **online workbook** to take a look at Summary of key concepts 4.5 to reinforce your understanding.

As we have discovered earlier, relevant costs are those costs that affect short-term decision making. Let us now see how marginal costing and relevant costs are used in decision making by businesses.

CONTRIBUTION ANALYSIS AND DECISION MAKING
Break-even point

Anna's first concern when setting up her business was to determine the selling price of her dining chairs. Her second concern (and the concern of many new businesses when they start up) is to calculate the number of units of production she will need to sell to cover all her costs, both fixed and variable. The point at which the revenue from sales = the total costs (Figure 4.2) is known as the break-even point, the level of sales that produces neither a profit nor a loss. Contribution analysis is relevant in determining break-even point. As we have seen, each additional unit of production and sales adds contribution towards the fixed costs so each sale is a further step towards covering those fixed costs. This is very similar to walking up a hill: the hill does not move (fixed costs) and each step you take (contribution) brings you closer to the top of the hill. Just as all your steps take you to the top, so the contribution from each sale takes an entity closer and closer to the break-even point.

This knowledge enables us to calculate the break-even point as:

$$\frac{\text{Total fixed costs}}{\text{Contribution per unit of sales}} = \text{Break-even point in sales units}$$

Figure 4.2 Break-even point: revenue = total costs

Anna's break-even point is calculated in Example 4.7.

How many dining chairs does Anna need to sell to break even? We know from our calculations in Example 4.1 that the contribution from the sale of one chair is £40. We also know from our examples in Chapter 3 that Anna's annual fixed costs for her workshop are £7,800 (annual rent of £6,000, annual business rates of £1,000 and heating and lighting costs of £800, see Example 3.4).

Using the break-even formula given previously, Anna's break-even point is thus:

$$\frac{£7,800}{£40} = 195\, \text{Dining chairs}$$

Anna needs to sell 195 chairs in order to break even. Using this figure, let's prove that she does in fact break even if she sells 195 chairs in the year.

	£	£
Sales of 195 dining chairs at £85 each		16,575
Materials cost for 195 dining chairs at £20 each	3,900	
Direct labour cost for 195 dining chairs at £25 each	4,875	
Total variable cost		8,775
Selling price – variable costs = contribution		7,800
Fixed costs (rent, rates, heating and lighting)		7,800
Profit/loss for the year		—

The above calculations prove that our formula for break-even point works and gives us the correct answer. For Anna, at the break-even point, her sales of £16,575 are exactly equal to her variable costs for the break-even level of sales (£8,775) plus the fixed costs that she is incurring during the year (£7,800). She makes neither a profit nor a loss at this point. Once she sells 196 chairs, the additional £40 of contribution is pure profit as there are no further fixed costs that must be covered before a profit can be made.

WHY IS THIS RELEVANT TO ME?   Break-even point

As an accounting professional knowledge of break-even point analysis will enable you to:

- Appreciate that a business breaks even when all of its costs, both fixed and variable, are exactly covered by the revenue from sales
- Calculate the break-even point in sales units and sales value in £s for different products and services
- Determine break-even points for new products or services that your company intends to introduce

SUMMARY OF KEY CONCEPTS   Are you certain that you can state the break-even formula and say what break-even represents? Go to the **online workbook** to take a look at Summary of key concepts 4.6 to test your knowledge.

MULTIPLE CHOICE QUESTIONS   Are you confident that you can calculate a break-even point from a given set of data? Go to the **online workbook** and have a go at Multiple choice questions 4.1 to try out your new knowledge.

Break-even point: graphical illustration

Just as we drew graphs to illustrate the behaviour of fixed, variable and total costs in Chapter 3, so, too, can we draw a graph to show the break-even point. Break-even charts require three lines to be drawn: the line representing sales revenue, the line representing fixed costs and the line representing total costs (fixed costs + variable costs). Fixed costs remain the same throughout the period under review just as we saw in Chapter 3 (Fixed costs), but sales revenue and total costs both rise directly in line with the level of sales and production activity. The point at which the sales revenue line and total costs line intersect is the break-even point as shown in Figure 4.3. Beneath the break-even point losses will be made while above the break-even point profits are made.

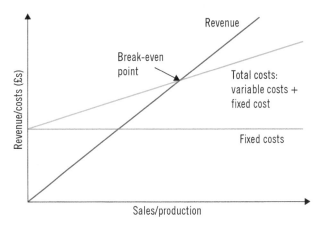

Figure 4.3 Graphical presentation of sales revenue, fixed costs, total costs and break-even point

The margin of safety

As we have seen, the break-even point in sales tells us how many units of production we have to sell in order to cover all our fixed costs and make neither a profit nor a loss. However, it also tells us how far our projected sales could fall before we reach a break-even position. In Anna's case, we found that she needs to sell 195 chairs before she breaks even. As her projected sales are 1,000 units for the year, she has a margin of safety of 1,000 − 195 = 805 chairs (Figure 4.4). This means that her projected sales could fall by 805 chairs before she reaches her break-even point. The higher the margin of safety, the less an organisation is exposed to the risk of a fall in

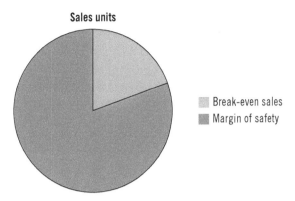

Sales units

☐ Break-even sales
■ Margin of safety

Figure 4.4 Anna's break-even sales units and margin of safety

4

sales that could result in a loss-making situation. In Anna's case, even if her projected sales fell to 500 units, she will still make a profit as sales of 500 chairs are still well above the break-even point of 195 chairs.

WHY IS THIS RELEVANT TO ME?   Margin of safety

To enable you as an accounting professional to:

- Calculate the margin of safety for a product or service
- Appreciate that the larger the margin of safety, the less likely it is that a business will make a loss

---

SUMMARY OF KEY CONCEPTS   Are you sure you can you say what the margin of safety represents? Go to the **online workbook** to take a look at Summary of key concepts 4.7 to test your knowledge.

MULTIPLE CHOICE QUESTIONS   Are you confident that you can calculate break-even point and the margin of safety? Complete Multiple choice questions 4.2 in the **online workbook** to reinforce your learning.

Sensitivity analysis

Knowledge of the break-even point enables us to determine the profit or loss from any given level of sales as illustrated in Example 4.8.

EXAMPLE 4.8

Anna knows that selling her chairs at £85 each will give her a contribution per chair of £40. Her break-even point is 195 chairs, so what will her profit or loss be if she sells 180 chairs or 300 chairs?

We could calculate individual profit and loss accounts for sales of 180 chairs and 300 chairs to determine profit or loss at the two sales levels. However, as we know that the break-even point is 195 chairs, we can calculate Anna's profit or loss by subtracting the break-even point from the projected sales units and then multiplying the difference by the contribution per unit of sales.

Thus, using our previous calculations, the loss at sales of 180 chairs will be $(180 − 195) \times £40 = £600$. Is this right? Contribution of £40 per chair will result in total contribution from sales of 180 chairs of $180 \times £40 = £7,200$. After deducting the fixed costs of £7,800, Anna's loss will be $£7,200 − £7,800 = £600$ so our calculation using the number of chairs from the break-even point is correct.

Similarly, at sales of 300 chairs, Anna's profit will be $(300 − 195) \times £40 = £4,200$. Proof: $300 \times £40 = a$ total contribution of £12,000. Deducting fixed costs of £7,800 gives a profit of $£12,000 − £7,800 = £4,200$.

WHY IS THIS RELEVANT TO ME?   Break-even point and sensitivity analysis

As an accounting professional knowledge of break-even point and sensitivity analysis will:

• Enable you to calculate the profit or loss at a given level of sales quickly

• Show you that the profit or loss depends on how far the level of sales differs from the break-even point

• Provide you with a useful analysis tool when evaluating the profit or loss from different levels of sales of products or services

SUMMARY OF KEY CONCEPTS   Are you certain that you can state the relationship between break-even point and the profit or loss at a given level of sales? Go to the **online workbook** to take a look at Summary of key concepts 4.8 to test your knowledge.

MULTIPLE CHOICE QUESTIONS   How accurately do you think you can you use break-even analysis to determine profits and losses at a given level of production? Complete Multiple choice questions 4.3 in the **online workbook** to reinforce your learning.

Target profit

Example 4.9 shows how break-even analysis can be used to calculate a target profit.

EXAMPLE 4.9

If Anna sells 1,000 chairs she will make a profit of £32,200 (Chapter 3, Example 3.7). However, she might consider that this profit does not compensate her sufficiently for the time and effort she has put into the business. She might decide that a profit of £40,000 is much more acceptable. How many chairs would she need to sell to achieve this target profit?

Break-even analysis will enable us to calculate the number of sales units required to achieve this target profit. Anna makes a contribution per chair sold of £40. Sales of her first 195 chairs will cover her fixed costs and enable her to break even. Therefore, she will need to sell a further $£40,000 \div £40 = 1,000$ chairs to make a net profit of £40,000. Adding these two figures together means that Anna will have to sell $1,000 + 195 = 1,195$ chairs to make a profit of £40,000.

Is this right? Let's check. 1,195 chairs produce a total contribution of $1,195 \times £40 = £47,800$. Deducting the fixed costs of £7,800 gives a net profit for the year of $£47,800 - £7,800 = £40,000$, so our calculations are correct.

WHY IS THIS RELEVANT TO ME?   Break-even point and target profit

As an accounting professional knowledge of break-even analysis will:

- Enable you to calculate a target profit
- Provide you with the technique to calculate the number of units of sales required to achieve a target profit

SUMMARY OF KEY CONCEPTS   Can you state the relationship between break-even point and the target profit? Go to the **online workbook** to take a look at Summary of key concepts 4.9 to test your knowledge.

MULTIPLE CHOICE QUESTIONS   Are you sure that you can use break-even analysis to determine a target profit? Complete Multiple choice questions 4.4 in the **online workbook** to reinforce your learning.

Cost-volume-profit analysis

The techniques we have considered so far in this chapter are examples of cost-volume-profit (CVP) analysis. CVP analysis studies the relationship between costs, both fixed and variable, the level of activity, in terms of sales, and the profit generated. Do entities actually use these techniques in practice? Give me an example 4.1 describes the findings of a CIMA sponsored survey into the use of management accounting practices in small and medium sized entities in the UK.

GIVE ME AN EXAMPLE 4.1   Break-even point and cost-volume-profit analysis

Management Accounting Practices of UK Small-Medium-Sized Enterprises published in July 2013 investigated the management accounting techniques and practices used by a sample of small and medium sized enterprises in the UK. All of the small and medium sized enterprises used break-even analysis with managers having a rough idea of their fixed costs and the level of sales revenue required to cover these. However, while all of the medium sized entities surveyed used cost-volume-profit analysis, this technique was only used by a few of the small organisations in the survey: the view was taken that, as small entities are unable to exercise much control over the selling price that they can charge or the variable costs that they pay for inputs, respondents considered that they would gain little benefit from trying to evaluate alternative scenarios based on selling and cost prices.

Source: www.cimaglobal.com

4

High and low fixed costs

Anna has very low fixed costs and, consequently, a high margin of safety given that she aims to make sales of 1,000 units in a year. However, many businesses have very high fixed costs with very low levels of variable costs. Such businesses will have a very high break-even point and, as a result, a very low margin of safety. Such businesses are thus very vulnerable during a downturn in the economy and, if they do not collapse, they will incur very large losses before the recovery enables them to reach their break-even level of sales. Example 4.10 provides an example of a high fixed costs industry.

EXAMPLE 4.10

Premier League football clubs are an example of businesses with very high fixed costs. Players' wages are a very high proportion of each club's total costs. These wages are fixed and do not vary in line with the number of customers who pay to watch the team each week. Therefore, Premier League clubs need to fill their stadia for every match in order to cover these fixed costs and still make some sort of profit. Thus, their margin of safety is very low and they have made regular losses in recent seasons. However, changes in the rules imposed by football's governing body have forced clubs into cutting costs in order to make a profit, as shown in Give me an example 4.2.

GIVE ME AN EXAMPLE 4.2   English football's top flight back in profit after 15 years

English top-flight football has long been a sink-hole for cash. In the past decade, the Premier League's 20 clubs have racked up £2.6bn in losses, with the proceeds of lucrative television rights largely being spent on ever higher salaries for players.

Last season marked the start of a turnaround. On Thursday, Deloitte, the accounting firm, released figures showing the Premier League clubs made a collective pre-tax profit last season for the first time in 15 years. The £190m in pre-tax profit in 2013–14 was almost four times higher than the previous record of £49m in 1997–98.

The figures, compiled from clubs' financial statements, showed that wage growth had slowed fol-lowing the introduction of rules designed to curb the spending of owners with deep pockets.

Wages increased just 6 per cent to £1.9bn, al-though the season included the first year of the lu-crative £3bn television rights deal signed in 2012. Wage costs as a proportion of revenue fell to their lowest level since the 1998–99 season.

According to Dan Jones, a partner at Deloitte's sports business group, the 'transformational' shift was due to new financial fair play rules, which re-quired clubs to break-even.

Source: Kadhim Shubber, 2015, *English football's top flight back in profit after 15 years*, the Financial Times, 28 March. Used under licence from the Financial Times. All Rights Reserved.

CONTRIBUTION ANALYSIS, RELEVANT COSTS AND DECISION MAKING

Marketing and selling price

Example 4.11 illustrates how contribution and relevant costs analysis can be used in making marketing and selling price decisions.

EXAMPLE 4.11

Anna is currently selling her chairs at £85 each. A friend who is in marketing and who knows the market well has looked at her chairs and has suggested that she should reduce the selling price to £70. Her friend estimates that this reduction in selling price will enable her to increase sales by 50 per cent. As the workshop has spare capacity, there would be no need to take on any additional workshop space and so fixed costs will not increase as a result of this decision. Similarly, the costs of materials and labour will not increase and will remain the same at £20 and £25 per chair respectively. Anna is now trying to decide whether this marketing strategy will increase her profits or not.

To help her make this decision, we can draw up two costing statements as follows to assess the profits produced by the two different strategies, one for the original level of sales of 1,000 chairs at £85 and one for the expected level of sales of 1,500 chairs (1,000 × 150 per cent) at £70.

	Selling 1,000 chairs at £85 each		Selling 1,500 chairs at £70 each	
	£	£	£	£
Sales 1,000 × £85/1,500 × £70		85,000		105,000
Materials 1,000 × £20/1,500 × £20	20,000		30,000	
Direct labour 1,000 × £25/1,500 × £25	25,000		37,500	
Total variable costs		45,000		67,500
Selling price − variable costs = contribution		40,000		37,500
Fixed costs (rent, rates, heating and lighting)		7,800		7,800
Profit for the year		**32,200**		**29,700**

However, if you have been following the argument so far, you will have realised that you could have used contribution analysis to solve this problem much more quickly. A selling price of £70 and a variable cost per chair of £45 gives a revised contribution of £70 − £45 = £25. Selling 1,500 chairs at £70 each would give a total contribution of 1,500 × £25 = £37,500. Fixed costs will not change, so the profit for the year after deducting fixed costs will be £37,500 − £7,800 = £29,700, lower than the current strategy of selling 1,000 chairs at £85.

How many chairs would Anna need to sell to make the new strategy as profitable as the current strategy? Again, contribution analysis will help us to determine the answer to this question. Current contribution from selling 1,000 chairs at £85 each is £40,000. The contribution per unit in the new strategy will be £70 − £45 = £25. To produce a total contribution of £40,000 from selling the chairs at £70 each would thus require sales of £40,000 ÷ £25 = 1,600 chairs. This is a large increase on current sales and Anna might well decide that she is quite happy selling 1,000 chairs at £85 each rather than taking the risk of trying to increase production by 60 per cent for no increase in the profit generated.

WHY IS THIS RELEVANT TO ME?   Relevant costs and evaluating the profitability of different marketing strategies

- As an accounting professional you will be involved in making pricing decisions for products
- Knowledge of relevant costs and contribution will enable you to evaluate different marketing strategies in terms of their relative profitability and to choose the profit maximising pricing strategy

GO BACK OVER THIS AGAIN!   Are you convinced that you can use contribution analysis to determine the profit that will arise from different marketing strategies? Have a go at Exercises 4.4 in the **online workbook** to make sure you can use contribution analysis in analysing such decisions.

Special orders

Thus far, we have assumed that selling prices will remain the same for all customers and for all of an organisation's output. In reality, this is rather unrealistic and most organisations will have different selling prices for different customers. When a new customer approaches an entity with a price they would be willing to pay for goods or services, the organisation has to decide whether to accept the new order or not at the customer's offered price. Again, contribution analysis will enable us to determine whether the new order is worth taking and whether it will add to our profit or not. Examples 4.12 and 4.13 illustrate the steps involved in decisions such as these.

EXAMPLE 4.12

Anna receives an enquiry from a charity that wishes to place an order for 50 dining chairs. They have seen examples of Anna's chairs and are very impressed by the quality of the workmanship and the sturdiness of the chairs, but they have been put off by the £85 selling price. They can only afford to pay £50 for each dining chair and have asked Anna whether she would be willing to sell the chairs at this price or not. Anna looks at her cost card for one chair (see Chapter 3, Example 3.6) and discovers that her absorption cost price per chair is £52.80. Her first thoughts are that if she sells the chairs at £50 each, she will be making a loss of £2.80 per chair. The workshop has spare capacity and the order could be accommodated without incurring any additional costs other than the variable costs of producing each chair. This additional order will not affect Anna's current production of 1,000 chairs. As the price offered by the charity is £2.80 less than the absorption cost per chair, Anna is considering refusing the order. Is she right to do so?

Let's see what Anna's total profit will be if she accepts the new order for 50 chairs at £50 each.

	£	£
Current sales: 1,000 chairs at £85 each		85,000
Additional sales: 50 chairs at £50 each		2,500
Total sales		87,500
Variable costs of production		
Materials: 1,050 chairs at £20 each	21,000	
Direct labour: 1,050 chairs at £25 each	26,250	
Total variable costs		47,250
Total contribution		40,250
Fixed costs (rent, rates, lighting and heating)		7,800
Profit for the year		**32,450**

Anna's original production level of 1,000 chairs produced a profit of £32,200. Accepting the new order alongside the current production of 1,000 chairs increases profit by £250 to £32,450. Anna expected to make a loss of £2.80 per chair (£50.00 selling price – £52.80 absorption cost per chair) so why is her profit not lower if she accepts the new order?

The answer again lies in the fact that the fixed costs are irrelevant to this decision; fixed costs are fixed for a given period of time and do not change with increased levels of activity. The only relevant costs are those that do change with the increase in the level of activity. These are the variable costs relating to production and the selling price for each additional chair produced. The selling price of £50 is £5 higher than the variable costs of production which are £45. Each additional chair in the new order adds £5 of contribution (and a total additional contribution and profit of £5 × 50 chairs = £250), the selling price less the variable costs, so, as the new order generates more profit for Anna, she should accept.

4

EXAMPLE 4.13

The decision above was made on the basis that Anna has spare capacity in her workshop and can easily add the new order to her existing level of production. Would your advice have been different if the additional order for 50 dining chairs had meant giving up 50 chairs of current production? Again, let's look at the effects of this decision and consider the relevant costs of making this decision to decide whether accepting the new order would be worthwhile in terms of the overall effect on profit.

If the new order were to be accepted and 950 full price chairs and 50 special price chairs produced, Anna's profit for the year would be as follows.

	£	£
Full price sales: 950 chairs at £85 each		80,750
Discounted sales: 50 chairs at £50 each		2,500
Total sales		83,250
Variable costs of production		
Materials: 1,000 chairs at £20 each	20,000	
Direct labour: 1,000 chairs at £25 each	25,000	
Total variable costs		45,000
Total contribution		38,250
Fixed costs (rent, rates, lighting and heating)		7,800
		30,450

Slide 49

the new order as profits fall by £1,750 from £32,200 for
chairs and 50 special price chairs. How has this fall oc-
tribution of £5 each, but to generate this contribution of
h of the 50 full price chairs that this order has replaced.
s: (£40 (contribution per chair given up) – £5 (contribu-
= £1,750. Thus, from a profitability point of view, no ad-
r should be declined. More profitable production would
ler so the charity would be turned away if there were no

> **WHY IS THIS RELEVANT TO ME?**   Relevant costs and special orders
>
> To enable you as an accounting professional to:
>
> - Use contribution analysis to evaluate the profitability of new orders with a selling price lower than the normal selling price
>
> - Appreciate that new orders should be accepted if they give rise to higher total contribution, add to total profits and make use of spare capacity
>
> - Understand that where more profitable production is given up, orders at a special price should not be accepted

> **SUMMARY OF KEY CONCEPTS**   Are you unsure whether to accept a special order or not? Go to the **online workbook** to take a look at Summary of key concepts 4.10 to review the criteria you should apply when evaluating such decisions.

> **NUMERICAL EXERCISES**   Do you think you can use contribution analysis to determine whether a special order should be accepted? Have a go at Numerical exercises 4.1 in the **online workbook** to test your grasp of the principles.

Special orders: additional considerations

Other than additional income and costs and the effects on overall profit, what other consider-ations should be taken into account when making these special order decisions? First, as we have seen, entities faced with this choice should have spare capacity with which to fulfil orders at a lower selling price. Entities operating at full capacity have no idle resources with which to meet new orders at lower selling prices and so will not accept them. To do so would be to replace production generating higher contribution with production generating lower contribution. As a result, profits after fixed costs will fall.

Second, entities must also consider how easily information about a special price for a new customer could leak into the market. If existing customers found out that dining chairs are be-ing supplied to a charity at £50 when they are paying £85, they are likely to demand a similar discount and this would have a very severe effect on Anna's profitability in the long run. Where information is likely to be available in the wider market, special orders should thus be declined as long-run profits will suffer as all customers will demand special prices.

In order to avoid rejected orders and hence lost profits, organisations can adopt a product differentiation strategy. Rather than producing and selling all their production under one label, producers have a quality label and an economy label to enable them to overcome the problem of all customers demanding the same reduced price. In the same way, supermarkets sell branded products from recognised manufacturers and they also sell goods with the supermarkets' own label at lower prices. Both quality and economy products might have been manufactured in the same production facility, but they are marketed in different ways.

On the positive side, should Anna accept the order from the charity, she might well receive some welcome publicity for her dining chairs as the charity recommends her business by word of mouth. This would amount to free advertising in return for her cutting the selling price for this special order and, in her attempts to expand her business, she might consider this short-term reduction in profits to be a worthwhile sacrifice for the longer-term growth of the business as a whole.

In such special order situations, after taking into account the additional considerations, the short-term decision will always be to accept the new order when this increases contribution and to reject the order when this results in a reduction in contribution.

WHY IS THIS RELEVANT TO ME?   Relevant costs and special orders: additional considerations

To enable you as an accounting professional to:

- Appreciate that additional profit is not the only consideration in deciding whether to accept a special order or not

- Understand the non-accounting, business related considerations involved in making special order decisions

- Discuss and evaluate the non-accounting aspects relating to special order decisions

4

Outsourcing (make or buy decisions)

Relevant costs can also be used in making decisions on whether it is more economical to buy goods and services from external parties or whether it will be more profitable to produce or provide these goods and services in-house. Again, when making this decision, only those costs that change with the level of activity will be considered. Think about this in Example 4.14.

EXAMPLE 4.14

Anna is expanding rapidly and has more orders for dining chairs than she can currently fulfil with two employees in her workshop. She has annual orders now for 1,500 dining chairs at a selling price of £85 each. She is considering whether to take on a third employee to help with these additional orders. Taking on this third employee will not increase her fixed costs as she has spare capacity in her workshop to accommodate another two workers and the new employee will be paid at the same rate for producing chairs as the existing employees. Another dining chair producer, Wooden Wonders, has offered to make the additional 500 dining chairs for Anna and to sell them to her at a cost of £49 each. Anna is delighted as this £49 cost is lower than her absorption cost per chair of £52.80, so she is expecting to make an additional profit of £1,900 (500 × (£52.80 −£49.00)) by buying in the chairs. She is ready to accept Wooden Wonders' offer, but, knowing how your advice has proved invaluable in the past, she has asked you whether it will be more profitable to take on the new employee or to contract out the manufacture of the dining chairs to Wooden Wonders.

Let us solve this problem in both a long and short way to show that both approaches give us the same answer and to provide you with a quick method of calculating the alternatives where profit maximisation is the objective. First, let us look at a comparison of Anna's sales, costs and profits if she either makes all of her production in-house or if she makes 1,000 chairs in her workshop and contracts out the additional 500 chairs to Wooden Wonders.

4

	Making and selling 1,500 chairs at £85 each		Making 1,000 chairs, buying in 500 chairs and selling 1,500 chairs at £85 each	
	£	£	£	£
Sales 1,500 × £85		127,500		127,500
Materials 1,500 × £20/1,000 × £20	30,000		20,000	
Direct labour 1,500 × £25/1,000 × £25	37,500		25,000	
Buying in 500 chairs at £49 each	—		24,500	
Total variable costs		67,500		69,500
Selling price − variable costs = contribution		60,000		58,000
Fixed costs (rent, rates, heating and lighting)		7,800		7,800
Profit for the year		**52,200**		**50,200**

Anna's expectation was of £1,900 more profit, gained by buying in 500 chairs at £49 each alongside the in-house production of 1,000 chairs. However, this option results in a profit for the year that is lower by £2,000 in comparison with making all the chairs in-house. How does this difference arise?

Using marginal costing and contribution analysis, you could have solved this problem much more quickly. Contribution from in-house production is £40 (£85 selling price less the £20 material costs less the £25 labour cost) whereas contribution from the bought in chairs is £36 (£85 selling price less the £49 purchase cost from Wooden Wonders). The difference in contribution per chair of £4 (£40 − £36) multiplied by the 500 chairs that are bought in from Wooden Wonders gives the £2,000 lower profit if the second alternative course of action is chosen.

Fixed costs are again irrelevant in making this decision as these do not change with the level of production: only those costs that change with the decision should be taken into account alongside the contribution that will be gained from each alternative. Anna had forgotten that the fixed costs had already been covered by the production of 1,000 chairs and that the only relevant costs in this decision were the additional variable costs that she would incur. These would either be £45 if she produces the chairs in her own workshop or £49 if she buys them in from an outside supplier. Given that the outside supplier charges more for the chairs than Anna's employees can make them for, Anna will engage the third employee in the workshop as this is the more profitable solution to her production problem.

WHY IS THIS RELEVANT TO ME?   Relevant costs and outsourcing (make or buy) decisions

To enable you as an accounting professional to:

- Use contribution analysis and relevant costs to determine whether outsourcing decisions are more or less profitable than in-house production

- Appreciate that where profit maximisation is the only consideration, products should be bought in when additional contribution is generated by outsourcing production

SUMMARY OF KEY CONCEPTS   Are you quite sure that you understand the relevant costs in making outsourcing decisions? Go to the **online workbook** to take a look at Summary of key concepts 4.11 to review the criteria you should apply when evaluating such decisions.

NUMERICAL EXERCISES   Are you convinced that you can use contribution analysis and relevant costs to determine whether production should be outsourced or not? Have a go at Numerical exercises 4.2 in the **online workbook** to test your grasp of the principles.

Outsourcing (make or buy decisions): additional considerations

4

While profit maximisation is a valid aim for many organisations, costs saved and additional profit will be only one of the considerations in an outsourcing (make or buy) situation. There are also various qualitative factors that have to be taken into account when making decisions of this nature as shown in Figure 4.5.

First, we will need to consider the products or services that the external provider will be offering us. Will these products or services meet our quality standards? Will the product or service be of the same quality or at the same level as our own in-house employees provide? Should the level of quality be lower, then further costs will arise. Products that use lower quality outsourced parts will break down more often and require more maintenance visits or refunds to dissatisfied customers. Services such as cleaning might not be carried out to the same exacting standards as

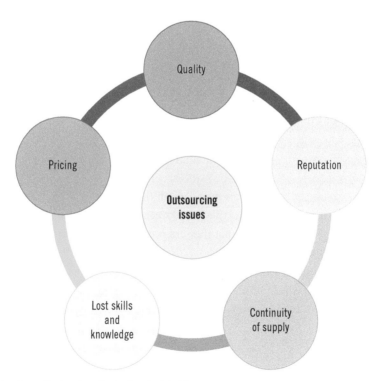

Figure 4.5 Factors to consider in outsourcing (make or buy) decisions

the organisation sets for its own staff, leading to an increase in complaints and a loss of customers as they go to other product or service providers who are providing the quality that customers demand.

While the product or service might look cheaper to buy in now, there are longer-term hidden costs that have to be considered. These longer-term costs might be much more damaging for the organisation in terms of loss of reputation and they will often outweigh the benefit of saving a few pounds at the present time. In Anna's case, she would need to determine whether the chairs bought in from Wooden Wonders will be made to the same standards and with the same care and attention as that given by her own employees. Where the chairs are not made to the same standards, Anna will want to ensure that her own reputation for quality chairs is maintained by producing all her chairs in-house.

Second, the price might be cheaper now, but will it always be cheaper? Once our new supplier has captured our custom and we have closed down our own production facility, will the price rise and wipe out all the previous savings? Contracts for the supply of goods and services have to be drawn up very carefully to ensure that a short-term advantage is not suddenly eroded by a change in price.

Organisations will also need to consider their willingness to be reliant upon another entity. In this case, one organisation relies upon the other to maintain continuity of supply and continuity of quality. This may not always happen and disruptions at a supplier very soon affect production and sales to customers. Where components are produced in-house, there is a much greater level of control over production and, hence, sales. Organisations might prefer to maintain their self-reliance rather than handing over responsibility for their parts, sales and production to other businesses.

Similarly, handing over production to another organisation will lead to a loss of skills within the business and an inability to reintroduce production at a later date should the current supply contract prove inadequate. Entities will lack in-house knowledge of how their products work and be unable to provide customers with advice on these products. When an organisation closes down part of its production facility and makes workers redundant, there is a knock-on effect on other workers. Job losses weaken employee morale, job satisfaction and productivity. These knock-on effects also have an effect on profitability as the current workforce becomes demoralised and more concerned about their own job security than completing the work in hand. Anna's two employees might become concerned about the continuity of their employment with Anna if production is outsourced. Concerned employees are distracted employees and they will not be concentrating on the quality of what they are producing but on whether they will still be employed in a year's time.

However, with the appropriate attention to detail and close cooperation and collaboration between the contracting parties, outsourcing can work very well indeed. Give me an example 4.3 shows how Toyota overcomes the potential difficulties of outsourcing through very close relationships with its suppliers.

GIVE ME AN EXAMPLE 4.3   Outsourcing at Toyota

The Japanese car company, Toyota, prizes high quality at a low price. However, the company outsources 70 per cent of the components for its cars to suppliers and produces just 30 per cent of the components in its own production facilities. In order to ensure the quality of the products produced by its suppliers, Toyota adopts a policy of strong relationships and collaboration with its suppliers through the Toyota Production System. Toyota's high quality has been achieved as a result of the collaborative advantage it enjoys with its suppliers. Toyota regularly evaluates its suppliers' performance and provides suggestions on how they could improve their operations. However, this is not a one way relationship: the company also invites its suppliers to evaluate Toyota and to provide their suggestions for operational improvement. This continuous improvement approach enables the Toyota Production System to deliver the high quality products demanded by both Toyota and its customers despite the fact that most of its car parts are not manufactured in-house.

Source: www.scribd.com/doc/53016595/Vertical-Integration-or-Outsourcing-Nokia-Ford-Toyota-IBM-Intel-Toshiba-Matsushita#scribd

WHY IS THIS RELEVANT TO ME?   Relevant costs and outsourcing (make or buy) decisions: additional considerations

As an accounting professional you should:

- Appreciate the additional strategic factors that must be taken into account when an outsourcing decision is being made
- Understand that cost reduction and profit are not the only grounds on which to base make or buy/outsourcing decisions
- Be able to discuss and evaluate non-accounting, business related considerations when undertaking make or buy/outsourcing decisions

Limiting factor (key factor) analysis

Contribution analysis can also be used in making decisions to maximise short-term profits where organisations are facing a shortage of direct material or direct labour. In this situation, contribution analysis can be used to determine which products generate the highest contribution per unit of material or labour input in order to maximise profits. Those products that generate the highest contribution per unit of limiting factor (key factor) will be produced, while those that produce a lower contribution per unit of limiting factor will be discontinued in the short term. Limiting factor analysis is only relevant where two or more products are produced. If only one product is produced, then there is no decision that has to be made, manufacturers will just produce their

4

one product up to the maximum number that they can based upon the limitations imposed by the shortage of direct materials or direct labour. Let us consider how this would work and the steps that would be undertaken to determine which products produce the highest level of contribution per unit of limiting factor in Example 4.15.

Anna's business has grown and is now a very successful producer of wooden dining chairs, small wooden coffee tables and wooden kitchen cabinets. However, a new government has come to power in the country from which she sources her supplies of wood. This new government has introduced restrictions on the export of timber as new environmental policies are put in place to preserve rather than exploit the local forests. Anna is thus currently facing a shortage of wood from her suppliers because of these restrictions. While she investigates new production methods to enable her to use wood from other sources, Anna is looking to maximise her short-term profit and needs help in deciding which products she should make to achieve this.

The selling price and variable costs for her three products are as follows:

	Dining chairs	Coffee tables	Kitchen cabinets
	£	£	£
Selling price	85.00	50.00	80.00
Materials: wood	(18.00)	(12.60)	(10.80)
Materials: other	(2.00)	(5.40)	(9.20)
Direct labour	(25.00)	(18.00)	(30.00)
Contribution	**40.00**	**14.00**	**30.00**

All three products use the same type of wood at a cost of £1.80 per kg. The new government in the country of her supplier has allocated Anna a maximum of 12,600 kgs of wood for the next three months. Anna has thought about the figures above and is considering diverting all her production into dining chairs as these provide the highest total contribution of the three products and she thinks that producing just chairs will maximise her profit for the period. Is Anna right? If she is not right, which (or which combination) of the three products should she produce to maximise her profits in the next three months?

In problems of this nature you should work through the following three steps.

Step 1: calculate the quantity of limiting factor used in the production of each product

In order to maximise contribution when there is a limiting factor, the first step is to determine the usage that each unit of production makes of that limiting factor. Given that wood costs £1.80 per kg and using the product costing details above, each of the three products uses the following amounts of material:

Dining chairs: material usage: £18.00 ÷ £1.80 = 10 kilograms
Coffee tables: material usage: £12.60 ÷ £1.80 = 7 kilograms
Kitchen cabinets: material usage: £10.80 ÷ £1.80 = 6 kilograms

Step 2: calculate the contribution per unit of limiting factor delivered by each product

The next step is to determine how much contribution each product generates per unit of limiting factor. This calculation divides the total contribution for each product by the number of units of limiting factor used in the production of each product. The products are then given a ranking: the highest contribution per unit of limiting factor is placed first and the lowest contribution per unit of limiting factor comes last.

Using the information about Anna and our calculations in Step 1, the three products generate the following contributions per unit of limiting factor:

	Contribution per unit of limiting factor	Ranking
Dining chairs	£40/10 kg per unit = £4 of contribution per unit of material used	2
Coffee tables	£14/7 kg per unit = £2 of contribution per unit of material used	3
Kitchen cabinets	£30/6 kg per unit = £5 of contribution per unit of material used	1

As the above calculations show, the highest contribution per unit of limiting factor is delivered by kitchen cabinets. These use 6 kg of material in each finished unit and deliver a total contribution of £30 per product. Dining chairs are ranked second with the second highest contribution per unit of limiting factor, while coffee tables are ranked last out of the three products, with a contribution per unit of limiting factor of only £2.

Step 3: calculate the contribution maximising production schedule

If Anna wishes to maximise her contribution and profit, she will now need to determine how much of the limiting factor is available to use and the most profitable products to produce. In Anna's business, if demand for each product is not limited, then she would just produce kitchen cabinets as each kitchen cabinet delivers £5 per unit of limiting factor used. A more likely scenario would be that demand for each product would be limited and so the contribution maximising production schedule will involve producing all of the product delivering the highest contribution per unit of limiting factor first, then producing the product delivering the second highest contribution per unit of limiting factor next and so on until all of the limiting factor is used up.

Anna estimates that demand for each product for the next three months will be as follows:

Dining chairs:	580 units
Coffee tables:	500 units
Kitchen cabinets:	900 units

What will the profit maximising production schedule be? As we have seen, Anna should produce as many kitchen cabinets as she can, as this product gives her the highest contribution per unit of limiting factor. She should then produce as many dining chairs as possible and finally produce coffee tables up to the total amount of material available, the limiting factor. Her production schedule and contribution will look like this:

Product	(a) Kgs of material per unit	(b) Quantity produced	(c) ((a) × (b)) Kgs of material used	(d) (12,600 − (c)) Kgs of material remaining	(e) Contribution per unit	(f) ((b) × (e)) Total contribution
	kg	units	kg	kg	£	£
Cabinets	6	900	5,400	7,200	30	27,000
Chairs	10	580	5,800	1,400	40	23,200
Tables	7	200	1,400	—	14	2,800
		Total material used (kg)	**12,600**		Total contribution	**53,000**

The above production schedule shows that demand for kitchen cabinets and chairs can be met in full as there is sufficient material to make the 900 kitchen cabinets and 580 chairs that customers require. However, there is only sufficient material remaining to produce 200 of the 500 coffee tables that customers are looking to buy, so production of these will be limited if Anna adopts a profit maximising strategy. This strategy will produce a total contribution of £53,000.

SHOW ME HOW TO DO IT!   Are you sure that you understand how the above allocation of limiting factor was made to the three products? View Video presentation 4.1 in the **online workbook** to see a practical demonstration of how this allocation between the three products is carried out.

What of Anna's intention to produce only chairs? How much contribution would this production scheme have produced? As there are 10 kgs of wood in each chair, 12,600 kgs of wood would have produced 1,260 chairs. The contribution from one chair is £40, so 1,260 chairs would produce a total contribution of 1,260 × £40 = £50,400. This is a good contribution, but it is not as high as the contribution forecast by using the contribution per unit of limiting factor calculated above. Given that demand for dining chairs is only 580 units, Anna will have a lot of chairs in stock at the end of the three months and these unsold chairs, too, will limit her profit for the three-month period.

The above production schedule shows what the maximum profit could be, given the limiting factor and the current maximum demand. However, in reality, it would be very difficult for Anna to stick to this schedule as her customers will be ordering her products in the expectation that she will fulfil all those orders. It would not be easy to refuse an order for coffee tables from a current customer on the grounds that she could not produce those products as they were not profitable enough. Such an excuse would lead to the loss of that customer, who would then source coffee tables from another supplier. In the longer term, the loss of customers could lead to a loss of reputation with all the attendant effects that this would have on sales and profits. Therefore, while the profit maximising schedule is a useful technique to determine what maximum profit could be in times of shortage, considerations other than cost and profit will tend to determine what is produced to meet customers' expectations of the organisation.

WHY IS THIS RELEVANT TO ME?   Relevant costs and limiting factor analysis

To enable you as an accounting professional to:

- Use contribution analysis and relevant costs to devise contribution and profit maximising strategies when resources are scarce

- Understand that this technique has certain limitations in the real world

4

SUMMARY OF KEY CONCEPTS   Do you remember the steps to follow when calculating profit maximising strategies in a limiting factor situation? Go to the **online workbook** to take a look at Summary of key concepts 4.12 to review the steps you should follow when making such decisions.

NUMERICAL EXERCISES   Do you think you could use contribution analysis and relevant costs to determine which products should be produced to maximise contribution when resources are scarce? Have a go at Numerical exercises 4.3 in the **online workbook** to test whether you have fully grasped the techniques involved.

RELEVANT COSTS, MARGINAL COSTING AND DECISION MAKING: ASSUMPTIONS

The decisions discussed and illustrated above all seem to be very straightforward and easy to apply. However, in practice, difficulties will be encountered. This is because of the assumptions upon which marginal costing analysis is based. These assumptions can be summarised as follows:

- First, it has been assumed that the variable costs of a product can be identified by a business with the required level of precision to enable accurate calculations to be made.

- Second, fixed costs for a period are assumed to be completely predictable and unchanging.

- Variable costs are assumed to be linear, that is, variable costs vary directly in line with production. In reality, the purchase of more materials will result in bulk discounts causing the average cost of materials used in each product to fall (see Chapter 3, Assumption 2: variable costs remain the same for all units of production). Similarly, additional units of production might well entail the payment of overtime premiums or bonuses to existing staff, causing the direct labour cost to jump when higher levels of production are reached.

- Prices have been assumed to be stable whereas, in reality, prices of materials change all the time depending on whether there is a shortage or an oversupply of those materials in the market. For example, in a delivery business, the price of fuel to run delivery vans changes on a daily basis.

- In break-even analysis, it is assumed that only one product is produced. Once two or more products are produced, the techniques behind break-even analysis are invalidated by the presence of two sets of variable costs and two contributions, making it impossible to determine the break-even point for one set of fixed costs.

Nevertheless, despite these limitations, relevant cost analysis does have some application in practice, as illustrated in Give me an example 4.4.

GIVE ME AN EXAMPLE 4.4   Relevant costing for decisions in practice

The July 2009 CIMA report, *Management accounting tools for today and tomorrow*, surveyed the current and intended usage by business of more than 100 management accounting and related tools based on a questionnaire completed by 439 respondents from across the globe. The findings indicated that relevant costing for decisions was used by small (43 per cent), medium (48 per cent), large (50 per cent) and very large (44 per cent) companies worldwide. However, product/service profitability analysis was the preferred profitability analysis tool across all companies surveyed. Of those intending to introduce relevant costing for decisions in the coming year, only a small percentage of UK respondents aimed to adopt this technique while much higher percentages of respondents across all regions were planning to introduce product/service profitability analysis.

Source: www.cimaglobal.com

WHY IS THIS RELEVANT TO ME?   Relevant costs, marginal costing and decision making: assumptions

To enable you as an accounting professional to:

* Appreciate the assumptions upon which marginal costing and decision-making analysis are based

* Develop an insight into the limitations posed by these assumptions

CHAPTER SUMMARY

You should now have learnt that:

* Contribution per unit = selling price per unit – variable costs per unit

* The concept of opportunity cost is used to determine the benefits lost by using a resource in one application rather than in another

* Fixed costs are not relevant when making short-term decisions as these costs do not vary with changes in the level of activity in the short term

* The only costs relevant in short-term decision making are those that change in line with levels of activity

* The break-even point is calculated by dividing fixed costs by the contribution per unit

* The margin of safety is the number of units of sales above the break-even point: the higher this number, the higher the margin of safety

* Knowledge of the break-even point enables entities to calculate the profit or loss from any given level of sales

- Contribution analysis enables entities to determine the effect of different pricing strategies on short-term profits
- Special orders should be accepted when they increase contribution
- Make or buy decisions can be made on the basis of the marginal costing technique
- Calculation of the contribution per unit of resource enables entities to devise profit maximising strategies when resources are limited
- Users of the costing techniques discussed in this chapter have to be aware of the advantages and limitations of marginal costing

4

QUICK REVISION   Test your knowledge with the online flashcards in Summary of key concepts and attempt the Multiple choice questions, all in the **online workbook**.

END-OF-CHAPTER QUESTIONS

Solutions to these questions can be found in the **online workbook**.

❯ DEVELOP YOUR UNDERSTANDING

❯ Question 4.1

Define the following terms

(a) Contribution

(b) Relevant costs

(c) Irrelevant costs

(d) Sunk costs

(e) Opportunity cost

(f) Break-even point

(g) Margin of safety

(h) Target profit

❯ Question 4.2

Podcaster University Press is a small publishing company producing a range of introductory text books on a variety of academic subjects for first year undergraduate students. The company's marketing department is considering reducing the selling price of text books to generate further sales and profit. The company's text books currently retail at £30 each. Variable production costs are £10 per book and Podcaster University Press has annual fixed costs of £3,000,000. Current sales of text books are 200,000 per annum. The marketing department has forecast that a £5 reduction in the selling price of each text book will boost annual sales to 275,000 books whereas decreasing the selling price to £21 would increase annual sales to 360,000 books.

Required

Using contribution analysis, evaluate the proposals of the marketing department and advise the company on whether the two proposals would be financially beneficial or not.

≫ TAKE IT FURTHER

≫ Question 4.3

Big Bucks University is planning to offer a series of professional accounting course classes. The fee payable for this professional accounting course is £400 per student per module. The university has already allocated lecturers currently employed at the university to each class and has determined that lecturers are being paid £60 per hour for the 60 hours required to deliver each module. The lecturers will be paid whether any students are enrolled on each module or not and they can be diverted to other classes if the professional accounting course modules do not run. Books and handouts are provided to each student at a cost of £100 per student per module. The university allocates £1,200 of central overhead costs for the year to the room used in the provision of each module. The university has asked for your help in deciding on the number of students that should be recruited to each module.

Required

(a) State which costs are relevant to the decision as to how many students to recruit to each module.

(b) Determine how many students the university should recruit to each module to ensure that each module breaks even.

(c) What is the margin of safety if the university recruits 25 students to each module?

(d) Calculate the profit or loss the university will make on each module if 14 students or 30 students are recruited to each module.

(e) What will the break-even point be if the university decides to charge £340 per module instead of £400?

≫ Question 4.4

Gurjit Limited produces and sells ink jet printers. The selling price and cost card for each printer are as follows:

	£	£
Selling price		40.00
Direct materials	9.50	
Direct labour	11.25	
Direct expenses	3.65	
Fixed overhead	5.60	
Total cost of one ink jet printer		30.00
Profit per ink jet printer sold		**10.00**

Currently, production and sales are running at 5,000 printers per annum. The fixed overhead allocated to each printer has been based on production and sales of 5,000 units. However, because of the popularity of the product and a strong advertising campaign, the directors of Gurjit Limited are expecting sales to rise to 10,000 units. The directors are currently reviewing the costs and profits made by printers along with their expectations of future profits from the increased sales. One option open to Gurjit Limited is to outsource production of their printers to another company. It is estimated that any outsourcing of production would lead to an increase in total fixed overheads of £40,000 to enable Gurjit Limited to ensure the quality of printers produced outside the company. The directors have a quote from Anand Limited to produce all 10,000 ink jet printers for £200,000. The directors of Gurjit Limited are considering whether to accept this offer and have asked for your advice.

In order to advise the directors of Gurjit Limited on whether to accept the offer from Anand Limited, you should:

(a) Calculate the current profit made at a level of sales and production of 5,000 ink jet printers per annum.

(b) Calculate the profit that will be made if sales and production rise to 10,000 printers per annum.

(c) Calculate the profit that will be made if sales and production rise to 10,000 printers and production of printers is outsourced to Anand Limited.

(d) Advise the directors of Gurjit Limited whether to outsource production to Anand Limited and what additional factors they should take into account in this decision other than costs and profit.

>> Question 4.5

Diddle Limited produces ornamental statues for gardens whose selling price, costs and contribution per unit are as follows:

	Clio	Diana	Athena
	£	£	£
Selling price	81	58	115
Materials (clay)	(30)	(12)	(42)
Direct labour	(15)	(27)	(30)
Variable overheads	(6)	(3)	(8)
Contribution	30	16	35

The same specialised clay is used in all three statues and costs £6 per kg. The company faces a shortage of this clay, with only 3,000 kg available in the next month. The board of directors is therefore considering which statues should be produced in order to maximise contribution in the coming month. The sales director has suggested that production should concentrate on Athena as this statue has the highest contribution of the three products. Is the sales director right?

Maximum predicted demand for the three products for the coming month is as follows:
Clio: 198 units
Diana: 900 units
Athena: 200 units

5

STANDARD COSTING AND VARIANCE ANALYSIS

LEARNING OUTCOMES

Once you have read this chapter and worked through the questions and examples in both this chapter and the online workbook, you should be able to:

- Appreciate that a standard cost is an expected cost rather than an actual cost
- Determine how a standard cost is calculated
- Calculate direct material total, price and usage variances
- Calculate direct labour total, efficiency and rate variances
- Calculate sales volume and price variances
- Calculate fixed overhead expenditure variance
- Calculate variable overhead total, expenditure and efficiency variances
- Discuss the function of standard costing as an accounting control device
- Understand that variances are merely an indication of a problem that requires further management investigation to establish and rectify the causes

INTRODUCTION

In the last two chapters we have looked at the different types of cost that organisations incur in their operations and how the distinction between fixed and variable costs can be used to make decisions that aim to maximise the short-term profitability of an organisation. It is now time to turn to the second function of management accounting: planning. Initially, this involves the use of accounting data to make predictions and forecasts for the future. Once actual outcomes are known, then comparison of actual results with these forecasts is used as a means to control an organisation's operations. The next chapter will consider budgeting in much greater detail and look at how the use of budgets and the comparison of outcomes with expectations enable an entity to control its operations, to enhance positive trends and to take action to correct problems as they arise. In this chapter we will consider the use of the related technique of standard costing and how the analysis of divergences from the standard can be used to identify problems requiring management's attention.

WHAT IS STANDARD COSTING?

As we saw in Chapter 3, the product costing process takes up a lot of time as information is gathered about the inputs of direct material, direct labour, direct expenses and indirect production overheads and as costs are allocated to products and services. This information is then used to determine selling prices for products so that a profit is made. However, prices of inputs change rapidly. The cost of materials rises and falls as users demand more or less of a particular raw material, wages rise each year, electricity and gas prices go up and down as the weather warms or cools. To change all these prices on a daily or weekly basis would be time consuming in the extreme and the task would eventually overwhelm the individuals performing this role. What is needed is an efficient, predictive tool that provides a reasonably accurate estimate of what the cost of a product or service should be over a given period of time. Variations from this estimate can then be analysed to determine whether the estimate needs revising or not. This reasonably accurate estimate can be provided by standard costing.

A standard cost card will include all the direct materials, direct labour, direct expenses, variable overheads and an allocation of fixed overheads that go into a product or service. These standard costs are the expected costs of that product and the standard cost card will also include the expected selling price for each product, along with the standard profit. Standard costs are derived from numerous observations of an activity over time and represent an expectation of costs incurred by and income generated from mass produced products and services. As the number of observations increases, so the standard is revised and the accuracy of the estimate becomes much closer to the actual cost of each product.

Standard costs recognise that goods are made up of a fixed set of inputs, whether materials, labour or overheads. These inputs are measured and costed and then summarised to present the total costs of producing one item of output. As an example, consider this book. Variable costs will include the paper, the ink, the covers, the binding, the power to drive the printing machinery and the handling of each book as it comes off the press. Fixed costs to be allocated across each print run will include typesetting, editing, development, website construction and maintenance, advertising and marketing. All these costs can be readily determined as a result of Oxford University Press's vast experience of printing books and the staff's detailed knowledge of the costs of book production. All the costs involved can be summarised to calculate the cost of one book and this is then the standard cost of that book. Management will set an expected selling price based on the costs incurred and the anticipated market for the book and this becomes the standard selling price.

WHY IS THIS RELEVANT TO ME?   Standard costing

To provide you as an accounting professional with:

• A basic understanding of what standard costing involves and how it works

• A predictive accounting tool you can use in the future to forecast the costs and profits of mass produced products and services

GO BACK OVER THIS AGAIN!   Confident you can say what standard costing is? Go to the **online workbook** and complete Exercises 5.1 to make sure you understand the aims and objectives of standard costing.

VARIANCE ANALYSIS

Standard costs just represent expectations, the expected costs and revenues from each product produced and sold. What happens when the reality turns out to be different from the expectation? When the actual costs and revenues are known, then a comparison of the standard expected results and the actual results is undertaken. The differences between the standard costs and revenues and the actual figures are known as variances. These variances are calculated and then used to explain the difference between anticipated and actual outcomes. In the case of book production, the cost of materials might be more than expected as a shortage of the expected quality of paper might have resulted in more expensive paper being used. Ink prices might have been higher or lower than forecast, a rise or fall in power costs might have resulted in changes to the anticipated printing cost, the selling price might have been set higher to cover these additional costs and so on. Explanations for variances will be sought as a means of controlling operations. Where actual costs are significantly different from the standard, the standard can be updated to produce more accurate information in the future.

What use do organisations across the world make of variance analysis? Give me an example 5.1 describes the findings of a 2009 CIMA survey.

The July 2009 CIMA report, *Management accounting tools for today and tomorrow*, surveyed the current and intended usage by business of more than 100 management accounting and related tools based on a questionnaire completed by 439 respondents from across the globe. The 4th most commonly used technique in practice was variance analysis. When used as a costing tool, variance analysis was undertaken by 73 per cent of respondents, the most popular costing tool in use. Over 60 per cent of small companies in the survey used variance analysis while more than 80 per cent of large companies employed this technique.

Source: www.cimaglobal.com

5

WHY IS THIS RELEVANT TO ME?   Variance analysis

To enable you as an accounting professional to:

- Understand how expected and actual costs and revenues are compared to explain deviations from forecast performance
- Appreciate that variances between expected and actual costs and revenues can lead to improvements in standards
- Appreciate the roles that standard costing and variance analysis perform in the control of business operations

GO BACK OVER THIS AGAIN!   How clearly have you understood what variance analysis involves? Go to the **online workbook** and complete Exercises 5.2 to make sure you understand how variance analysis works and what it aims to achieve.

DIFFERENT STANDARDS

The different types of standards are shown in Figure 5.1. Setting standards requires thought about expectations and what you want to achieve through the use of standards. You might hope that your favourite sports team will win all its matches, win all the trophies for which they are competing and play perfectly in every match. This would be an ideal standard, the best that can be achieved. However, ideal standards are unrealistic and unachievable as they would only ever be attained in a perfect world. In the real world, your team will lose some matches and draw others, play poorly yet win and play well but still lose. Therefore, a degree of realism is required in setting standards. Attainable standards are those standards that can be achieved with effort and you might set your team the attainable standard of winning one trophy during the coming season: it can be done, but winning

Figure 5.1 The hierarchy of different standards

that trophy will require focus, concentration and special effort. Alternatively, you might just set a normal standard, which is what a business usually achieves. Your team might finish in the middle of the table each year, avoiding relegation yet not playing particularly well or winning any trophies and you might settle for this as this is what is normally achieved. Anything beyond this is a bonus!

In the same way, businesses will set standards based on what they consider to be achievable under normal circumstances, with anything beyond this basic level of achievement being seen as a bonus for the business. Alternatively, directors can set performance targets to encourage staff to put in more effort to generate higher levels of productivity. Staff will be incentivised with the prospect of additional rewards to work towards these attainable standards.

> **WHY IS THIS RELEVANT TO ME?**   Different standards
>
> To enable you as an accounting professional to appreciate the different performance standards that can be set by businesses and what these different performance standards involve.

GO BACK OVER THIS AGAIN!   Are you sure you can summarise what ideal, attainable and normal standards are? Go to the **online workbook** and complete Exercises 5.3 to make sure you understand the different standards of performance that can be set.

SETTING THE STANDARD

We have already considered Anna's cost card, the revenue and costs for one dining chair. This is reproduced on the next page. This cost card can be seen as an example of a standard cost card, the expected costs of each input into each chair along with the revenue that each chair is expected to generate.

Standard cost card: wooden dining chair	£
Variable costs	
Wood	18.00
Glue	0.60
Screws	1.00
Sandpaper	0.40
Direct labour	25.00
Prime cost (total variable cost)	45.00
Rent	6.00
Business rates	1.00
Heating and lighting	0.80
Total production cost of one chair	52.80
Standard selling price	85.00
Standard profit per dining chair	**32.20**

The standard cost card shows the direct inputs into a product, together with an allocation of fixed overhead to each product. Anna will use this standard cost card to measure actual outcomes and to analyse variances from her expectations. These variances could be positive (favourable variances) resulting in lower costs or more revenue than expected, or negative (unfavourable variances) arising from higher costs or lower revenue than anticipated. Unfavourable variances are sometimes called adverse variances but we will stick with the term unfavourable in this book.

To illustrate how standard costing and variance analysis work, let us consider a comprehensive example (Example 5.1).

EXAMPLE 5.1

Anna has completed her first year of dining chair production. Things have gone well and her workshop has made and sold 1,100 chairs over the first 12 months of operations. While happy with her success, Anna is puzzled. She has used her original standard cost card to produce a forecast of the profit she should have made based on production and sales of 1,100 chairs. This calculation is shown in Illustration 5.1. However, her actual results are somewhat different from this forecast and these actual results are shown in Illustration 5.2.

Illustration 5.1 Anna: expected sales income, costs and profit for the first year of trading based on the standard cost card for sales and production of 1,100 dining chairs

	£	£
Sales 1,100 chairs at £85		93,500
Direct materials: wood 1,100 chairs at £18	19,800	
Direct materials: other 1,100 chairs at £2	2,200	
Direct labour 1,100 chairs at £25	27,500	
Total variable costs		49,500
Total contribution (sales – variable costs)		44,000
Fixed costs		
Rent	6,000	
Rates	1,000	
Heating and lighting	800	
Total fixed costs		7,800
Expected profit for the year		**36,200**

Illustration 5.2 Anna: actual sales income, costs and profit for the first year of trading from the production and sale of 1,100 dining chairs

	£	£
Sales		92,400
Direct materials: wood	19,720	
Direct materials: other	2,200	
Direct labour	28,644	
Total variable costs		50,564
Total contribution (sales – variable costs)		41,836
Fixed costs		
Rent	6,000	
Rates	1,000	
Heating and lighting	600	
Total fixed costs		7,600
Actual profit for the year		**34,236**

Given that her calculations show that she should have made a profit of £36,200 from the sale of 1,100 dining chairs, Anna is disappointed that her actual sales income and costs statement above shows a profit of only £34,236, a difference of £1,964. She has asked you to investigate how this difference has arisen.

A comparison of the two statements will enable us to determine where the differences between expected and actual profit lie. A comparison table can be drawn up as shown in Illustration 5.3. What is this comparison telling us? We can summarise our conclusions as follows:

Illustration 5.3 Anna: comparison of actual and expected sales, expenses and profit for the first year of trading from the production and sale of 1,100 dining chairs

	Actual for 1,100 chairs £	Expected for 1,100 chairs £	Total variance £
Sales	92,400	93,500	(1,100)
Less:			
Direct materials: wood	19,720	19,800	80
Direct materials: other	2,200	2,200	—
Direct labour	28,644	27,500	(1,144)
Rent	6,000	6,000	—
Rates	1,000	1,000	—
Heating and lighting	600	800	200
Profit for the year	**34,236**	**36,200**	**(1,964)**

- Sales revenue from the sale of the 1,100 chairs is £1,100 lower than it should have been had Anna sold all her output at £85 per chair.

- The wood for chairs cost £80 less than it should have done based on a wood cost per chair of £18.

- Direct labour cost Anna £1,144 more than it should have done for the production of 1,100 chairs.

- Heating and lighting cost £200 less than expected.

- All other expenses (direct materials: other, rent and rates) cost exactly what Anna had expected them to.

- The positive reductions in spending on wood and heat and light are deducted from the lower sales income and the overspend on direct labour to give the net difference between the two profits of £1,964.

WHY IS THIS RELEVANT TO ME?   Expected costs v. actual costs and calculation of total variances

As an accounting professional you will be expected to understand:

- How standard costs can be used to calculate a statement of expected revenue and costs at any given level of production and sales
- How to compare actual revenue and costs with expected revenue and costs
- How to produce a variance statement comparing actual and expected outcomes
- That each total variance is the difference between the expected revenue and costs of actual production and sales and the actual revenue and costs of actual production and sales

---

NUMERICAL EXERCISES   Are you completely confident that you could use a standard cost card to:

- Produce a statement of expected costs and revenue
- Compare this to a statement of actual costs and revenue and
- Calculate total variances from this comparison?

Go to the **online workbook** and attempt Numerical exercises 5.1 to make sure you can undertake these tasks.

You explain these differences to Anna, but she is still not satisfied. Why has sales revenue fallen from what she expected it to be and why has so much more been spent on labour than she expected? You ask Anna for her accounting records for the year in order to investigate these differences. Once you have undertaken your investigations, you make the following discoveries:

- The average selling price for each dining chair was not £85, but £84.

- The wood was bought in at a cost of £1.70 per kg instead of the expected cost of £1.80 per kg (Chapter 4, Example 4.15).

- The expected usage of wood for 1,100 chairs should have been 10 kg per chair (Chapter 4, Example 4.15 Step 2) × 1,100 chairs = 11,000 kg whereas actual usage was 11,600 kg.

- Anna expected each chair to take two hours to make and she expected to pay her employees £25 for each chair produced. In fact, she decided to pay her employees an hourly rate of £12.40 instead of a payment for each chair produced.

- The 1,100 chairs should have taken 2,200 hours to produce (1,100 × 2), but her wages records show that her two employees were paid for a total of 2,310 hours.

- Because of the autumn and winter weather being milder than anticipated, the heating costs came in at £200 lower than expected.

How can this information be used to explain the differences between the actual results and the expected results based on the increased levels of production and sales?

DIRECT MATERIAL PRICE AND USAGE VARIANCES

We saw in Illustration 5.3 that the wood for 1,100 chairs cost £19,720 against an expected cost of £19,800 (1,100 × £18 per chair in Anna's original estimates). This gave a total variance of £80. This is a favourable variance as Anna spent £80 less than expected on the wood used in production of her dining chairs. However, our additional investigations revealed two facts relating to the wood used in the chairs. First, the purchase price of wood was £1.70 per kg instead of the expected £1.80 and 11,600 kg of wood were used instead of the expected 11,000 kg. So the material was cheaper than expected but the usage was more than expected. Do these two differences explain the total variance of £80?

Figure 5.2 Direct material variances

Standard costing calls these two differences the direct material price variance and the direct material usage variance (Figure 5.2). The price variance shows how much of the difference is due to a higher or lower cost for direct material while the usage variance shows how much of the difference is due to the quantity of material used varying from what the standard says should have been used.

The direct material price variance is calculated in the following way:

	£
11,600 kg of wood should have cost (11,600 × £1.80)	20,880
11,600 kg of material actually cost	19,720
Direct material price variance	1,160

Does this make sense? The standard cost for wood is £1.80 per kg, whereas Anna paid £1.70 per kg, a difference of £0.10 per kg. Anna's employees used 11,600 kg of wood, so 11,600 × £0.10 = £1,160, the same answer as above.

Is this variance favourable or unfavourable? To answer this question you should ask whether the cost is higher or lower than the standard cost says it should be. In this case, the actual quantity of material used cost less than the standard cost says it should have done, so this is a favourable variance. Anna has spent less on wood for her chairs than the standard says she should have done.

However, while Anna has spent less on wood for her chairs than her standard says she should have spent, her craftsmen have used more material than anticipated in the standard. Each chair should use 10 kg of wood and so 1,100 chairs should have used 11,000 kg in total. As actual usage was 11,600 kg, Anna's employees have used 600 kg more than expected. The usage variance is calculated as follows:

	Kg
1,100 chairs should have used 10 kg of wood × 1,100 chairs	11,000
1,100 chairs actually used	11,600
Direct material usage variance in kg	(600)
	£
Direct material usage variance in kg × standard price per kg (600) × £1.80	(1,080)

Again, we can ask whether this variance is favourable or unfavourable. More material has been used than the standard says should have been used, so this variance is unfavourable. Anna's craftsmen have used more wood than they should have done and this has meant that her profit has been reduced as a result of this over usage.

DIRECT MATERIAL TOTAL VARIANCE

How do the price and usage variances relate to the total variance that we calculated earlier? This total variance was a favourable variance of £80 (£19,720 actual cost of the wood compared to £19,800 expected cost of wood for 1,100 chairs). Summarising our two variances above will give us this £80 total variance thus:

	£	Favourable/(Unfavourable)
Direct material price variance	1,160	Favourable
Direct material usage variance	(1,080)	(Unfavourable)
Direct material total variance	**80**	Favourable

WHY IS THIS RELEVANT TO ME?   Direct material price variance, direct material usage variance and direct material total variance

To enable you as an accounting professional to:

- Appreciate that variations in both the price and the usage of material should be used to explain the total direct material variance
- Calculate the direct material price variance and direct material usage variance
- Demonstrate that the total direct material variance is the sum of the direct material price variance and the direct material usage variance

SUMMARY OF KEY CONCEPTS   Are you confident you can state the formulae for the direct material variance and the two sub-variances, direct material price variance and direct material usage variance? Go to the **online workbook** to revise these variances with Summary of key concepts 5.1.

MULTIPLE CHOICE QUESTIONS   Do you think that you could calculate the direct material variance and the sub-variances, direct material price variance and direct material usage variance? Go to the **online workbook** and have a go at Multiple choice questions 5.1 to test out your ability to calculate these figures.

DIRECT MATERIAL VARIANCES: INFORMATION AND CONTROL

We have calculated our variances, but what do they tell Anna and what use can she make of them? Our investigations and calculations show that cheaper material has been purchased and that this has saved Anna money on the material acquired. However, this money seems to have been saved at a cost. While the material is cheaper, more has been used than should have been and this suggests that the wood may not have been of the expected quality. Lower quality materials tend to lead to more wastage as they require more work to shape and fit them into the final product. This additional working has resulted in a higher usage as material was lost in the production process. Anna now needs to conduct further investigations to determine whether this lower cost material really is of lower quality. If so, she should in future demand only material of the requisite quality to minimise wastage and to guarantee the quality of the finished product.

Alternatively, Anna's employees might just have been careless in the way they handled the wood. More careful handling and more thoughtful workmanship might have resulted in less wastage and bigger savings from using this cheaper material. If this is the case, then her workers may need additional advice or training on how to make the best use of the material they are provided with so that wastage is reduced and profits increased. Price and usage variances thus point the way towards the areas that require further investigation to determine the reasons behind these variances and the means to resolve the problems arising.

WHY IS THIS RELEVANT TO ME?   Direct material variances: information and control

To enable you as an accounting professional to appreciate that:

- Unfavourable material variances are only indicators of problems that require management investigation, intervention and action to correct them

- Management must consider possible reasons for the variances that have arisen, along with potential solutions to ensure that unfavourable material variances do not persist

---

GO BACK OVER THIS AGAIN!   How confident are you that you can identify reasons for changes in the direct material price and usage variances? Go to the **online workbook** and complete Exercises 5.4 to test your skill in this area.

DIRECT LABOUR RATE AND EFFICIENCY VARIANCES

Our summary table of expected and actual costs in Illustration 5.3 shows that direct labour cost £28,644 against an expected cost to produce 1,100 chairs of £27,500. This is an unfavourable variance as Anna has incurred £1,144 more in direct labour costs than she expected to. Let's look first at the additional information uncovered by our investigations. Anna's employees were paid

Figure 5.3 Direct labour variances

not for the dining chairs that they produced but at a fixed rate per hour. This hourly rate was £12.40 instead of the expected £12.50 and the actual hours used in producing 1,100 chairs were 2,310 against an expected 2,200. Again, can these two differences explain the total variance of £1,144?

Just as for direct material, we can also calculate sub-variances for direct labour (Figure 5.3). The direct labour rate variance performs the same function as the direct material price variance by taking into account the unit cost of each hour paid for production. The direct labour efficiency variance looks at the time taken to make the actual goods and compares this with the hours that were expected to be used for that level of production. Where the hours taken are lower than they should have been, workers have been more efficient in producing goods. However, where more hours have been used to make the production than were expected, this will mean that labour has been less efficient than expected. In just the same way, the standard time to work through this chapter might be set at 10 hours, but different students will have very different experiences of how long studying this chapter will take them!

Direct labour rate variance is calculated in the following way:

	£
2,310 labour hours should have cost (2,310 × £12.50)	28,875
2,310 labour hours actually cost	28,644
Direct labour rate variance	**231**

Direct labour cost is lower than the standard cost says it should be for the hours actually worked, so this variance is favourable. This would be expected as the actual rate at which labour is paid is £12.40 per hour compared to the standard rate of £12.50 per hour. Thus you could have calculated this variance by taking the difference between the two hourly rates of £0.10 (£12.50 − £12.40) and multiplied this by 2,310 hours to give you the same answer of £231 less than 2,310 standard hours should have cost.

Again, while Anna has spent less on labour for her chairs than her standard says she should have done, her craftsmen have also used more hours than they should have spent in making the actual production. Each chair should use two hours of direct labour and so 1,100 chairs should have used 2,200 labour hours. As actual labour hours were 2,310, Anna's employees have taken 110 hours more than expected to make the actual production. The direct labour efficiency variance is calculated as follows:

	Hours
1,100 chairs should have used 1,100 × 2 hours	2,200
1,100 chairs actually used	2,310
Direct labour efficiency variance in hours	(110)

	£
Direct labour efficiency variance in hours × standard rate/hour (110) × £12.50	(1,375)

This variance is unfavourable as more labour hours have been used than the standard says should have been used in the production of 1,100 chairs. This means that Anna has incurred more cost and made a lower profit as a result of this increased usage and lower than expected efficiency of the workforce.

DIRECT LABOUR TOTAL VARIANCE

The sum of the direct labour rate and direct labour efficiency variances should equal the total variance that we calculated in Illustration 5.3. This total variance was £1,144 (£28,644 actual cost of direct labour compared to a £27,500 expected direct labour cost for 1,100 chairs). Summarising our two variances above will give us this £1,144 total variance thus:

	£	Favourable/Unfavourable
Direct labour rate variance	231	Favourable
Direct labour efficiency variance	(1,375)	(Unfavourable)
Direct labour total variance	**(1,144)**	(Unfavourable)

WHY IS THIS RELEVANT TO ME?   Direct labour rate variance, direct labour efficiency variance and direct labour total variance

To enable you as an accounting professional to:

- Appreciate that variations in both the rate at which labour is paid and the speed at which employees work should be used to explain the total direct labour variance
- Calculate the direct labour rate variance and the direct labour efficiency variance
- Realise that the total direct labour variance is the sum of the direct labour rate variance and the direct labour efficiency variance

SUMMARY OF KEY CONCEPTS   Are you sure you know how to calculate the direct labour total variance and its associated sub-variances, direct labour rate variance and direct labour efficiency variance? Go to the **online workbook** to check your understanding of how these variances are calculated with Summary of key concepts 5.2.

MULTIPLE CHOICE QUESTIONS   Are you convinced that you can calculate the direct labour total variance and its associated sub-variances, direct labour rate variance and direct labour efficiency variance? Go to the **online workbook** and attempt Multiple choice questions 5.2 to check your ability to calculate these figures.

DIRECT LABOUR VARIANCES: INFORMATION AND CONTROL

Again, merely calculating the variances is not enough: these variances have to be investigated and the causes, once identified, used to improve operations with a view to improving efficiency and making additional profit.

It seems that Anna can employ craftsmen at a slightly lower hourly rate than she had expected. This is helpful as a small amount shaved off the labour rate means additional profit for the business. Unfortunately, her craftsmen have taken rather longer than they should have done to make the 1,100 chairs over the course of the year. Why might this be? Under our analysis of the direct material variance (this chapter, Direct material variances: information and control), we suggested that the wood used in the chairs might be of lower quality and hence require more working and shaping before it could be incorporated into the finished chairs. If this were the case, then the additional hours taken in the production of the chairs could be accounted for by this additional working and shaping. Anna should therefore discuss this issue with her employees to find out why these additional hours were worked and whether there is a problem with the wood that is being used. A lower price for direct materials is always welcome, but if this lower price is causing additional costs to be incurred elsewhere in the production cycle, then higher quality materials at a higher price should be acquired. In this way, the higher quality materials will pay for themselves as lower labour costs will be incurred in making goods and more profit will be generated. Alternatively, Anna's craftsmen might just have worked more slowly to increase the number of hours they worked, thereby increasing their pay. To avoid this problem, Anna needs to think about incentivising her staff to work to the standard while still producing goods of the expected quality.

WHY IS THIS RELEVANT TO ME?   Direct labour variances: information and control

As an accounting professional you should understand:

- That direct labour rate and efficiency variances are only indicators of problems that require management investigation, intervention and action

- How to suggest possible reasons for the labour variances that have arisen, along with potential solutions to ensure that unfavourable variances do not persist

---

GO BACK OVER THIS AGAIN!   How easily do you think you can identify reasons for changes in the direct labour rate and efficiency variances? Go to the **online workbook** and complete Exercises 5.5 to test your skill in this area.

VARIABLE OVERHEAD VARIANCES

Anna does not incur any variable overheads in her business. If she did incur such overheads, the variances between standard and actual would be calculated in exactly the same way as for direct material and direct labour. First, there would be the variable overhead total variance, the total cost of variable overheads for actual production compared to the standard cost of variable overheads for actual production. This total variance would then be split down into the variable overhead expenditure variance and the variable overhead efficiency variance. To avoid disrupting the flow of our comparison and analysis of Anna's actual and expected profit, further discussion and an example of variable overhead variances is given at the end of this chapter (this chapter, Appendix: variable overhead variances).

FIXED OVERHEAD EXPENDITURE VARIANCE

Fixed overheads are, of course, fixed. Therefore, the only relevant consideration in analysing this variance is the expected expenditure compared to the actual expenditure (Figure 5.4). In Anna's case, she expected her fixed costs to be £7,800 (rent: £6,000, rates: £1,000, heating and lighting: £800) whereas the actual outcome was £7,600 (rent: £6,000, rates: £1,000, heating and lighting: £600). As we discovered from our investigations into Anna's accounting records, £200 less was spent on heating and lighting during the year as a result of milder than expected winter weather. This £200 fixed overhead expenditure variance is favourable as less was spent on fixed costs than was expected.

Figure 5.4 Fixed overhead expenditure variance

SUMMARY OF KEY CONCEPTS   Do you think you can calculate the fixed overhead expenditure variance? Go to the **online workbook** to check your understanding of how these variances are calculated with Summary of key concepts 5.4.

FIXED OVERHEAD EXPENDITURE VARIANCE:
INFORMATION AND CONTROL

As fixed overheads are fixed, businesses usually experience only small variations between expected and actual fixed costs. Organisations will not usually investigate fixed overhead expenditure variances in depth. There is little that can be done to reduce fixed costs that are mostly imposed from outside the business. On the other hand, since materials, labour and variable overheads are driven directly by internal business activity, time will be spent on investigating these variances as much more can be done to reduce unfavourable variances arising from operations under the direct control of management.

> ### WHY IS THIS RELEVANT TO ME?   Fixed overhead expenditure variance
>
> As an accounting professional you should appreciate that:
>
> - Fixed overhead expenditure variance is the difference between total forecast expenditure on fixed overheads and actual fixed overhead expenditure
> - Fixed overheads are largely outside the control of businesses
> - Management time and effort will therefore focus upon investigating unfavourable material, labour and variable overhead variances as businesses can take action to control and eliminate or exploit these variances

SALES VARIANCES

Our final variances relate to income, the sales variances.

Sales price variance

The first of these is the sales price variance (Figure 5.5). Anna's expectation was that she would sell her dining chairs for £85 each. However, further investigation revealed that her average selling price was only £84, a reduction of £1 per chair sold. Anna sold 1,100 chairs, so her sales price variance was 1,100 × £1 = £1,100. This is unfavourable as she received less income per chair than budgeted.

Figure 5.5 Sales price variance

Sales volume variance

We have now explained all the variances between Anna's expected and actual profit from the sale of 1,100 chairs as shown in Illustration 5.3, but there is one more variance we need to consider. Anna's original expectation was that she would sell 1,000 chairs and make a profit of

£32,200. Her actual results show that she sold 1,100 chairs and made a profit of £34,236. The additional sales of 100 chairs give rise to another variance, the sales volume variance (Figure 5.6). This variance takes the additional standard contribution from each sale and multiplies this by the additional number of units sold to reflect the increased contribution arising from higher sales. This is logical as each additional sale will increase revenue by the selling price of one unit, but will also increase variable costs by the standard cost of direct material, direct labour and variable overhead for each additional unit of production and sales. Therefore, the contribution, the selling price less the variable costs, is used in this calculation. This variance is calculated as follows:

	Units
Actual units sold	1,100
Budgeted sales in units	1,000
Sales volume variance	100
	£
Sales volume variance at standard contribution 100 × £40	4,000

Is this variance favourable or unfavourable? As more sales have been made and more contribution earned, this is a favourable variance.

Anna will want to know why she is selling more chairs than budgeted and so she will investigate this increase with a view to selling even more. Similarly, she will also be keen to find out why her selling price is lower than budgeted and what factors in the market are pushing her selling price down.

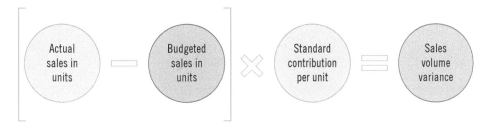

Figure 5.6 Sales volume variance

WHY IS THIS RELEVANT TO ME?   Sales price variance and sales volume variance

To enable you as an accounting professional to:

- Appreciate that variations in the selling price and in the volume of sales will have an impact upon the actual profit made compared to the expected profit
- Calculate the sales price variance and sales volume variance

SUMMARY OF KEY CONCEPTS   Are you sure you know how to calculate the sales price variance and the sales volume variance? Go to the **online workbook** to check your understanding of how these variances are calculated with Summary of key concepts 5.5.

MULTIPLE CHOICE QUESTIONS   Are you confident that you can calculate the sales price variance and the sales volume variance? Go to the **online workbook** and attempt Multiple choice questions 5.3 to check your ability to calculate these figures.

VARIANCES:SUMMARY

We can now summarise all our variances and reconcile Anna's forecast to her actual profit as follows. Anna's original expectation was that she would sell 1,000 dining chairs at £85 each and generate a profit of £32,200 so our starting point is this original expected profit.

	Unfavourable £	Favourable £	Profit £
Expected profit from selling 1,000 chairs at £85			32,200
Sales price variance	(1,100)		
Sales volume variance		4,000	
Direct material price variance		1,160	
Direct material usage variance	(1,080)		
Direct labour rate variance		231	
Direct labour efficiency variance	(1,375)		
Fixed overhead expenditure variance		200	
Total variances	(3,555)	5,591	
Add: favourable variances			5,591
Deduct: unfavourable variances			(3,555)
Actual profit for the year			**34,236**

WHY IS THIS RELEVANT TO ME?   Summary of variances and reconciliation of expected to actual profit

To enable you as an accounting professional to:

- Present all your variances in summary form to explain the difference between expected and actual profit

NUMERICAL EXERCISES   How confident do you feel handling extensive variance analysis questions? Go to the **online workbook** and have a go at Numerical exercises 5.2 to see how effectively you have absorbed the lessons of this chapter and how well you understand standard costing and variance analysis.

SHOW ME HOW TO DO IT   This chapter has involved a lot of tricky calculations and ideas. View Video presentation 5.1 in the **online workbook** to reinforce your knowledge of how standard costing and variance analysis is undertaken.

STANDARD COSTING: LIMITATIONS

Standard costing is a useful technique in comparing expected with actual financial performance. Where variances arise, these can be investigated to determine their causes and to identify ways in which unfavourable variances can be reduced and favourable variances maintained or enhanced. While setting standards encourages improvement and change for the better over time, standard costing also suffers from the following limitations:

- You will agree, I am sure, that this is a very complicated system and that this complexity can be discouraging when you first come across standard costing and variance analysis.

- It is also a time consuming system: a great deal of time will be needed to gather information from which to set the standards, to collect data from which to monitor standards against actual performance and to produce and evaluate variances.

- Time will also be needed to update standards for changes in costs owing to rising or falling material prices, wage costs, changes in overheads and selling prices.

- The information produced by variance analysis can be extensive and management may be overwhelmed by the volume of data presented to them.

- Standard costing systems tend to be rigid and inflexible: lack of flexibility should be avoided in the modern, ever changing business environment.

- However, modern computer systems should be able to assist management with the production of standard costs and variance analysis and in highlighting those variances that indicate that operations are out of control rather than within set tolerance limits. Profitability improvement depends upon careful cost control and such cost control is one of the key functions of business managers.

GIVE ME AN EXAMPLE 5.2   Adoption of standard costing variance analysis by small and medium sized companies in the UK

Management Accounting Practices of UK Small-Medium-Sized Enterprises published in July 2013 investigated the management accounting techniques and practices used by small and medium sized enterprises. While all the organisations surveyed undertook product costing, break-even analysis and working capital measures, none of the respondents engaged in standard cost variance analysis. However, the researchers considered that the failure to use this technique was appropriate for small and medium sized enterprises on cost benefit grounds as the costs of obtaining the information were substantial while the benefits gained were very limited.

Source: www.cimaglobal.com

Given these limitations, it is probably not surprising to find that small and medium sized companies make no use of standard costing variance analysis. Give me an example 5.2 describes this failure to adopt this approach.

APPENDIX: VARIABLE OVERHEAD VARIANCES

Variable overheads are absorbed into products on the basis of the number of hours of activity incurred to produce one unit of production. The standard cost for variable overheads will estimate the number of hours products take to produce on either a labour or machine hour basis (see Chapter 3, Absorption costing: overhead allocation, to refresh your memory on how absorption cost bases work) and then allocate the variable overhead to each product on the basis of the standard number of hours required to produce one unit multiplied by the standard variable overhead cost per hour.

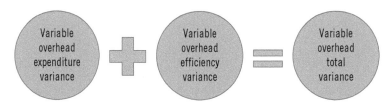

Figure 5.7 Variable overhead variances

Variable overhead variance calculations divide the total variance into variable overhead expenditure and variable overhead efficiency variances (Figure 5.7), in much the same way that the total direct labour variance is divided into labour rate and labour efficiency variances. The expenditure variance measures the difference between the variable overhead that should have been incurred for the level of production achieved and the actual expenditure. The variable overhead efficiency variance compares the difference between the actual hours taken to produce the actual production and the standard hours that actual production would have been expected to take. Think about how these variances are calculated in Example 5.2.

EXAMPLE 5.2

The Ultimate Chef Company manufactures food processors. Variable overhead incurred in the production of each food processor is set at 2½ hours at £6 per hour. During September, 1,000 food processors were produced. The employees of the Ultimate Chef Company were paid for 2,450 hours. The variable overhead cost for September was £14,540. Calculate:

- The variable overhead total variance
- The variable overhead expenditure variance
- The variable overhead efficiency variance

State whether each variance is favourable or unfavourable.

Variable overhead total variance

This is what the actual production should have cost and what it did cost.

	£
1,000 food processors should have cost 1,000 × 2½ hours × £6	15,000
1,000 food processors actually cost	14,540
Variable overhead total variance	**460**

Variable overhead expenditure variance

This is what the variable overhead should have cost compared with what it did cost for the actual hours worked.

	£
2,450 hours should have cost (2,450 × £6.00)	14,700
2,450 hours actually cost	14,540
Variable overhead expenditure variance	**160**

The variable overhead expenditure variance is favourable as less cost was incurred than expected for the actual number of hours used in production.

Variable overhead efficiency variance

This is how many hours should have been worked and how many were actually worked for the actual level of production.

	Hours
1,000 food processors should have used 1,000 × 2½ hours	2,500
1,000 food processors actually used	2,450
Variable overhead efficiency variance in hours	50

	£
Variable overhead efficiency variance in hours × standard rate/hour 50 × £6.00	**300**

The variable overhead efficiency variance is favourable as fewer hours were used than expected for the level of production achieved.

The variable overhead expenditure variance and the variable overhead efficiency variance can be summarised as follows to give the variable overhead total variance:

	£	Favourable/Unfavourable
Variable overhead expenditure variance	160	Favourable
Variable overhead efficiency variance	300	Favourable
Variable overhead total variance	**460**	Favourable

WHY IS THIS RELEVANT TO ME?   Variable overhead expenditure variance, variable overhead efficiency variance and variable overhead total variance

As an accounting professional you should now:

• Appreciate that variations in both the variable overhead expenditure and the speed of working should be used to explain the variable overhead total variance

• Be able to calculate the variable overhead total variance, variable overhead expenditure variance and variable overhead efficiency variance

• Understand that the variable overhead total variance is the sum of the variable overhead expenditure variance and the variable overhead efficiency variance

SUMMARY OF KEY CONCEPTS   Are you sure you know how to calculate the variable overhead total variance and the associated sub-variances, variable overhead expenditure variance and variable overhead efficiency variance? Go to the **online workbook** to check your understanding of how these variances are calculated with Summary of key concepts 5.3.

MULTIPLE CHOICE QUESTIONS   Are you confident that you can calculate the variable overhead total variance and its associated variances, variable overhead expenditure and variable overhead efficiency variances? Go to the **online workbook** and attempt Multiple choice questions 5.4 to check your ability to calculate these figures.

CHAPTER SUMMARY

You should now have learnt that:

• Selling price, material, labour, direct expenses, variable overhead and fixed overhead are the components that make up a standard cost

• Standard cost is an expected rather than an actual cost

• Standard costs are used in the planning and evaluation of operations

• Total variances between what should have been achieved and what was achieved explain the difference between actual and expected profits

• Variance analysis splits total variances into their constituent sub-variances arising from:

— Price (material), rate (labour) and expenditure (variable overhead) and

— Usage (material) and efficiency (labour and variable overhead)

- Sales variances are split into sales price and sales volume variances

- Variances help identify problems requiring further investigation and analysis to assist in the control of operations

---

QUICK REVISION   Test your knowledge with the online flashcards in Summary of key concepts and attempt the Multiple choice questions, all in the **online workbook**.

END-OF-CHAPTER QUESTIONS

Solutions to these questions can be found in the **online workbook**.

❯ DEVELOP YOUR UNDERSTANDING

❯ Question 5.1

There are 30 apple trees in the orchard attached to Bill's farm. Bill reckons that each tree will be given five doses of fertiliser each year at a cost of £4 per tree and that 10 hours of labour per tree will be required to pick the apples from and prune each tree. Workers are paid £7.50 per hour.

At the end of the apple picking season, Bill calculates that the 30 trees only received four doses of fertiliser, although these cost £4.50 for each tree, and that the picking and pruning was undertaken at a cost of £8 per hour for 270 hours of labour.

Required

Calculate:

(a) The total expected costs of the orchard for the past year.

(b) The actual total costs of the orchard for the past year.

(c) Material total, price and usage variances.

(d) Labour total, rate and efficiency variances.

State whether the variances are favourable or unfavourable.

❯ Question 5.2

Fred bakes cakes. His budget indicates that he will produce and sell 1,000 cakes during March at a selling price of £15 each. At the end of March he calculates that his selling price was £15.50 for each cake produced and sold and that he has generated £14,725 in sales. His standard cost card for each cake shows that his variable cost of production is £6 per cake.

Required

Calculate for Fred for March:

(a) The sales price variance.

(b) The sales volume variance.

State whether the variances are favourable or unfavourable. Assuming that Fred's actual production costs are £6 per cake, prove that the sales price and sales volume variances explain fully his additional contribution for March.

>> TAKE IT FURTHER

>> Question 5.3

Sanguinary Services carries out blood tests for local hospitals, surgeries and doctors. The standard cost card for each blood test is given below.

	£
Chemicals used in blood tests: 10 millilitres at 50 pence/ml	5.00
Laboratory worker: 15 minutes at £16 per hour	4.00
Fixed overhead of the testing centre	2.00
Total cost	11.00
Charge for each blood test	15.00
Standard profit per blood test	**4.00**

The centre has fixed overheads of £72,000 per annum and plans to carry out 36,000 blood tests every year at the rate of 3,000 tests per month.

In April, the following results were recorded:

	Number
Blood tests carried out	**3,600**

	£
Chemicals used in blood tests: 33,750 millilitres at 48 pence/ml	16,200
Laboratory workers: 925 hours at £16.20 per hour	14,985
Fixed overhead of the testing centre	7,500
Total cost	38,685
Charge for each blood test 3,600 at £15.50	55,800
Profit for April	**17,115**

Required

(a) Calculate the profit that the centre expected to make in April, based on the original forecast of 3,000 blood tests in the month.

(b) Calculate the following:

- Sales volume variance
- Sales price variance
- Direct material total variance
- Direct material price variance
- Direct material usage variance
- Direct labour total variance
- Direct labour rate variance
- Direct labour efficiency variance
- Fixed overhead expenditure variance

Stating whether each variance is favourable or unfavourable.

(c) Prepare a statement reconciling the expected profit to the actual profit for April.

≫ Question 5.4

Smashers Tennis Club runs coaching courses for its junior members. Each course lasts for ten weeks and is priced at £70 for each junior member. Smashers expects each course to attract 12 junior members. Each course is allocated 20 tennis balls for each participating junior at an expected cost of £10 for 20 balls. A professionally qualified tennis coach undertakes each hour-long coaching session over the ten weeks at a cost of £30 per hour.

The club administrator is reviewing the costs and income for the latest junior coaching course and she is trying to understand why the surplus from the course is £438 instead of £420. She tells you that the course actually attracted 16 juniors instead of the 12 expected and that a total of 400 balls had been allocated to and used by juniors on the course. Balls for the latest coaching course had cost 60 pence each. The coach had received an increase in her hourly rate to £33 per hour. The price for each course had been reduced by 10 per cent on the original price in order to attract additional participants.

Required

(a) Calculate the original expected surplus from the coaching course.

(b) Calculate the expected surplus from the coaching course given that 16 juniors were enrolled.

(c) Calculate the actual income and costs for the course.

(d) Calculate variances for income and expenditure and present these in tabular form to reconcile the original expected surplus to the actual surplus.

Vijay Manufacturing produces garden gnomes. The standard cost card for garden gnomes is as follows:

	£
Plastic: 2 kg at £2.25 per kg	4.50
Labour: 0.5 hours at £8 per hour	4.00
Variable overhead: 4 machine hours at £0.75 per hour	3.00
Fixed overhead	1.00
Total cost	12.50
Selling price to Plastic Gnome Painters Limited	15.00
Standard profit per garden gnome	**2.50**

Fixed overheads total £24,000 and are allocated to production on the basis that 24,000 gnomes will be produced each year, 2,000 each month.

Vijay is reviewing the actual production and sales for the month of June. The weather has been wet and garden gnome sales have fallen from their normal levels. Consequently, the company has had to reduce the selling price in June to £14 per gnome in order to keep production and sales moving. Production and sales for the month were 1,800 gnomes. The input price per kg of plastic was £2.50 as a result of a sharp rise in the oil price but, because of reduced wastage and careful material handling, only 3,500 kg of plastic were used in June. Owing to the high level of unemployment in the area, Vijay has been able to pay his employees at the rate of £7.50 per hour. Total labour hours for the month were 950. Total machine hours for the month were 7,000 and the fixed and variable overheads totalled £1,600 and £5,500 respectively. Vijay has been trying to understand why his profit has fallen from its expected level for the month and has asked for your help. You are meeting him later on today to discuss his figures and to show him how his expected profit has fallen to the actual profit for the month.

Required

Draft figures for your meeting later on today with Vijay. Your figures should include:

(a) Calculations to show the profit Vijay expected to make from the production and sale of 2,000 garden gnomes in the month of June.

(b) Calculations to show the profit Vijay might have expected to make from the production and sale of 1,800 garden gnomes for the month of June.

(c) Calculations to show the profit Vijay actually did make for the month of June.

(d) A reconciliation statement showing all the necessary favourable and unfavourable variances to explain the difference between the expected profit for June calculated in (a) and the actual profit calculated in (c).

BUDGETING

6

LEARNING OUTCOMES

Once you have read this chapter and worked through the questions and examples in both this chapter and the online workbook, you should be able to:

- Discuss the ways in which budgets involve planning, communicating, coordinating, motivating and control functions

- Prepare budgeted monthly statements of profit or loss for an entity

- Determine the timing of cash inflows and outflows from budgeted income and expenditure

- Prepare a month-by-month cash budget for an entity

- Draw up a budgeted statement of financial position at the end of a projected accounting period

- Undertake comparisons between budgeted and actual income and expenditure to highlight variances in expected and actual financial performance

- Undertake sensitivity analysis to assess the effect that any changes in budget assumptions will have

INTRODUCTION

The word budget is all around us, every day. There are constant reminders of the national budget, individuals' budgets and business budgets. You yourself may have drawn up a budget for what you expected to spend during your first year at university. This budget might have been quite basic to start with, but, as you thought more about the costs you would be likely to incur, your budget would have been refined and become a more realistic means of planning your anticipated expenditure and its timing. However, budgeting can occur at a much simpler level. When you go out for the evening, the amount of money you take with you is your budget for that evening. In both cases, actual expenditure is likely to be very different from your original plan due to unforeseen costs—an expensive book or field trip for your course or a taxi home when you missed the last bus. This does not mean that the exercise was not worthwhile: planning ahead is important for both individuals and business organisations. Experience helps us to refine our future budgets so that the actual outcomes gradually become closer to our budgeted expectations.

WHAT IS BUDGETING?

For business people, a budget is the expression of a plan in money terms. That plan is a prediction of future income, expenditure, cash inflows and cash outflows. Once each stage of the plan is completed, then the actual results can be compared to expectations to determine whether actual outcomes are better, worse or the same as anticipated. As we saw in Chapter 5 on standard costing, such comparisons are a means of controlling an organisation's operations and taking action to reduce or eliminate unfavourable divergences from the plan while finding out the ways in which better than expected performance can be maintained and built upon.

WHY IS THIS RELEVANT TO ME?   What is budgeting?

As an accounting professional:

* You should appreciate that all businesses undertake budgeting
* You will be expected to play a significant role in the annual budgeting process
* Building an awareness of what budgeting is, what it involves and how to budget in practice will be essential knowledge

---

SUMMARY OF KEY CONCEPTS   Are you convinced you can define budgeting? Go to the **online workbook** to revise the definition with Summary of key concepts 6.1.

Give me an example 6.1 highlights the importance accorded to budgeting and forecasting by the business community.

The July 2009 CIMA report, *Management accounting tools for today and tomorrow*, surveyed the current and intended usage by business of more than 100 management accounting and related tools based on a questionnaire completed by 439 respondents from across the globe. The most commonly used technique in practice was financial year forecasting with 86 per cent of respondents engaging in this activity. The third most popular technique was cash forecasting which was used by 78 per cent of those businesses surveyed. These two activities were the most popular budgeting tools across every size of company in the survey from small to very large. These findings indicate the very high priority that is accorded to budgeting and forecasting in the business community.

Source: www.cimaglobal.com

BUDGET OBJECTIVES AND THE BUDGETING PROCESS

Everyone has objectives, both individuals and organisations. It is not enough to have a vague hope that everything will work out and that objectives will be achieved without any planning or positive actions and a great deal of hard work being undertaken. Thus, individuals and organisations have to decide how they will achieve their objectives through careful planning on a step-by-step basis. A well-known phrase among university tutors is 'failing to plan is planning to fail'. This is just as true when you are writing an essay as it is when making projections for what a business will achieve in the next 12 months.

Budgets and the budgeting process thus assist organisations to focus upon achieving and the means to achieve their objectives in the ways shown in Table 6.1.

Table 6.1 The objectives of the budgeting process

Planning	Budgeting forces entities to look ahead and plan. Planning helps organisations think about the future and what they want to achieve, as well as helping them anticipate problems to determine how these will be overcome.
Communication	The directors will have plans to achieve certain objectives. However, if they do not tell everyone else involved in the organisation about those objectives, then they will not be achieved. Budgets communicate information to those persons and departments involved in achieving objectives to tell them what level of performance they have to attain to fulfil their part in reaching the desired goal.
Coordination and integration	Different departments have to work together to achieve objectives. The directors have to tell marketing what level of sales they need to achieve to reach the profit goal. Marketing then have to liaise with production to make sure that production can produce this number of goods and to the required timescale. Production has to make sure that purchasing is buying in the necessary raw materials to enable production to take place on schedule while personnel have to recruit the necessary workers to make the goods. Budgets thus coordinate and integrate business activities to give the organisation the best chance of achieving its goals.

→

Control	Budgeting enables an organisation to control its activities and check its progress towards achieving objectives by regularly comparing actual results with budgeted outcomes. Differences can then be investigated and action taken either to bring operations back on track or to exploit favourable trends further.
Responsibility	Responsibility for different parts of the budget is delegated to individual managers. One person alone cannot achieve everything on their own, so various managers work as part of a team, each with their own responsibility for hitting the targets assigned to them in the budget. These managers are then assessed and rewarded on the basis of their ability to meet their agreed objectives. Breaking down one big task into various smaller tasks and then making several managers responsible for achieving each of these smaller targets is a very good way to get things done.
Motivation	Budgets are used as motivating devices. Something too easy is not motivating and managers need to be challenged to achieve more. In the same way, your degree is challenging so that achieving your qualification motivates you and makes it worthwhile. As an incentive to achieve challenging budget targets, managers will be rewarded with bonuses. However, it is important to make sure that the targets are not completely unrealistic as impossible targets will result in managers giving up before they have even started.

WHY IS THIS RELEVANT TO ME?   Budgeting objectives and the budgeting process

As an accounting professional you should be aware of:

- What the objectives of the budgeting process are
- The roles budgeting plays in setting and achieving organisational goals
- What the budgeting process will expect of you

SUMMARY OF KEY CONCEPTS   Are you certain that you can summarise the objectives of budgeting and the budgeting process? Go to the **online workbook** to revise these objectives with Summary of key concepts 6.2.

GO BACK OVER THIS AGAIN!   Are you convinced that you understand the objectives of budgeting and the budgeting process? Go to the **online workbook** and attempt Exercises 6.1 to make sure you have fully grasped the principles.

GO BACK OVER THIS AGAIN!   Are you quite sure you understand how the budgeting objectives and the budgeting process work in practice? Go to the **online workbook** Exercises 6.2 and consider the scenario there to see how budgeting objectives and the budgeting process operate in everyday life.

BUDGETING: COMPREHENSIVE EXAMPLE

Now that we have defined a budget and considered what the organisational objectives in preparing budgets are, let's look in detail at the process of actually setting a budget through a practical example. This process involves several steps, which we will think about one by one.

Anna is considering the expansion of her business. She is planning to move her operations to a bigger workshop and has asked her bank for a loan with which to finance this expansion. In connection with her application for the loan, the bank has asked Anna to produce a budget covering sales, costs and cash flows for the next 12 months, together with a budgeted statement of financial position at the end of those 12 months. Anna has made a start on her budgets and has produced information for the first three months of the next financial year. However, she is finding budgeting difficult and has asked for your assistance in helping her to complete the remainder of the required information.

Step 1: setting the strategy and deciding on selling prices

Anna first has to decide what she wants to achieve and whether there are any obstacles she must overcome or which will stand in the way of her achieving her goals. She wants to expand, but she feels that the lack of finance is holding her back. However, her products are selling well and her customers are pleased with the quality of her output. Will she be able to finance her proposed expansion from current operations if the bank is not willing to help her? Budgeting will help her to answer this question. Figure 6.1 illustrates the first step in the budgeting process.

Figure 6.1 Budgeting step 1: setting the strategy and the selling prices

Her first decision will be to set her selling prices. Should she raise these, leave them at the same level or reduce the selling prices of each product? She has gone back to the costings for her three products that she presented in Chapter 4 (Limiting factor (key factor) analysis). These are reproduced in Illustration 6.1. Can she justify raising her selling prices? This will first depend on whether her costs are rising.

Illustration 6.1 Anna: selling prices and variable costs for dining chairs, coffee tables and kitchen cabinets

	Dining chairs	Coffee tables	Kitchen cabinets
	£	£	£
Selling price	85.00	50.00	80.00
Materials: wood	(18.00)	(12.60)	(10.80)
Materials: other	(2.00)	(5.40)	(9.20)
Direct labour	(25.00)	(18.00)	(30.00)
Contribution	**40.00**	**14.00**	**30.00**

Anna tells you that she has discussed the price of wood and other materials with her suppliers. They have reassured her that there are no price rises or material shortages anticipated in the next 12 months. This tells Anna that there will be no supply difficulties which will need to be planned for over the course of the coming year. At the same time she now knows that there are no expected increases in the cost of inputs to her products which would need to be built into her selling prices to pass on these cost increases to her customers.

Her workforce is loyal and they have stated that they have no intention of leaving in the next 12 months. Anna has looked into the current rates she is paying her workers and these are in line with market rates. The furniture makers' trade association informs her that labour costs are likely to remain steady over the course of the next year. Again, Anna now knows that she should not encounter any shortages of labour or pay rises which she would have to build into her budget for the coming year.

As her direct costs should remain unchanged for the next 12 months, it will be difficult for Anna to change her selling prices. She is happy with the levels of profit her sales are currently generating and, as she does not want to lose her customers through pitching her selling prices too high, she decides to leave the selling prices of each of her three products at the same level for the next 12 months.

WHY IS THIS RELEVANT TO ME?　Setting the strategy

To enable you as an accounting professional to appreciate that:

- Before the detailed budgeting process can begin, businesses have to decide what their objectives and strategy are

- The strategy is directly responsible for the budgeted income and costs, cash inflows and cash outflows

- Setting targets for sales, profits or market share will determine the selling prices of products and services and these targets in turn will feed into the costs of providing those products and services

---

Step 2: the sales budget

Now that the pricing decision and the supply of materials and labour are clear, Anna's next thoughts will focus on her sales. Once decisions on strategy and prices have been made, this is exactly the right place to start the budgeting process as so many other costs and cash flows depend upon the volume of sales achieved. As we discovered in Chapters 3 and 4, Anna's direct costs for wood, other materials and labour will depend directly upon the number of products she sells: the more products she makes and sells, the more direct materials and direct labour cost she will incur. However, she will be unable to produce her material and labour budgets until she has set her sales budget in terms of units produced and sold. Figure 6.2 outlines this process.

Figure 6.2 Budgeting step 2: setting the sales budget

Illustration 6.2 Anna: budgeted sales in units of product for January, February and March

	January number	February number	March number	Total number
Dining chairs	150	200	350	700
Coffee tables	100	250	300	650
Kitchen cabinets	300	350	400	1,050

Anna has been talking to her customers to see how many of her products they propose buying in the near future. She has managed to determine that orders from customers for the first three months of the year are likely to be as shown in Illustration 6.2.

From these budgeted units of sales, Anna can now produce a sales budget in £s. This sales budget is presented in Illustration 6.3.

Illustration 6.3 Anna: budgeted sales in £s for January, February and March

	January £	February £	March £	Total £
Dining chairs	12,750	17,000	29,750	59,500
Coffee tables	5,000	12,500	15,000	32,500
Kitchen cabinets	24,000	28,000	32,000	84,000
Total sales for month	41,750	57,500	76,750	176,000

How did Anna arrive at the above figures? Monthly sales of each product are calculated by multiplying the monthly expected sales in units in Illustration 6.2 by the selling price for each product in Illustration 6.1. Thus, Anna expects to sell 150 dining chairs in January at a selling price of £85. This gives her a sales figure of 150 × £85 = £12,750 for this product line in January.

WHY IS THIS RELEVANT TO ME?   The sales budget

To enable you as an accounting professional to understand:

- How a sales budget is prepared
- The influence of projected sales on the direct costs of making and selling products and providing services

---

NUMERICAL EXERCISES   Are you confident that you can produce a sales budget? Work your way through the figures in Illustrations 6.1, 6.2 and 6.3 again to confirm your understanding of how the monthly sales figures for each product were calculated and then go to the **online workbook** and attempt Numerical exercises 6.1 to make sure you can produce a sales budget from monthly budgeted sales units and budgeted selling prices.

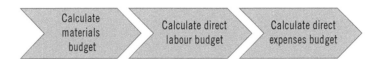

Figure 6.3 Budgeting step 3: setting the direct costs budget

Step 3: calculate the direct costs of budgeted sales

Now that the sales budget has been set, the direct costs associated with those sales can be calculated. As already noted, direct costs are dependent upon the level of sales. In Anna's case, the more units of each product her workshop makes, the more wood will be used, the more other materials will be consumed and the more direct labour will be needed. Figure 6.3 outlines this process.

Budgeted sales income for each month was calculated by multiplying the selling price by the number of units produced and sold. In the same way, budgeted direct costs are found by multiplying the direct materials and direct labour by the number of units of sales. This gives the budgeted material costs for wood shown in Illustration 6.4.

Illustration 6.4 Anna: budgeted costs for wood in January, February and March

	January £	February £	March £	Total £
Direct materials: wood				
Dining chairs	2,700	3,600	6,300	12,600
Coffee tables	1,260	3,150	3,780	8,190
Kitchen cabinets	3,240	3,780	4,320	11,340
Total direct materials (wood) for month	7,200	10,530	14,400	32,130

Illustration 6.2 tells us that Anna expects to sell 150 dining chairs in the month of January, while Illustration 6.1 shows us that the wood for each chair costs £18.00; 150 chairs × £18.00 gives a total cost of wood for dining chairs in January of £2,700. Using the budgeted sales in Illustration 6.2 for each product and the product costs for wood in Illustration 6.1, check the calculation of the materials costs for wood in Illustration 6.4 to reinforce your understanding of how we arrived at these costs.

In the same way and using the information in Illustrations 6.1 and 6.2, the budgeted costs for other materials and direct labour for each product for each month have been calculated in Illustrations 6.5 and 6.6. Other materials used in dining chairs amount to £2 per chair. Multiplying this cost of £2 per chair by the 150 chairs Anna expects to sell in January gives us a cost for other materials of £300 in that month. Similarly, labour costs of £25 per dining chair are multiplied by the 150 chairs budgeted for January to give a total labour cost for dining chairs in that month of £3,750.

Illustration 6.5 Anna: budgeted costs for other materials in January, February and March

Direct materials: other	January £	February £	March £	Total £
Dining chairs	300	400	700	1,400
Coffee tables	540	1,350	1,620	3,510
Kitchen cabinets	2,760	3,220	3,680	9,660
Total direct materials (other) for month	3,600	4,970	6,000	14,570

Illustration 6.6 Anna: budgeted costs for direct labour in January, February and March

Direct labour	January £	February £	March £	Total £
Dining chairs	3,750	5,000	8,750	17,500
Coffee tables	1,800	4,500	5,400	11,700
Kitchen cabinets	9,000	10,500	12,000	31,500
Total direct labour for month	14,550	20,000	26,150	60,700

WHY IS THIS RELEVANT TO ME?   The direct costs of budgeted sales

To provide you as an accounting professional with the knowledge and techniques to:

• Prepare budgets for direct costs based on budgeted sales

• Understand how direct cost budgets are compiled

NUMERICAL EXERCISES   Do you think you can produce a direct costs budget for materials and labour? Work your way through the figures in Illustrations 6.1, 6.2, 6.4, 6.5 and 6.6 again to confirm your understanding of how we arrived at the budgeted materials and labour cost figures for each product and then go to the **online workbook** and attempt Numerical exercises 6.2 to see if you can produce a direct materials and direct labour budget from monthly budgeted sales units and budgeted cost prices per unit.

Step 4: set the budget for fixed costs

The fixed costs budget will be different for every organisation and will depend upon what sort of resources are consumed by each entity as shown in Figure 6.4.

Anna expects her fixed costs and her capital expenditure for the next three months to be as follows:

• Rent on the new workshop of £3,000 will be paid in January to cover the months of January, February and March.

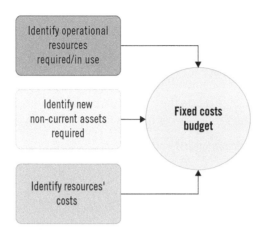

Figure 6.4 Budgeting step 4: setting the fixed costs budget

- New machinery and tools will cost £15,000 and will be delivered and paid for in January. These new non-current assets will have an expected useful life of five years and will be depreciated on the straight line basis.

- Anna anticipates that she will receive and pay an electricity bill in March covering the period 1 January to 15 March. She expects that this bill will be for around £1,500. Anna estimates that the new workshop will use a further £300 of electricity between 16 and 31 March. Each month of operation should be allocated an equal amount of electricity cost.

- An invoice for business rates of £1,200 on the new workshop will be received and paid on 15 February. These rates will cover the six-month period to 30 June.

- The insurance company requires a payment of £1,500 on 1 January to cover all insurance costs for the whole year to 31 December.

Step 5: draw up the budgeted monthly statement of profit or loss

Anna can now draw up her budgeted monthly statement of profit or loss from the information gathered together in steps 1–4 (Figure 6.5). This budgeted statement of profit or loss is presented in Illustration 6.7.

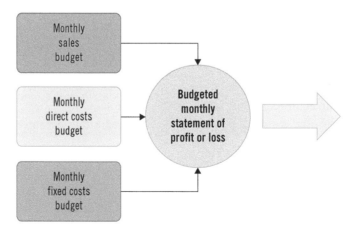

Figure 6.5 Budgeting step 5: draw up the budgeted monthly statement of profit or loss

Illustration 6.7 Anna: budgeted statement of profit or loss for January, February and March

	January £	February £	March £	Total £	Note
Sales	41,750	57,500	76,750	176,000	1
Cost of sales					
Direct material: wood	7,200	10,530	14,400	32,130	2
Direct material: other	3,600	4,970	6,000	14,570	3
Direct labour	14,550	20,000	26,150	60,700	4
Cost of sales	25,350	35,500	46,550	107,400	
Gross profit (sales – cost of sales)	16,400	22,000	30,200	68,600	
Expenses					
Rent	1,000	1,000	1,000	3,000	5
Rates	200	200	200	600	6
Machinery and tools depreciation	250	250	250	750	7
Electricity	600	600	600	1,800	8
Insurance	125	125	125	375	9
Net profit (gross profit – expenses)	14,225	19,825	28,025	62,075	

How did Anna calculate the budgeted results in Illustration 6.7? The following notes will help you understand how she determined the numbers in her budgeted statement of profit or loss:

1. The monthly sales are derived from Illustration 6.3.

2. Similarly, the direct materials for wood are given in Illustration 6.4.

3. Figures for other direct materials are given in Illustration 6.5.

4. Direct labour costs were calculated in Illustration 6.6. Check back to Illustrations 6.3–6.6 to make sure that the numbers in the statement of profit or loss have been correctly transferred from these workings.

5. While the rent of £3,000 was paid in January, this payment relates to three months, so the total expense is spread equally over the three months to which it relates as required by the accruals basis of accounting.

6. In the same way, the rates payment relates to the six months from January to June. The total cost of £1,200 is therefore divided by six months and £200 allocated as the rates cost to each month. The total cost for rates for the three months amounts to £600. How is the remaining £600 (£1,200 paid – £600 charged to the statement of profit or loss) classified in the accounts? This is a prepayment, an expense paid in advance that belongs to a future accounting period.

7. The total cost of £15,000 is divided by five years, giving an annual depreciation charge on these new assets of £3,000. As there are 12 months in a year, a monthly depreciation charge of £3,000 ÷ 12 = £250 is allocated to each of the three months considered here.

8. The total electricity charge for the three months will be the £1,500 bill received and paid in the middle of March plus the £300 that has been used in the last two weeks of March. This £300 will

be treated as an accrual, an expense incurred by the end of an accounting period giving rise to a liability and an expense that has not been paid by that period end date. The total electricity expense for the three months is thus £1,800. Dividing this figure by three gives us an expense of £600 for each month in the budgeted statement of profit or loss.

9. While the total insurance payment is £1,500, this cost covers the whole 12-month period. Therefore, the monthly charge for insurance in our budgeted statement of profit or loss will be £1,500 ÷ 12 = £125 per month, the remaining £1,125 (£1,500 − £375) being treated as a prepayment at the end of March.

WHY IS THIS RELEVANT TO ME?   The budgeted monthly statement of profit or loss

To enable you as an accounting professional to understand how:

- Budgeted statements of profit or loss you will be presented with have been drawn up
- To prepare your own budgeted monthly statements of profit or loss

NUMERICAL EXERCISES   Do you think you could put together a budgeted statement of profit or loss for a given time period using budgeted sales, materials, labour and fixed overheads? Work through Illustration 6.7 again to confirm your understanding of how we arrived at the figures in the budgeted statement of profit or loss and then go to the **online workbook** and attempt Numerical exercises 6.3 to make sure you can produce a budgeted statement of profit or loss from the sales, materials, labour and fixed overhead budgets.

SHOW ME HOW TO DO IT   Are you quite sure you understand how this budgeted statement of profit or loss in Illustration 6.7 was put together? View Video presentation 6.1 in the **online workbook** to see a practical demonstration.

Step 6: calculating cash receipts from sales

The budgeted statement of profit or loss for the first three months of the year in Illustration 6.7 shows that Anna expects to make a healthy profit of £62,075. However, the main concern of both entities and their banks will always be the cash flowing in and the cash flowing out, so it is important in any budgeting exercise to prepare the cash budget alongside the budgeted statement of profit or loss (Figure 6.6).

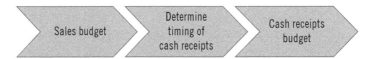

Figure 6.6 Budgeting step 6: cash receipts from sales budget

Under the accruals basis of accounting, sales are recognised as income in the months in which they occur, but cash from those sales will not necessarily be received in those same months. Where goods are purchased on credit, there is a time lag between the date of the sale and the day on which cash from that sale is received.

Based on her past experience and knowledge, Anna expects 30 per cent of her customers to pay in the month of sale and the remaining 70 per cent to pay in the following month. These expected monthly cash receipts from sales are shown in Illustration 6.8.

Illustration 6.8 Anna: budgeted cash receipts from sales in January, February and March

	January £	February £	March £	Total £
30% of sales received in month	12,525	17,250	23,025	52,800
70% of sales received next month	—	29,225	40,250	69,475
Total cash receipts per month	12,525	46,475	63,275	122,275

How were these cash receipts calculated? Anna expects to make total sales in January of £41,750 (Illustration 6.3); 30 per cent of £41,750 is £12,525 received in January, the month of sale. Cash from the remaining 70 per cent of January's sales will be received in the following month, February. This amounts to £29,225. You could calculate this number as 70 per cent of £41,750 or just deduct the £12,525 already received from £41,750 to give you the same result. Work through the other budgeted sales and cash receipts in Illustrations 6.3 and 6.8 to ensure that you understand how the cash inflows from sales were calculated on the basis of Anna's expectations of when her customers will pay for the goods they have received.

Anna expects to make sales of £176,000 in the three months to the end of March (Illustrations 6.3 and 6.7). However, she has only collected £122,275 in cash (Illustration 6.8), a difference of £53,725. What does this difference represent and where should it be recorded in the budgeted accounts? This figure represents trade receivables due to the company, a current asset, which will be posted to Anna's budgeted statement of financial position at 31 March.

WHY IS THIS RELEVANT TO ME? Calculating cash receipts from sales

To enable you as an accounting professional to understand:

- That, unless an entity sells for cash, sales do not equal cash receipts in the months in which the sales are recognised
- How to prepare budgets for receipts of cash from sales made to customers on credit terms

Are you convinced that you could produce a statement of budgeted cash inflows from sales? Work through Illustration 6.8 again to confirm your understanding of how we arrived at the budgeted cash receipts from sales and then go to the **online workbook** and attempt Numerical exercises 6.4 to make sure you can produce a statement of budgeted cash inflows from sales.

Step 7: calculating cash payments to direct materials suppliers and direct labour

Just as Anna's customers do not pay for their goods immediately, so Anna, as a customer of her materials suppliers, does not pay for all her direct materials in the month she receives them. Therefore, cash payments to suppliers have to be worked out in the same way as cash receipts from customers (Figure 6.7).

Figure 6.7 Budgeting step 7: cash payments from direct costs budget

Anna expects to pay for her purchases of wood as follows:

- 50 per cent of the wood used in each month will be paid for in the actual month of use
- 30 per cent of the wood used in each month will be paid for one month after the actual month of use
- 20 per cent of the wood used in each month will be paid for two months after the actual month of use

Illustration 6.9 shows Anna's cash payments for wood.

Illustration 6.9 Anna: budgeted cash payments for wood for January, February and March

	January £	February £	March £	Total £
50% of wood used in month	3,600	5,265	7,200	16,065
30% of wood used one month ago	—	2,160	3,159	5,319
20% of wood used two months ago	—	—	1,440	1,440
Total cash payments per month	**3,600**	**7,425**	**11,799**	**22,824**

How were these cash payments for wood calculated? Anna's direct materials budget (Illustrations 6.4 and 6.7) shows that she expects to use wood costing £7,200 in January. This will be paid for as follows:

- 50 per cent in month of use (January): £7,200 × 50 per cent = £3,600
- 30 per cent one month after the month of use: £7,200 × 30 per cent = £2,160

- 20 per cent two months after the month of use: £7,200 × 20 per cent = £1,440
- Check: £3,600 + £2,160 + £1,440 = £7,200

On top of these payments for January's wood made in February and March are payments for wood used in those months, as well as March's payment for the wood used in February.

Illustration 6.9 shows that Anna will be paying £22,824 in cash for her wood purchases in the three months to 31 March, while her statement of profit or loss (Illustration 6.7) shows that she is incurring total direct materials costs for wood of £32,130. She therefore still has £9,306 to pay (£32,130 − £22,824), made up of £2,106 (20 per cent of February's usage (£10,530 × 20 per cent)) and £7,200 (50 per cent of March's usage (£14,400 × 50 per cent)). This figure of £9,306 represents a liability incurred and due to be paid to her suppliers. This amount will be recorded as a trade payable in Anna's budgeted statement of financial position at 31 March.

As well as her suppliers of wood, Anna also buys in other direct materials for use in producing her furniture. She intends to pay the suppliers of these other materials in the month in which these materials are used in production. Similarly, she will be paying her employees in the month in which production and sales are made. The cash outflows for other direct materials and direct labour in her monthly cash budget will be the same as the expenses already presented in Illustrations 6.5, 6.6 and 6.7.

WHY IS THIS RELEVANT TO ME?   Calculating cash payments for direct materials and direct labour

To enable you as an accounting professional to understand:

- That, unless an entity pays cash for all its direct materials and other purchases, direct materials do not equal cash payments in the months in which the costs are recorded
- How to prepare budgets for payments of cash to suppliers of direct materials and other purchases where these goods are purchased on credit terms

---

NUMERICAL EXERCISES   Are you confident that you could put together a budgeted statement of cash payments for direct materials and direct labour? Work through Illustration 6.9 again to confirm your understanding of how we calculated the budgeted cash payment figures for direct materials and direct labour and then go to the **online workbook** and attempt Numerical exercises 6.5 to see how accurately you can produce a budgeted statement of cash payments for direct materials and direct labour.

Step 8: draw up the monthly cash budget

Anna now has all the information from which to draw up her month-by-month cash budget. To do this she will look at the timing of her cash inflows from sales, the timing of her cash payments for direct materials and labour, together with any other payments or inflows of cash, as shown in Figure 6.8. Details of other payments of cash were given in step 4, the budget for fixed costs. In addition, Anna decides that she will be paying £10,000 of her own money into her business bank account on 1 January and that she will be drawing out £2,000 a month for her own personal expenses.

Her monthly cash budget for January, February and March is presented in Illustration 6.10.

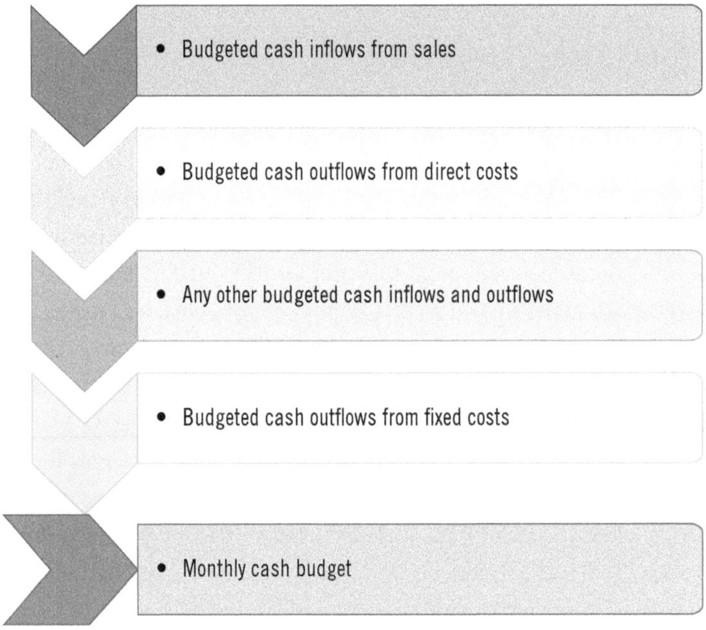

Figure 6.8 Budgeting step 8: draw up the monthly cash budget

Illustration 6.10 Anna: budgeted cash inflows and outflows for January, February and March

	January £	February £	March £	Total £	Note
Cash received					
Sales	12,525	46,475	63,275	122,275	1
Capital introduced	10,000	—	—	10,000	2
Total cash receipts	**22,525**	**46,475**	**63,275**	**132,275**	
Cash paid					
Direct material: wood	3,600	7,425	11,799	22,824	3
Direct material: other	3,600	4,970	6,000	14,570	4
Direct labour	14,550	20,000	26,150	60,700	5
Rent	3,000	—	—	3,000	6
Machinery and tools	15,000	—	—	15,000	7
Electricity	—	—	1,500	1,500	8
Rates	—	1,200	—	1,200	9
Insurance	1,500	—	—	1,500	10
Drawings: personal expenditure	2,000	2,000	2,000	6,000	11
Total cash payments	**43,250**	**35,595**	**47,449**	**126,294**	
Cash receipts – cash payments	(20,725)	10,880	15,826	5,981	12
Cash at the start of the month	—	(20,725)	(9,845)		13
Cash at the end of the month	(20,725)	(9,845)	5,981		14

How did Anna produce her monthly cash budget for January, February and March? The following notes explain the numbers in each line of the cash budget.

1. The budgeted cash receipts from sales were calculated in Illustration 6.8.

2. Anna is paying in £10,000 of her own money on 1 January as noted.

3. The budgeted cash payments to suppliers of wood were presented in Illustration 6.9.

4. Anna is paying her suppliers of other direct materials in the month in which the other direct materials are used, so the cash payments to these suppliers are the same as the budgeted costs in Illustrations 6.5 and 6.7.

5. Likewise, direct labour is paid in the month in which production and sales take place so these cash payments are the same as the costs given in Illustrations 6.6 and 6.7.

6. Step 4 tells us that the rent is paid on 1 January. Although the cost of this rent is spread across the three months to which it relates in the statement of profit or loss (Illustration 6.7), the actual cash payment is budgeted to take place in January, so the whole £3,000 is recognised in the January cash payments.

7. In the same way, the cash outflow to buy the machinery and tools occurs in January so the whole of the £15,000 cash payment is recognised in January. Remember that depreciation is not a cash flow, just an accounting adjustment that spreads the cost of non-current assets over the periods benefiting from their use, so depreciation does not appear in a cash budget. The actual outflow of cash to pay for the machinery and tools is £15,000 and this occurs in January so, just like the rent, this is the month in which this cash payment for these non-current assets is recognised.

8. Step 4 explains that the electricity bill received in March will be for £1,500 and that this electricity bill is paid in that month. Thus, £1,500 is the amount of cash that leaves the bank in March. The additional £300 accrual in the statement of profit or loss will be paid in a later period so no cash outflow is recognised in these three months for this amount which has not yet been paid.

9. Step 4 notes that the rates bill is paid in February and the full £1,200 payment is recognised in the cash budget as this is the actual amount paid in February regardless of the amounts that are allocated to each month in the budgeted statement of profit or loss.

10. Similarly, the insurance for the year is paid in January, so the whole cash outflow of £1,500 is shown in January's column even though the cost in the statement of profit or loss is spread over the next 12 months.

11. Anna withdraws £2,000 a month from which to meet her personal expenditure so she recognises this as a cash outflow each month.

12. After totalling up the cash receipts (inflows) and the cash payments (outflows), the receipts – payments line is presented. For January, total receipts in Illustration 6.10 are £22,525 while payments total £43,250. Thus, £22,525 – £43,250 = – £20,725, which means that there is a shortfall of cash in January and Anna's bank account will be overdrawn.

January thus shows greater payments than receipts of cash, while both February and March show a net inflow of cash, receipts in both months being greater than payments.

13. Cash at the start of the month is the cash balance at the end of the previous month. In the first month of a new business venture, as in Anna's case, this will be £Nil. In continuing businesses, this will be the budgeted or actual figure at the end of the last financial period.

14. The cash at the end of the month is the net cash inflow or outflow for the month plus or minus the cash or overdraft at the start of the month. In January, the net outflow for the month is £20,725 while the cash at the start of January is £Nil so (£20,725) +/− £Nil = (£20,725). At the end of February, there is a net cash inflow of £10,880 (total cash inflows of £46,475 − total cash outflows of £35,595). Adding this positive inflow of £10,880 to the negative balance at the start of the month (£20,725) gives us a lower overdraft at the end of February (£9,845), which then forms the opening balance at the start of March.

WHY IS THIS RELEVANT TO ME?   The monthly cash budget

To enable you as an accounting professional to understand:

• How cash budgets you will be presented with have been drawn up

• How to prepare your own monthly cash budgets

NUMERICAL EXERCISES   Are you sure that you could draw up a cash budget? Work through the figures in Illustration 6.10 again to confirm your understanding of how the cash budget was constructed and then go to the **online workbook** and attempt Numerical exercises 6.6 to make sure you can produce these budgeted statements.

SHOW ME HOW TO DO IT   How easily did you follow the preparation of Anna's monthly cash budget? View Video presentation 6.2 in the **online workbook** to see a practical demonstration of how the monthly cash budget in Illustration 6.10 was put together.

The importance of cash flow forecasts

The cash budget is the most important budgeted statement that you will ever produce. Cash generation is the critical task for businesses as, without adequate cash inflows, a business will be unable to meet its liabilities as they fall due and will collapse. Give me an example 6.2, from the Entrepreneur column in the *Financial Times*, emphasises how business professionals must continue to produce cash budgets no matter how high up an organisation they climb. If they do not, they are risking the very survival of their organisations.

GIVE ME AN EXAMPLE 6.2 Custodians of finance make the difference

The weak link in many failed companies is the finance director. Better custody of borrowed or invested money by them would so often have prevented disaster. In most cases their words betray them as much as the numbers. I am indebted to John Dewhirst of Vincere, the turnaround specialists, for collecting some of the classic lines I discuss below.

'I don't do cash forecasts. I've never found them useful.'

A lack of focus on cash is perhaps the greatest sin. A finance professional who does not prepare reasonably accurate projections of liquidity on a rolling basis is guilty of dereliction of duty. Often FDs drop such nitty gritty as they ascend the ranks, while some have historically enjoyed a cash cushion and never felt the pressure. They are the ones exposed when conditions deteriorate.

Source: Luke Johnson, 2011, Custodians of finance make the difference, the Financial Times, 19 January. Used under licence from the Financial Times. All Rights Reserved.

6

WHY IS THIS RELEVANT TO ME?   The importance of cash budgets

To emphasise to you as an accounting professional:

* The critical importance of budgeting cash on a regular basis
* The risks you run if you do not undertake regular cash budgeting

Step 9: draw up the budgeted statement of financial position

The final step in the budgeting process is to draw up the budgeted statement of financial position at the end of the budgeted period using the budgeted information already produced as shown in Figure 6.9. We have already looked at all the numbers that will go into Anna's statement of financial position when we prepared the budgeted statement of profit or loss and cash budget. Anna's budgeted statement of financial position is presented in Illustration 6.11, together with notes reminding you of the sources of the figures.

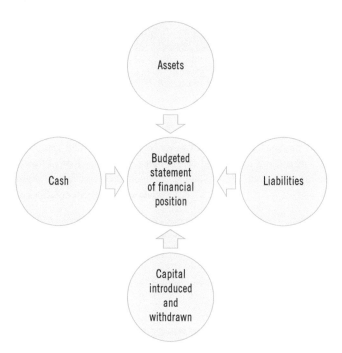

Figure 6.9 Budgeting step 9: draw up the budgeted statement of financial position at the period end

Illustration 6.11 Anna: budgeted statement of financial position at 31 March

	£	Note
Non-current assets		
Machinery and tools	**14,250**	1
Current assets		
Trade receivables	53,725	2
Insurance prepayment	1,125	3
Rates prepayment	600	4
Cash at bank	5,981	5
Total current assets	**61,431**	
Total assets	**75,681**	
Current liabilities		
Trade payables for wood	9,306	6
Electricity accrual	300	7
Total current liabilities	**9,616**	
Net assets: total assets − total liabilities (£75,681 − £9,616)	**66,075**	
Capital account		
Capital introduced	10,000	8
Net profit for the three months	62,075	9
Drawings	(6,000)	10
	66,075	

Notes to Anna's budgeted statement of financial position

1. Machinery and tools cost £15,000. Depreciation of £750 has been charged to the statement of profit or loss for the three months to the end of March (Illustration 6.7), so the carrying amount (cost – depreciation) of these assets is therefore £15,000 – £750 = £14,250.

2. The cash not collected from customers by the end of March. We calculated this figure in Step 6.

3. The payment of £1,500 covers 12 months of insurance; £375 has been charged against profits as the insurance cost for the three months in the budgeted statement of profit or loss to the end of March (Illustration 6.7), so there is an insurance prepayment of nine months. Therefore, the insurance prepayment is £1,500 × 9/12 = £1,125.

4. Similarly, the payment of £1,200 covers six months of rates expenditure. At 31 March only three of the six months paid for have been used up and charged as an expense in the budgeted statement of profit or loss (Illustration 6.7), so there is a prepayment at 31 March of £1,200 × 3/6 = £600. This £600 represents the rates cost to be charged as an expense in the statement of profit or loss for April, May and June.

5. The cash at bank must equal the closing cash figure in the cash budget (Illustration 6.10).

6. This trade payables figure was calculated in Step 7.

7. The electricity accrual is the expense incurred but not yet paid.

8. Anna introduced £10,000 into the business on 1 January in the cash budget.

9. Net profit for the three months is read off the budgeted statement of profit or loss in Illustration 6.7.

10. Drawings are the total amount that Anna has withdrawn from the business bank account for her own personal expenditure over the course of the three months. This figure appears in the cash budget in Illustration 6.10.

WHY IS THIS RELEVANT TO ME?   The budgeted statement of financial position

To enable you as an accounting professional to understand how:

• The budgeted statement of financial position is compiled from the budgeted statement of profit or loss and cash budget

• To prepare your own budgeted statements of financial position

---

NUMERICAL EXERCISES   Are you convinced that you could draw up a budgeted statement of financial position? Work through the above example again to confirm your understanding of how the statement of financial position was constructed and then go to the **online workbook** and attempt Numerical exercises 6.7 to make sure you can produce this statement.

SHOW ME HOW TO DO IT   How clearly did you understand how Anna's budgeted statement of financial position was put together? View Video presentation 6.3 in the **online workbook** to see a practical demonstration of how this statement was prepared.

Conclusions: financing expansion

What has Anna learnt from her budgeting exercise? At the start of the process, she had approached the bank for finance to start her new workshop. The bank asked her to undertake a budgeting exercise. By producing her budgets she now knows that, if everything goes exactly to plan, she will need to borrow a maximum of £20,725 (Illustration 6.10) from the bank as a result of her expansion. Happily, her cash budget also shows that this maximum borrowing of £20,725 will be paid off by the end of March, so any financing she needs will be very short term. A short-term overdraft with the bank would be the most appropriate form of financing for Anna.

Budgeting flowchart summary

We have now looked in detail at the budgeting process, the steps that are followed and the order in which those steps proceed. We can summarise the budgeting process in a flow chart. This flow chart is shown in Figure 6.10. Look back at the earlier sections of this chapter and relate each step to what you have learnt during our study of the budgeting process so far.

WHY IS THIS RELEVANT TO ME?   Budgeting flowchart summary

To provide you as an accounting professional with a:

- Map to help you draw up budgets and budgeted financial statements
- Logical step-by-step guide to the production of budgeted information
- Quick overview of the budgeting process to determine where each activity fits into the overall budgeting framework

GO BACK OVER THIS AGAIN!   A copy of this budgeting flowchart summary (Figure 6.10) is available in the **online workbook**: you might like to keep this on screen or print off a copy for easy reference while you revise the material in this chapter to provide you with a route map through the budgeting process.

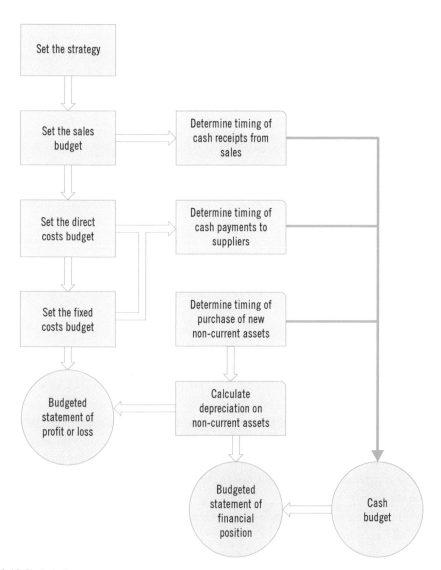

Figure 6.10 The budgeting process

BUDGETARY CONTROL: STATEMENT OF PROFIT OR LOSS

As we noted earlier in this chapter, budgets are used for control purposes. Once each month of actual activity is complete, comparisons are made between what was budgeted to occur and what actually happened. Figure 6.11 illustrates the budgetary control process. It is important to undertake this comparison activity every month so that variances from the budget can be determined and their causes investigated. It would be pointless waiting to complete a whole year of activity

Figure 6.11 The budgetary control process

before any comparisons were made. By then it would be too late to undertake the necessary action to correct budget deviations. In the same way, you do not wait until the end of the academic year to review feedback on your coursework, but instead look at the feedback on each assignment as it is returned so that you can make the necessary improvements in your next piece of assessment.

Monthly comparisons are an example of relevant accounting information (Chapter 1, What qualities should accounting information possess?). Monthly data is provided on a timely basis with a view to influencing managers' economic decisions in terms of, for example, what products to continue selling, whether to discount products that are not selling or to seek out cheaper sources of material if direct material prices from the current supplier are now too high. Comparisons are also confirmatory as well as predictive. The closer budgeted figures are to actual results in a month, the more likely budgeted figures for future months are to predict future outcomes accurately.

As an example, let's look at Anna's budgeted and actual results for January. These are shown in Illustration 6.12.

Illustration 6.12 Anna: budgeted v. actual statements of profit or loss for January

	January budget £	January actual £	January variances £
Sales	41,750	43,000	1,250
Cost of sales			
Direct material: wood	7,200	8,000	(800)
Direct material: other	3,600	3,550	50
Direct labour	14,550	14,500	50
Cost of sales	**25,350**	**26,050**	**(700)**
Gross profit (sales – cost of sales)	16,400	16,950	550
Expenses			
Rent	1,000	1,000	—
Rates	200	200	—
Machinery and tools depreciation	250	300	(50)
Electricity	600	600	—
Insurance	125	125	—
Net profit (gross profit – expenses)	**14,225**	**14,725**	**500**

In Illustration 6.12, numbers in brackets in the January variances column are classified as unfavourable, those variances that have reduced the budgeted profit, whereas figures without brackets are favourable, those variances that have increased the budgeted profit.

Now that we have produced our budget v. actual comparison, we can make the following observations.

Higher sales

* Sales are higher than budgeted. This suggests that the original estimates of product sales were a little lower than they should have been. If more products have been sold, Anna should find out why this has occurred and determine whether she can continue to exploit this favourable trend to make higher sales in the future.

* Alternatively, selling prices might have been higher than budgeted because of increased demand pushing prices up. Anna should do her best to maintain any higher selling prices as she will make more profit as a result.

* As there are two possible explanations for this sales variance, Anna will have to conduct further investigations to determine which of the two options is correct or whether it is a combination of both. The sales variance tells her to investigate further, but does not tell her the cause of this variance.

Direct costs

* The cost of wood used in production of goods sold rose in January. This, in itself, is not a surprise as higher production and sales will require more raw material input. However,

Anna will need to investigate whether the price of wood has increased or more wood than expected was used in production.

- Other direct material cost less than expected, suggesting lower prices than budgeted or more efficient usage by the workforce.

- Similarly, the cost of labour was lower despite the increased production and sales, suggesting that the workforce has been more productive than budgeted.

- Anna should try to encourage more efficient working as this will increase productivity and lower the costs per unit of production, resulting in the generation of higher profits.

- To encourage this higher productivity, Anna might introduce a bonus scheme for her workers to give them a share in any increased profits. However, she will need to make sure that the bonus scheme does not encourage the workforce to work with less care and attention to detail so that the finished production, while taking less time to produce, is of lower quality.

Fixed costs

- Rent and insurance overheads should be as budgeted as these costs should be easily predictable in advance.

- The rates and electricity budget and actual figures are currently the same as we do not have any actual bills to work from. Remember that the rates bill is expected in February and the electricity bill will arrive in March. Once the actual bills are received Anna will be able to determine whether these costs are higher or lower than budgeted.

- The higher than budgeted depreciation figure suggests that the machinery and tools cost Anna more than anticipated, resulting in a higher monthly depreciation charge. Anna will need to check the actual payment for machinery and tools.

Net profit

- Overall, actual profits for January were higher than budgeted by £500.

- Based upon her investigations of the causes of the variances in January, Anna will aim to correct any unfavourable variances in the cost and usage of wood, while attempting to exploit the favourable variances in the sales to sell more goods or to sell goods at a higher price.

WHY IS THIS RELEVANT TO ME?   Budgetary control: actual v. budget comparisons: statement of profit or loss

As an accounting professional you will be expected to:

- Take on responsibility for any departmental budget you hold and to explain variations between budgeted and actual results

- Produce actual v. budget comparisons on a monthly basis

- Ask relevant questions when evaluating actual v. budget comparisons

GO BACK OVER THIS AGAIN!   Do you think you could suggest reasons for changes in budgeted v. actual sales and costs? Go to the **online workbook** and have a go at Exercises 6.3.

BUDGETARY CONTROL: CASH BUDGET

As well as comparing her budgeted and actual statements of profit or loss, Anna will also undertake a comparison of her budgeted and actual cash flows. As we noted at the start of this chapter, Anna needs additional finance from the bank to expand her business and move into the larger workshop. Her initial cash budget suggested that she would only need to borrow a maximum of £20,725. Because of the critical nature of cash inflows and outflows in her business operations, both Anna and her bank will be watching her cash position very closely to make sure that she does not exceed her borrowing capacity or her borrowing limits.

Anna produces her budgeted and actual cash flow comparisons for January in Illustration 6.13.

Illustration 6.13 Anna: budgeted v. actual cash inflows and outflows for January

	January budget £	January actual £	January variances £
Cash received			
Sales	12,525	13,760	1,235
Capital introduced	10,000	10,000	—
Total cash receipts	**22,525**	**23,760**	**1,235**
Cash paid			
Direct material: wood	3,600	4,000	(400)
Direct material: other	3,600	3,550	50
Direct labour	14,550	14,500	50
Rent	3,000	3,000	—
Machinery and tools	15,000	18,000	(3,000)
Electricity	—	—	—
Rates	—	—	—
Insurance	1,500	1,500	—
Drawings – personal expenditure	2,000	2,000	—
Total cash payments	**43,250**	**46,550**	**(3,300)**
Cash receipts – cash payments	(20,725)	(22,790)	(2,065)
Cash at the start of the month	—	—	—
Cash at the end of the month	(20,725)	(22,790)	(2,065)

6

What does this budgeted v. actual cash flow comparison tell Anna? She can draw the following conclusions:

- Her customers are paying more quickly than she expected. While she anticipated that 30 per cent of her customers would pay in the month of sale, 32 per cent of actual sales have paid in January (£13,760 ÷ £43,000 (actual sales from the statement of profit or loss in Illustration 6.12) × 100 per cent). Anna should try to persuade her customers to continue paying more quickly as this will improve her cash inflows and thereby reduce her borrowings more rapidly.

- While £400 more has been paid out for wood, this is consistent with Anna's intention that she would pay for 50 per cent of the wood she used in the month of usage. As her actual usage was £8,000 (Illustration 6.12), she has paid half this amount in January.

- Payments for both other materials and labour are £50 less than expected, but these are the actual amounts used in January according to the budgeted v. actual statement of profit or loss (Illustration 6.12). Cash payments are thus in line with Anna's policy of paying in full for labour and other materials in the month in which they were used.

- Machinery and tools were budgeted to cost £15,000 but in fact cost £18,000. This is consistent with the increase in depreciation shown in the statement of profit or loss in Illustration 6.12. The machinery and tools are expected to have a five-year life, which gives an annual depreciation charge of £3,600 per annum (£18,000 ÷ 5) which equates to £300 per month (£3,600 ÷ 12). Anna tells you that the machinery and tools had been imported from Germany and that the increased cost was because of a fall in the value of the pound against the euro at the time the machinery and tools were bought and paid for.

- All other inflows and outflows of cash were as budgeted.

- As a result of the above differences in her planned cash inflows and outflows, Anna has borrowed an additional £2,065 from the bank in January. The sole cause of this problem was the payment for her machinery and tools. Her aim now will be to pay off this additional borrowing as quickly as possible by encouraging her customers to pay more promptly or trying to sell more products each month to increase her cash inflows while keeping outflows of cash as low as possible.

WHY IS THIS RELEVANT TO ME?   Budgetary control: actual v. budget comparisons: cash flow

As an accounting professional you must appreciate that:

- Cash is the lifeblood of business and without it businesses will run out of money and collapse
- Monitoring budgeted v. actual cash is thus just as (if not more) important than comparing budgeted v. actual profits

NUMERICAL EXERCISES Are you sure that you could produce a comparison of budgeted v. actual cash flows? Go to the **online workbook** and have a go at Numerical exercises 6.8.

SENSITIVITY ANALYSIS

Anna has produced her budgets for the first three months of operations and predicted her maximum borrowings from the bank. However, what if her budgets don't turn out as she expects? How will this affect her profits and her cash flows? Given questions such as these, it is usual when budgeting to conduct sensitivity analysis to assess how profits and cash flows would turn out if certain expectations are changed. Thus, for example, a reduction in budgeted sales units might be applied, or an increase in direct costs of 10 per cent or a fall in selling price of 10 per cent. Spreadsheets make these 'what if?' calculations easy to undertake.

As an example, let's see what would happen to profits and cash flows if budgeted unit sales of Anna's products fell by 10 per cent while keeping selling prices the same. We will adopt various short-cuts in producing our figures here, but all the calculations will be available in the online workbook.

First, let's look at the statement of profit or loss showing a 10 per cent fall in numbers of products sold compared with Anna's original plans. This is shown in Illustration 6.14.

Illustration 6.14 Anna: budgeted statement of profit or loss for January, February and March assuming a 10 per cent fall in the number of products sold while keeping selling prices the same

	January £	February £	March £	Total £	Note
Sales	37,575	51,750	69,075	158,400	1
Cost of sales	22,815	31,950	41,895	96,660	2
Gross profit (sales − cost of sales)	14,760	19,800	27,180	61,740	
Expenses					
Fixed costs	2,175	2,175	2,175	6,525	3
Net profit (gross profit − expenses)	**12,585**	**17,625**	**25,005**	**55,215**	

Notes on the above budgeted statement of profit or loss:

1. Sales volumes reduce by 10 per cent, which results in sales 10 per cent lower than those shown in Illustrations 6.3 and 6.7.

2. As sales volumes fall by 10 per cent, cost of sales (direct costs) also falls by 10 per cent as Anna's direct costs in producing 10 per cent fewer goods will be 10 per cent lower.

3. Budgeted fixed costs are made up of £1,000 (rent) + £200 (rates) + £250 (depreciation) + £600 (electricity) + £125 insurance to give total budgeted fixed costs per month of £2,175.

6

These are the same costs that we used in Illustration 6.7. Remember that fixed costs do not change with different levels of sales and production, so these costs are the same for the original budgeted sales and the revised budgeted sales volumes of 10 per cent lower than originally planned.

Anna's original budgeted profit of £62,075 in Illustration 6.7 has now fallen to £55,215 given a 10 per cent fall in sales volumes.

However, Anna's main concern was with finance and how much she would need to borrow from the bank. Surely the effect of this fall of 10 per cent in sales volumes will increase the size of her projected overdraft? The effect of the 10 per cent fall in sales volumes on the cash budget is shown in Illustration 6.15.

Illustration 6.15 Anna: budgeted cash inflows and outflows for January, February and March assuming a 10 per cent fall in the number of products sold while keeping selling prices the same

	January £	February £	March £	Total £
Cash received				
Sales	11,273	41,827	56,947	110,047
Capital introduced	10,000	—	—	10,000
Total cash receipts	**21,273**	**41,827**	**56,947**	**120,047**
Cash paid				
Direct material: wood	3,240	6,683	10,619	20,542
Direct material: other	3,240	4,473	5,400	13,113
Direct labour	13,095	18,000	23,535	54,630
Rent	3,000	—	—	3,000
Machinery and tools	15,000	—	—	15,000
Electricity	—	—	1,500	1,500
Rates	—	1,200	—	1,200
Insurance	1,500	—	—	1,500
Drawings: personal expenditure	2,000	2,000	2,000	6,000
Total cash payments	**41,075**	**32,356**	**43,054**	**116,485**
Cash receipts – cash payments	(19,802)	9,471	13,893	3,562
Cash at the start of the month	—	(19,802)	(10,331)	
Cash at the end of the month	(19,802)	(10,331)	3,562	

Budgeted payments for rent, machinery and tools, electricity, rates, insurance and drawings across the three months under review do not change, so these stay the same in both Illustrations 6.10 and 6.15. Receipts from sales fall, but planned payments for wood, other materials and direct labour fall by more than the reduction in sales receipts. This has the effect of actually reducing the expected borrowings at the end of January from £20,725 to £19,802, so, even with lower sales volumes, Anna is borrowing less. Her cash balance at the end of three months is lower at £3,562 compared to the £5,981 shown in Illustration 6.10, but she still pays off the borrowings by the end of March as in her original budget.

The assumptions on which Anna's original budgets were based can be relaxed further to see what effect these changes will have on her budgeted statement of profit or loss, cash budget and projected statement of financial position and you can have a go at some of these in the online workbook.

The following extract, in Give me an example 6.3, from the Audit Committee's report in the annual report and accounts of Greggs plc, shows how sensitivity analysis is used in practice to test the assumptions on which financial plans and forecasts are based and to determine whether these forecasts and plans are realistic and achievable.

6

GIVE ME AN EXAMPLE 6.3   Sensitivity analysis

The significant areas of judgement considered by the Committee in relation to the financial statements for the 52 weeks ended 28 December 2013 are set out below. These significant areas of judgement are principally borne out of the strategic review which took place during the year, the results of which were announced in August 2013. The strategic review took place as a response to declining like-for-like sales and reduced profitability. The impact of the suggested measures was reflected in a five-year financial plan and liquidity forecasts which were presented to the Board along with sensitivities for each scenario. The assumptions underlying each scenario were challenged robustly by the Committee which concluded that they represented an appropriate and prudent position.

Source: *Greggs plc Annual Report and Accounts for the year ended 28 December 2013,* page 44

WHY IS THIS RELEVANT TO ME?   SENSITIVITY ANALYSIS

To enable you as an accounting professional to:

- Appreciate that original budgets will be subjected to sensitivity analysis to determine the effect of changes in budgeted numbers on budgeted profits and cash flows
- Undertake sensitivity analysis on budgeted information prepared by yourself and others

GO BACK OVER THIS AGAIN! How readily did you understand how the figures for Anna were calculated for the reduction in sales volumes of 10 per cent? Visit the **online workbook** Exercises 6.4 to view all the calculations involved in this exercise.

NUMERICAL EXERCISES Are you convinced that you could undertake sensitivity analysis on a set of budgeted figures? Go to the **online workbook** and have a go at Numerical exercises 6.9 to see what effect various changes would have on Anna's budgeted statement of profit or loss and cash budget for January, February and March.

CHAPTER SUMMARY

You should now have learnt that:

- Budgets perform planning, communicating, coordinating, motivating and control functions within organisations
- The sales budget is the starting point for all other budgeted figures and statements
- Entities prepare budgeted statements of profit or loss and cash budgets on a monthly basis
- Monthly comparisons are made between budgeted income and expenditure and budgeted cash inflows and outflows to ensure that operations are under control
- Businesses undertake comparisons between budgeted and actual income and expenditure to highlight variances in expected and actual financial performance
- Sensitivity analysis is applied to assumptions made in budgeted financial statements to determine how easily an entity could make a loss or require overdraft financing

QUICK REVISION Test your knowledge with the online flashcards in Summary of key concepts and attempt the Multiple choice questions, all in the **online workbook**.

END-OF-CHAPTER QUESTIONS

Solutions to these questions can be found in the **online workbook**.

❯ DEVELOP YOUR UNDERSTANDING

❯Question 6.1

Dave is planning to start up in business selling ice cream from a van around his local neighbourhood from April to September. He wants to open a business bank account, but the bank manager has insisted that he provides a cash budget together with a budgeted statement of profit or loss for his first six months of trading and a budgeted statement of financial position at 30 September. Dave is unsure how to put this information together, but he has provided you with the following details of his planned income and expenditure:

* Dave will pay in £5,000 of his own money on 1 April to get the business started.

* He expects to make all his sales for cash and anticipates that he will make sales of £3,500 in April, £5,500 in May, £7,500 in each of the next three months and £2,500 in September.

* He will buy his ice cream from a local supplier and expects the cost of this to be 50 per cent of selling price. Dave has agreed with his supplier that he will start paying for his ice cream in May rather than in the month of purchase.

* Dave intends to sell all his ice cream by the end of September and to have no inventory at the end of this trading period.

* Ice cream vans can be hired at a cost of £1,500 for three months. The £1,500 hire charge is payable at the start of each three-month period.

* Van running costs are estimated to be £250 per month payable in cash each month.

* Business insurance payable on 1 April will cost £500 for six months.

* Dave will draw £1,000 per month out of the business bank account to meet personal expenses.

Required

Provide Dave with:

* A cash budget for the first six months of trading.

* A budgeted statement of profit or loss for the first six months of trading.

* A budgeted statement of financial position at 30 September.

> Question 6.2

Hena plc has a division that manufactures and sells solar panels. Demand for solar panels has picked up recently and the company is looking to increase its output. Hena plc's branch currently manufactures 600,000 solar panels annually and is looking to double this capacity. A new factory has become available at an annual rent of £600,000 payable quarterly in advance. New plant and machinery would cost £1.8 million, payable immediately on delivery on 1 January. This new plant and machinery would have a useful life of 10 years and would be depreciated on a straight line basis with £Nil residual value. The directors of Hena plc are now wondering whether they should go ahead with the new solar panel factory. They have produced the following projections upon which to base their budgets.

Hena plc sells each solar panel for £150. Demand for the increased output is expected to be as follows:

* January: 20,000 panels

* February and March: 30,000 panels per month

* April: 40,000 panels

6

- May to August: 80,000 panels per month
- September: 60,000 panels
- October and November: 40,000 panels per month
- December: 20,000 panels
- All panels are sold to credit customers, 10 per cent of whom pay in the month of sale, 60 per cent in the month after and the remaining 30 per cent two months after the month of sale.

Details of production costs are as follows:

- Materials cost is 30 per cent of the selling price of the panels. Materials suppliers are paid in the month after production and sales have taken place.
- Production labour is 20 per cent of the selling price; 70 per cent of this amount is payable in the month of sale and the remainder, representing deductions from production wages for tax and national insurance, is paid to HM Revenue and Customs one month after production and sales have taken place.
- Other variable production costs of 10 per cent of selling price are paid in the month of sale.

Fixed costs are estimated to be £50,000 per month and are to be treated as paid in the month in which they were incurred. Hena plc manufactures to order and sells all its production and has no inventories of solar panels at the end of the year.

Required

Using a spreadsheet of your choice, prepare the following statements for the next 12 months:

- A sales budget.
- A production costs budget.
- A monthly cash budget.
- A monthly budgeted statement of profit or loss.
- A budgeted statement of financial position at the end of the 12 months.

Advise the directors of Hena plc whether they should go ahead with the proposed expansion or not.

> Question 6.3

The directors of Hena plc are impressed with your spreadsheet and your recommendation. However, they have new information that they would like you to build into your projections. The directors now expect that the selling price of panels will fall to £120 in the near future because of new competitors entering the market. Production materials, due to high levels of demand, will rise to 58 per cent of the new selling price, while employees will have to be given a 5 per cent pay rise based on production labour costs originally calculated in Question 6.2 to encourage them to stay. Other variable production costs will now fall to 10 per cent of the new selling price. All other expectations in Question 6.2 will remain the same. The directors are now wondering if your recommendation would be the same once you have incorporated the above changes into your budget projections.

Required

Using the spreadsheet you have prepared for Question 6.2, prepare the following statements for the next 12 months on the basis of the directors' new expectations:

- A sales budget.

- A production costs budget.

- A monthly cash budget.

- A monthly budgeted statement of profit or loss.

- A budgeted statement of financial position at the end of the 12 months.

Advise the directors of Hena plc whether they should go ahead with the proposed expansion or not given the new information that has come to hand.

≫ TAKE IT FURTHER

≫ Question 6.4

It is now August 2020. You have been asked by your head of department to prepare the monthly budgeted statement of profit or loss, the monthly cash budget and the budgeted statement of financial position for the 12 months ending 31 December 2021. You have been provided with the following details to help you in this task:

(a) Positive cash balances at the end of each month will earn interest at the rate of 0.5 per cent of the month end balance and this interest will be receivable in the following month.

(b) Negative cash balances at the end of each month will be charged interest at the rate of 2 per cent of the month end balance and this interest will be payable in the following month.

(c) Cash of £30,000 will be spent in March 2021 on new plant and equipment. The new plant and equipment will be brought into use in the business in the month of purchase.

(d) Your company produces three products: shirts, dresses and skirts. The cost cards for each product are as follows:

	Shirts £	Dresses £	Skirts £
Direct materials	10.00	12.00	6.00
Direct labour	12.00	15.00	7.50
Variable overhead	3.00	5.00	1.50
Total variable cost	**25.00**	**30.00**	**15.00**

(e) Selling prices are 140 per cent of total variable cost. Payments for direct labour are made in accordance with note (i). 60 per cent of the cost of materials is paid for one month after the month in which the materials were used in production, with the other 40 per cent of materials being paid for two months after the month in which they were used in production. Where purchases of direct materials are greater than £20,000 in any one month, a 2½ per cent discount is given on all purchases of direct materials in that month. When purchases of direct materials are greater than £25,000 in any one month, a 3½ per cent discount is given on all purchases of direct materials in that month. Variable overhead is paid for in the following month.

(f)　The marketing department has estimated that sales of each product for the year will be as follows:

2021	Shirts Number	Dresses Number	Skirts Number
January	500	300	800
February	600	350	900
March	750	400	700
April	900	700	650
May	1,000	800	500
June	1,000	1,200	400
July	800	1,000	350
August	700	600	200
September	950	400	500
October	650	300	600
November	850	450	750
December	1,100	600	850
Total	**9,800**	**7,100**	**7,200**

Your company sells its products directly to retailers. Retailers pay for the goods purchased as follows: 10 per cent on delivery, 25 per cent one month after delivery, 50 per cent two months after delivery and the remaining 15 per cent three months after delivery. All goods produced in the month are sold in the month and there are no inventories of finished goods or raw materials at the start or end of each month.

(g)　The company rents its factory and offices and currently pays a total of £30,000 a year in rent. A rent review in March 2021 is expected to increase the annual factory rent to £36,000 from 1 August 2021. Quarterly rental payments in advance will be made on 1 February, 1 May, 1 August and 1 November 2021.

(h)　Business rates for the six months to March 2021 will be paid on 1 October 2020 and the prepayment relating to January, February and March is shown in the forecast statement of financial position at 1 January 2021 in note (k). Business rates of £7,500 per half year will be payable on 1 April 2021 and 1 October 2021. These business rates will cover the year from 1 April 2021 to 31 March 2022.

(i)　Administrative and supervisory staff salaries are expected to total up to £9,000 a month. 68 per cent of staff salaries and direct labour costs are payable in the month in which they are incurred with the remaining 32 per cent representing deductions for tax and national insurance being paid to HM Revenue and Customs in the following month.

(j)　An insurance premium of £6,000 is payable on 1 May 2021 covering all the insurance costs of the business for the year to 30 April 2022.

(k)　The forecast statement of financial position at 1 January 2021 is as follows:

	£
Non-current assets	
Plant, equipment and fittings: cost	120,000
Plant, equipment and fittings: accumulated depreciation	(36,000)
	84,000
Current assets	
Trade receivables (owed by customers)	122,000
Rent prepayment	2,500
Rates prepayment	3,600
Insurance prepayment	1,800
Bank interest receivable	17
Cash at bank	3,395
	133,312
TOTAL ASSETS	**217,312**
Current liabilities	
Trade payables (materials)	29,400
Trade payables (variable overhead)	7,200
Tax and national insurance (direct labour)	8,570
Tax and national insurance (admin and supervisory salaries)	2,752
Corporation tax payable	3,200
Dividend payable	5,000
Total liabilities	**56,122**
Net assets	**161,190**
Equity	
Share capital	50,000
Retained earnings	111,190
	161,190

Notes to the forecast statement of financial position at 1 January 2021:

(i) Plant, equipment and fittings have a useful economic life of five years. Depreciation on these assets is charged monthly on the straight line basis.

(ii) Sales for October, November and December 2020 are budgeted to be £60,000, £70,000 and £75,000 respectively.

(iii) Purchases of materials are budgeted to cost £20,000 in November 2020 and £21,400 (net of the 2½ per cent discount) in December 2020.

(iv) The dividend payable is scheduled for payment in April 2021 and the corporation tax is due for payment on 1 October 2021.

Required

Prepare the budgeted statement of profit or loss and cash budget for your company for the 12 months ended 31 December 2021 together with a budgeted statement of financial position at 31 December 2021.

>> **Question 6.5**

Your friend is proposing to make a bid for a manufacturing business that has come onto the market. The business makes white plastic patio chairs. The purchase price for this business is £240,000. This purchase price is made up of plant, equipment and fittings (£180,000) with a useful life of five years, an inventory of raw materials (£20,000) and finished goods (£40,000). A delivery van will be purchased for £24,000 as soon as the business purchase is completed. The delivery van will be paid for in full in the second month of operations.

The following plans have been made for the business following purchase:

(a) Sales of plastic patio chairs, at a mark up of 60 per cent (before discounts) on production cost (see (b) below), will be:

Month	January	February	March	April	May	June	July
Planned sales (units)	10,000	12,000	14,000	20,000	24,000	22,000	18,000

Thirty per cent of sales will be for cash. The remaining sales will be on credit with 60 per cent of credit sales being paid in the following month and the remaining 40 per cent paying what is owed two months after the month of sale. A discount of 10 per cent will be given to selected credit customers, who represent 25 per cent of gross sales.

(b) Production cost is estimated at £5.00 per unit. The estimated production cost is made up of:

- Raw materials: £4.00
- Direct labour: £1.00

Production will be arranged so that closing inventory of finished goods at the end of every month is sufficient to meet 60 per cent of sales requirements in the following month. The valuation of finished goods purchased with the business is based upon the planned production cost per unit given in (a) above.

(c) The single raw material used in production will be purchased so that inventory at the end of each month is sufficient to meet half of the following month's production requirements. Raw material inventory acquired on purchase of the business is valued at the planned cost per unit as given in (b) above. Raw materials will be purchased on one month's credit.

(d) Costs of direct labour will be paid for as they are incurred in production.

(e) Fixed overheads are as follows: annual rent: £21,000, annual business rates: £8,100, annual heating and lighting: £7,500 and annual insurance: £1,500. Rent is payable quarterly in advance from 1 January. The business rates bill for January to March has been estimated at £1,800 and will be payable on 15 February while the rates bill from April to September has been estimated at £4,200 and will be payable by monthly instalments from 1 April. Heating and lighting will be payable quarterly in arrears at the end of each three-month period. Annual insurance will be payable on 1 January.

(f)   Selling and administration overheads are all fixed, and will be £114,000 in the first year. These overheads include depreciation of the delivery van at 25 per cent per annum on a straight line basis.

(g)   Selling and administration overheads will be the same each month and will be paid in the month in which they are incurred.

Required

Prepare a monthly cash budget and a monthly budgeted statement of profit or loss for the first six months of operations together with a budgeted statement of financial position at the end of June. As part of your budget, you should also produce a monthly production budget to calculate raw material purchases and a monthly sales budget to calculate both monthly sales and monthly cash receipts from sales.

6

7

PROCESS COSTING

LEARNING OUTCOMES

Once you have read this chapter and worked through the questions and examples in both this chapter and the online workbook, you should be able to:

- Describe what is meant by the term process costing

- Complete the basic process account

- Describe how losses can arise during a process

- Account for normal losses arising during a process

- Account for abnormal losses and abnormal gains

- Value the outputs from processes

- Apply the equivalent units approach in calculating output from a process during an accounting period

- Value closing work in progress at the end of an accounting period using both the first in first out and weighted average cost methods of valuing units of finished production and work in progress

INTRODUCTION

Our review of cost and management accounting thus far has focused on the costs and selling prices for solid units of production. The inputs to the production of wooden furniture in terms of materials and labour are easily distinguishable one from another. Likewise, the finished products are tangible and readily visible as individual units of production. However, what of products which are made in processes which involve the input and output not just of solid materials but of liquids or gases? These are processes in which the final output may not be immediately produced in readily divisible units. The production process for, for example, soft drinks or paints is continuous and it is very difficult to identify separate units of production until they are put into bottles, cans or tins. The outputs from one process can become the inputs to another process with the finished goods only being produced in the final process. Process costing is the costing method that is used to value the inputs and outputs from the oil, chemical, paper, food and drink industries. This chapter will therefore look at the ways in which process costing works in order to give a cost to units of production. In addition, we shall consider the way in which inventory is valued under process costing. Anna was able to value her wooden furniture on the basis of the material and labour inputs to each product together with an allocation of a proportion of production overhead (Chapter 3, Absorption costing and inventory valuation). By counting up her inventory of finished products and multiplying the total number of units by the cost price per unit she was able to derive a value for her inventory at the end of each accounting period very quickly and easily. But how should inventory for processes be valued at the end of each financial period? This valuation is made more difficult as a result of the continuous nature of the production process: at the end of the relevant period, some of the production may be only partially complete. How should this work in progress (WIP) be valued?

THE PROCESS ACCOUNT

As with all cost accounting techniques, the first step in process costing is to accumulate the costs in the cost account. In process costing, a process account is used to gather up these costs. The process account is a T account which gathers together the costs of inputs to a process. The inputs to the process, as in any other manufacturing operation, are materials, labour and overhead (Figure 7.1). Inputs to the process are posted to the debit (left hand) side of the process account while outputs appear on the credit (right hand) side. An example of a process account is shown in Illustration 7.1. Note that material inputs and outputs are expressed in money and unit terms, whereas labour and overhead are presented purely as costs expressed without any reference to quantities. In process costing, labour and overhead are known as conversion cost and this conversion cost is added to units of production. As always with T accounts, the totals on the two sides must be the same. In process costing, this means that both the quantities and the costs must be equal. From the example in Illustration 7.1, we can see that the cost per litre of output is the total cost of £60,000 divided by the total output of 5,000 litres = £12.

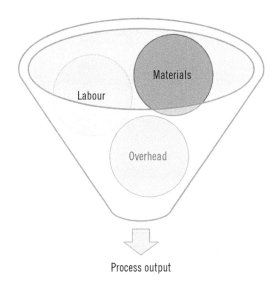

Process output

Figure 7.1 The process accounted for in the process account

Illustration 7.1 The process account

Process inputs   Process outputs

Process 1 account

	Litres	£		Litres	£
Materials	5,000	25,000	Transfer to process 2	5,000	60,000
Labour		20,000			
Overhead		15,000			
	5,000	**60,000**		**5,000**	**60,000**

WHY IS THIS RELEVANT TO ME?   The process account

To enable you as an accounting professional to understand:

● How the process account works

● The industrial situations in which process accounting is used to accumulate the cost of process inputs and to value process outputs

---

GO BACK OVER THIS AGAIN!   Are you sure that you understand how the process account works and what it is for? Go to the **online workbook** and have a go at Exercises 7.1 to check your understanding.

NORMAL LOSSES IN A PROCESS

In many if not all processes, the quantity of materials input to the process will not be the same as the quantity of materials of output from the process. This is as a result of evaporation, losses arising from chemical reactions or natural spoilage during the process (Figure 7.2). Lengthy experience and observation of these losses over time will enable entities to determine the normal level of losses that will be incurred each time the process is repeated. Normal losses are expected losses and are allowed for in the budget for each process. Normal losses in a process are usually expressed as a percentage of the quantity of materials input to the process. Normal losses are *never* given a value and are always valued at £Nil. The cost of normal losses is rolled up into the units of expected output from the process and valued as part of the units transferred to the next process or as units of finished product. Illustration 7.2 shows the way in which normal losses are accounted for in the process T account. In this case, the normal losses are expected to be 200 litres, leaving 4,800 litres of output transferred to process 2 (5,000 litres of input material – 200 litres of normal losses = 4,800 litres). While the normal loss is not valued in the process T account, the number of litres of normal loss is still added in to the credit side of the account as a deduction from the litres of input material to leave the number of litres transferred to process 2. Again, the two sides of the T account must balance: the 5,000 litres of input material is turned into 4,800 litres of output to process 2 + 200 litres of normal loss. From Illustration 7.2, we can see that the value of each litre of output to process 2 is now £60,000 divided by 4,800 litres = £12.50. The normal losses are thus valued as part of the output from the process and the value of these normal losses is carried forward in the cost of the output transferred to process 2.

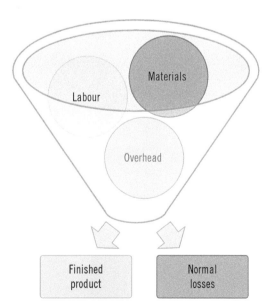

Figure 7.2 Process outcomes: finished product + normal losses

Illustration 7.2 The process account showing accounting for normal losses

Process 1 account					
	Litres	£		Litres	£
Materials	5,000	25,000	Transfer to process 2	4,800	60,000
Labour		20,000	Normal loss	200	–
Overhead		15,000	Normal losses: quantified in units but not valued in £s		
	5,000	**60,000**		**5,000**	**60,000**

ABNORMAL LOSSES

Figure 7.3 presents the additional complication of abnormal losses. Abnormal losses arise when there are losses that exceed the expected normal loss. These abnormal losses are valued in the process account and are accounted for separately. Abnormal losses are not part of normal production so are not rolled up into the cost of expected finished production units from a process.

Illustration 7.3 presents the process account showing the normal losses of 200 litres and an abnormal loss of 100 litres. Normal losses are still not valued, being recorded as the expected number of litres of lost input material at £Nil value. Abnormal losses are valued at the unit cost of the expected finished output transferred from the process. As we saw in Illustration 7.2, the cost per litre of output transferred to process 2 is £12.50 (£60,000 ÷ 4,800 litres = £12.50 per litre). The cost of the 4,700 litres transferred to process 2 is thus 4,700 × £12.50 = £58,750 while the

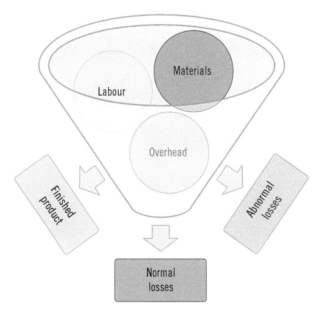

Figure 7.3 Process outcomes: finished product + normal losses + abnormal losses

abnormal loss of 100 litres is allocated a value of 100 litres × £12.50 (the unit cost of the expected finished output transferred from the process) = £1,250. Both sides of the process account must add up to 5,000 litres and £60,000 in total process inputs and total process costs.

Illustration 7.3 The process account showing the accounting for normal and abnormal losses

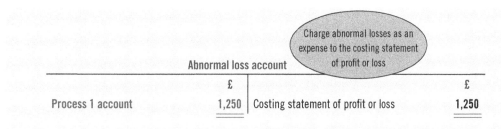

Process 1 account

	Litres	£		Litres	£
Materials	5,000	25,000	Transfer to process 2	4,700	58,750
Labour		20,000	Normal loss	200	–
Overhead		15,000	Abnormal loss	100	1,250
	5,000	**60,000**		**5,000**	**60,000**

Abnormal losses: quantified and valued at the cost of expected production

In the cost accounting system, the £1,250 of abnormal loss is transferred to an abnormal loss account as shown in Illustration 7.4. This abnormal loss represents a loss of expected finished production from a process and is charged as an expense to the costing statement of profit or loss at the end of the accounting period in which it arose. Highlighting this expense in this way reports the loss to the business and will encourage management to investigate the abnormal loss to determine whether it can be prevented in future or whether the loss was incurred as a result of a unique set of circumstances which will not be repeated.

Illustration 7.4 The abnormal loss account

Abnormal loss account

Charge abnormal losses as an expense to the costing statement of profit or loss

	£		£
Process 1 account	1,250	Costing statement of profit or loss	1,250

ABNORMAL GAINS

As well as abnormal losses, processes can experience abnormal gains. Abnormal gains arise when the actual losses from the process are lower than the expected normal losses (Figure 7.4). As was the case with abnormal losses, abnormal gains are valued in the process account and accounted for separately. Illustration 7.5 presents the entries to the process account when abnormal gains arise. What has happened here? Instead of the expected 4,800 litres of output, 4,880 litres have been transferred to process 2. The output transferred to process 2 is valued at £12.50 per litre

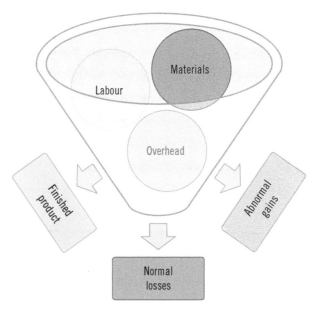

Figure 7.4 Process outcomes: finished product + normal losses + abnormal gains

giving a total transfer value of £61,000. The normal loss is still included at 200 litres and £Nil value. But there are now 5,080 litres and £61,000 on the credit side of the process account so the abnormal gain is added to the debit side to balance the account. Eighty litres is the abnormal gain and this is valued at the finished production price per litre of £12.50 to give a total abnormal gain of £1,000.

Illustration 7.5 The process account showing normal losses and abnormal gains

Process 1 account					
	Litres	£		Litres	£
Materials	5,000	25,000	Transfer to process 2	4,880	61,000
Labour		20,000	Normal loss	200	–
Overhead		15,000			
Abnormal gains	80	1,000			
	5,080	61,000		5,080	61,000

Abnormal gains: quantified and valued at the cost of expected production

In the cost accounting system, the £1,000 of abnormal gain is transferred to an abnormal gain account as shown in Illustration 7.6. This abnormal gain is then credited as income to the costing statement of profit or loss in the period in which it was incurred. Highlighting this additional income in this way will indicate to management that there may be ways in which to reduce the expected normal loss in the process. They will therefore be encouraged to investigate the gain to determine whether it can be maintained in the future or whether the gain arose as a result of an unrepeatable set of circumstances.

Illustration 7.6 The abnormal gain account

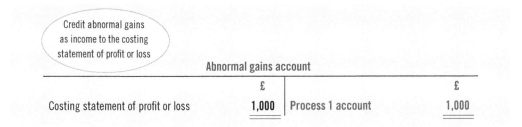

WHY IS THIS RELEVANT TO ME?   Normal losses, abnormal losses and abnormal gains

To enable you as an accounting professional to understand:

• How losses and gains in processes are accounted for

• That normal losses are expected losses from a process

• That normal losses are quantified in units but are never given a value in £s

• That valuing and accounting for abnormal losses and gains separately encourages management to investigate the causes of these abnormal gains and losses

MULTIPLE CHOICE QUESTIONS   Are you convinced that you could account correctly for normal losses, abnormal losses and abnormal gains? Go to the **online workbook** and have a go at Multiple choice questions 7.1 to check your abilities in these areas.

SUMMARY OF KEY CONCEPTS   Can you remember what normal losses, abnormal losses and abnormal gains mean? Go to the **online workbook** to check your recollection with Summary of key concepts 7.1 to 7.3.

SHOW ME HOW TO DO IT   How certain are you that you have followed all the steps so far in completing the process account? View Video presentation 7.1 in the **online workbook** to see in detail the accounting entries involved in writing up the process account, recording normal losses, abnormal losses and abnormal gains.

DISPOSAL COSTS
Normal losses

Rather than just disappearing as a result of the evaporation of input materials, the losses from a process may take the form of actual waste products. These waste products will have to be disposed of and this disposal may incur a cost. Figure 7.5 shows that where the disposal of waste products does incur a cost, the disposal cost of normal losses has to be added to the process account thereby increasing the cost of finished production from the process. Illustration 7.7 presents the process account and the disposal cost account to reflect the cost of disposal of normal losses. In this illustration, each litre of waste product arising from the normal losses produced by the process incurs a disposal cost of £1.20. 200 litres of normal loss therefore incur a total disposal cost of 200 × £1.20 = £240. This cost is debited to the process account as an

Figure 7.5 Accounting for the disposal costs of normal losses

additional cost of the process, with the credit posting being made to the disposal costs account. The credit to the disposal costs account records the liability for disposal costs, a liability that will be discharged when the payment is made from the bank account (debit disposals cost account, credit bank account). Note that the normal loss is still not valued in the process account. The value of each litre of production transferred from process 1 to process 2 is now £60,240 total costs ÷ 4,800 litres of production from process 1 = £12.55.

Illustration 7.7 Accounting for the disposal cost of normal losses

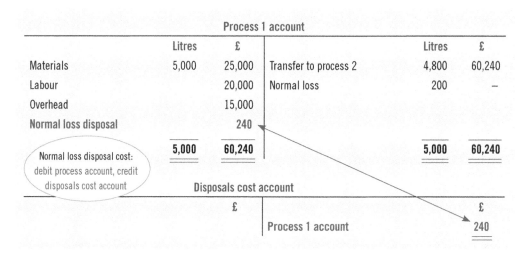

Process 1 account					
	Litres	£		Litres	£
Materials	5,000	25,000	Transfer to process 2	4,800	60,240
Labour		20,000	Normal loss	200	–
Overhead		15,000			
Normal loss disposal		240			
	5,000	**60,240**		**5,000**	**60,240**

Normal loss disposal cost: debit process account, credit disposals cost account

Disposals cost account		
	£	£
	Process 1 account	240

MULTIPLE CHOICE QUESTIONS   Do you think you can account correctly for situations in which normal losses have a disposal cost? Go to the **online workbook** and have a go at Multiple choice questions 7.2 to check your understanding.

Abnormal losses

When there is a charge to dispose of waste products from a process, then both abnormal and normal losses will incur these disposal costs. How should we account for the disposal costs of abnormal losses? Whereas the cost of the disposal of normal losses is included in the calculation of total process costs, the cost of disposal of abnormal losses is not valued in the process account. Instead, the cost of disposal of abnormal losses is added to the abnormal loss account (Figure 7.6) and rolled up with the cost of any abnormal losses incurred in the process during each period. The cost of each unit of abnormal loss is valued on the basis of the cost of each unit of expected finished product from the process as before (this chapter, Abnormal losses). Illustration 7.8 presents

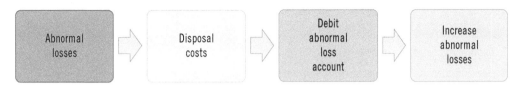

Figure 7.6 Accounting for the disposal costs of abnormal losses

the process account, the disposal cost account and the abnormal loss account to illustrate these entries. The expected production from the process is 4,800 litres (5,000 litres of input material – 200 litres normal loss = 4,800 litres). The cost per litre of expected finished production is £60,240 ÷ 4,800 litres = £12.55 per litre. The value of the abnormal loss is thus 100 litres × £12.55 per litre = £1,255 while production transferred to process 2 is 4,700 litres × £12.55 per litre = £58,985. As before (this chapter, Abnormal losses), the total abnormal losses are reported separately as a cost in the costing statement of profit or loss for the period in which the abnormal losses arise. However, when disposal costs arise, the loss is not just the lost production but the additional costs of disposing of these abnormal losses as well. This separate reporting encourages management to investigate these losses further to determine whether they can be prevented in future or whether the loss arose as a result of a unique set of circumstances which will not be repeated. The disposal cost account now shows a liability of £360 (£240 for the disposal of normal losses + £120 for the disposal of abnormal losses) which will be extinguished when the disposal cost is paid from the bank account (again, debit disposal cost account, credit bank account).

Illustration 7.8 Accounting for the disposal cost of normal and abnormal losses

Process 1 account

	Litres	£		Litres	£
Materials	5,000	25,000	Transfer to process 2	4,700	58,985
Labour		20,000	Normal loss	200	–
Overhead		15,000	Abnormal loss	100	1,255
Normal loss disposal		240			
Abnormal losses: debit abnormal loss account, credit process account	**5,000**	**60,240**		**5,000**	**60,240**

Abnormal loss account

	£		£
Process 1 account	1,255	Costing statement of profit or loss	1,375
Disposal cost account 100 × £1.20	120		
	1,375		**1,375**

Disposal cost account

	£		£
Abnormal loss disposal cost: debit abnormal loss account, credit disposal cost account		Process 1 account	240
		Abnormal loss account	120

SELLING LOSSES FROM A PROCESS
Normal losses

While organisations may incur a cost when disposing of the waste products from a process, it is just as likely that those waste products can be collected and sold to another entity for use in their own processes. Figure 7.7 summarises the way in which organisations should account for this income from the sale of losses from a process. As we shall see, the approach is very similar to the different accounting treatments for disposal costs for both normal and abnormal losses.

Figure 7.7 Accounting for the disposal proceeds from the sale of normal losses

Illustration 7.9 Accounting for the sale of normal losses from a process

Process 1 account

	Litres	£		Litres	£
Materials	5,000	25,000	Transfer to process 2	4,800	59,808
Labour		20,000	Normal loss scrap value	200	192
Overhead		15,000			
	5,000	**60,000**		**5,000**	**60,000**

Scrap account

	£		£
Process 1 account – normal loss	192		

Normal loss sale proceeds: debit scrap account, credit process account

Illustration 7.9 presents the process account and the scrap account for the normal losses arising in our process. In this example, each litre of waste product can be sold for 96 pence (£0.96). As normal losses amount to 200 litres, this means that the normal losses from the process can be sold for £192 (200 × £0.96). The sale of the normal losses from the process creates an asset, a receivable. Money will be received from the sale of the normal losses (and any other losses) from the process. Therefore, the scrap account is debited with the sale proceeds from the normal losses to reflect the creation of this asset. The corresponding credit entry is to the process account. This may seem surprising as we have so far insisted that normal losses are not valued. However, normal losses are still not valued in the process account. The credit of £192 is not a valuation of the normal losses but of the scrap value of those normal losses. The money receivable from the sale of the normal losses reduces the total costs of the process by £192. The cost of each litre of finished product transferred to process 2 is now £12.46 ((£60,000 – £192) ÷ 4,800 litres of expected output from the process). Whereas the disposal costs of the normal losses increased the costs of the process in Illustration 7.7, the sale proceeds from the sale of the normal losses reduce the costs of the process in Illustration 7.9.

Abnormal losses

Illustration 7.10 presents the accounting entries to record the treatment of abnormal losses in a process and the sale proceeds arising from the sale of those abnormal losses when losses from the process can be sold. Abnormal losses continue to be valued at the expected cost of production from the process. As the cost of each litre of product has now been determined at £12.46 (this chapter, Illustration 7.9) after taking into account the sale proceeds from normal losses, the 100 litres of abnormal losses are valued at 100 × £12.46 = £1,246. The scrap value of the abnormal losses is not included in the process account. As in the case of the sale of normal losses (Illustration 7.9), the sale proceeds of the abnormal losses create an asset, a receivable, which is debited to the scrap account. The corresponding credit entry is made to the abnormal loss account and this

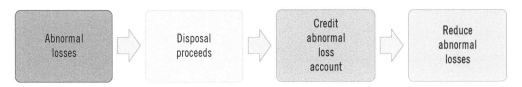

Figure 7.8 Accounting for the disposal proceeds from the sale of abnormal losses

has the effect of reducing the abnormal loss (Figure 7.8) that is charged to the costing statement of profit or loss for the period in which the abnormal losses arise. The abnormal loss continues to be reported separately to prompt management investigations to ensure that action is taken to avoid these abnormal losses in the future.

Illustration 7.10 Accounting for the sale of abnormal losses from a process

Process 1 account

	Litres	£		Litres	£
Materials	5,000	25,000	Transfer to process 2	4,700	58,562
Labour		20,000	Normal loss scrap value	200	192
Overhead		15,000	Abnormal loss account	100	1,246
	5,000	**60,000**		**5,000**	**60,000**

Abnormal losses: debit abnormal loss account, credit process account

Abnormal loss account

	£		£
Process 1 account	1,246	Scrap account	96
		Costing statement of profit or loss	1,150
	1,246		**1,246**

Abnormal loss sale proceeds: debit scrap account, credit abnormal loss account

Scrap account

	£		£
Process 1 account – normal loss	192		
Abnormal loss	96		

WHY IS THIS RELEVANT TO ME?   Selling the waste products arising from normal and abnormal losses from a process

To enable you as an accounting professional to understand:

- That losses from processes can be sold to other organisations resulting in additional income for the entity
- How the sale proceeds from both normal and abnormal losses in processes are accounted for

MULTIPLE CHOICE QUESTIONS   Do you think you can account correctly for the disposal proceeds from the sale of normal and abnormal losses? Go to the **online workbook** and have a go at Multiple choice questions 7.4 to check your ability in applying this technique.

SUMMARY OF KEY CONCEPTS   Can you remember how to account for the disposal proceeds from the sale of normal and abnormal losses? Go to the **online workbook** to revise the accounting with Summary of key concepts 7.5.

SHOW ME HOW TO DO IT   How certain are you that you have completely understood how to account for the sale proceeds from the sale of normal and abnormal losses in process accounting? View Video presentation 7.3 in the **online workbook** to see in detail how the sale proceeds from the sale of normal and abnormal losses are accounted for.

VALUING WORK IN PROGRESS AT THE END OF AN ACCOUNTING PERIOD

So far in this chapter we have assumed that processes all begin and end in an accounting period with no incomplete units of production at the start or at the end of the financial period. In real life situations, processes do not come to a complete stop at the end of each month or year with all processes completed and products transferred to finished goods or to the next process. Figure 7.9 shows that processes will usually generate finished product in a period but that the continuous nature of processes will give rise to partially completed production at the month or year end. This partially completed production is called work in progress, an asset that is in-

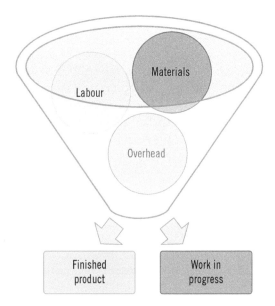

Figure 7.9 Process outcomes: finished product during the period + work in progress (production started but not yet finished) at the end of the period

cluded in inventory in the statement of financial position and as a deduction from production costs (cost of sales) in the statement of profit or loss. Work in progress represents products or processes that have been started but not completed by the period end date.

As an example of work in progress, consider a builder who might have started the construction of a house three months ago. By the end of the accounting year, all the foundations have been completed, the walls have been built and the roof beams have been added, but there are no roof tiles, no windows or doors and no internal plastering or internal fittings have been started. This house would be classified as work in progress at the end of the financial year. To value this house, the builder will add up all the costs of materials, of labour and of overhead incurred up to the year-end date to determine a cost for the work done up to that point. The cost of this work in progress will be added to the closing inventory in both the statement of profit or loss and the statement of financial position. The cost or net realisable value (not selling price) of inventory at the end of an accounting period is a deduction from cost of sales with that inventory being carried forward to the next accounting period in the statement of financial position. In the next financial year, the house will be completed and sold to a buyer. All the costs incurred in building the house (the work in progress at the start of the year + all the materials, labour and overhead costs incurred in completing the house) will then be matched with the selling price to give the total profit on the sale.

In the same way, when a process is partially complete at the end of the month or year, the costs that have been incurred up to that point have to be calculated in order to determine the cost of this work in progress so that the current asset can be recognised and carried forward to the next accounting period. How is this valuation of work in progress in a process carried out? In process costing, this valuation is based on equivalent units. Equivalent units are an estimate of the whole number of units of complete output representing the incomplete process. This sounds confusing, so let's consider this in Example 7.1.

EXAMPLE 7.1

Scary Chemicals Limited operates a process in which 1,000 units of production are left in the process at the end of the month. However, these units are only 60 per cent complete with respect to materials, labour and overhead. Therefore, the equivalent units are 1,000 × 60 per cent = 600 complete units. The completed units + the equivalent work in progress units are added together to find the number of units completed during the month. This total number of units is then used to determine the cost per unit for finished production and abnormal gains and losses (remember that normal losses are not valued). Figure 7.10 illustrates the equivalent units calculation.

Figure 7.10 The equivalent units calculation

EXAMPLE 7.2

Scary Chemicals Limited input 20,000 units of material to a new process at the beginning of September. At the end of the month, 16,000 units of finished production have been completed and there were 4,000 units of work in progress which is assessed as being 50 per cent complete. The costs of the inputs to the process during the month were as follows:

- Materials: £43,200
- Labour: £51,300
- Overhead: £13,500

The following steps will be completed to determine the costs for finished production and work in progress.

Step 1: Calculate the equivalent units of production

At this stage, the total costs of the process are irrelevant. The first stage in calculating the cost of each unit of output is to determine the number of equivalent units produced in the month. Illustration 7.11 presents the calculation of the equivalent units of production during September. 16,000 units are 100 per cent complete, so this gives a total of 16,000 equivalent units (16,000 × 1.00). The remaining 4,000 units started in the month are 50 per cent complete, so the equivalent units here are 4,000 × 0.50 = 2,000. The total equivalent units of production are thus 16,000 fully completed units + 2,000 units of work in progress = 18,000.

Illustration 7.11 Scary Chemicals Limited: equivalent units of production for September

	Total units	× % complete	= Equivalent units
Step 1: Output completed	16,000	100%	16,000
Step 1: Work in progress	4,000	50%	2,000
Total units	**20,000**		**18,000**

Step 2: Calculate the cost per equivalent unit of output and work in progress

Total costs now become relevant. In Example 7.2, total costs for September are £43,200 (materials) + £51,300 (labour) + £13,500 (overhead) = £108,000. Producing 18,000 equivalent units (Step 1) has cost £108,000. Therefore, the cost per equivalent unit of production is £6 (£108,000 total costs divided by 18,000 equivalent units).

Step 3: Calculate the total cost of output and work in progress

Each equivalent unit of production and work in progress has a cost of £6, so we can now value our finished production and work in progress as follows:

Cost of output of completed production: 16,000 units × £6 per unit (Step 2) = £96,000

Cost of work in progress 2,000 units × £6 per unit (Step 2) = £12,000

£96,000 + £12,000 = £108,000, the total cost of production for September

Step 4: Complete the process account

Illustration 7.12 presents the completed process account for the month. The units of output started in September in terms of materials are 20,000 of which 16,000 were completed during the month with 4,000 units of work in progress at the end of the month, so both units columns total up to 20,000. The cost of materials, labour and overhead are debited to the process account and add up to £108,000. The credits to the account are £96,000, the completed production transferred to the production account, together with £12,000 work in progress, inventory carried forward to October. This work in progress will be completed in October to produce finished goods ready for transfer to the production account.

Illustration 7.12 Scary Chemicals Limited process account for September (Example 7.2)

Scary Chemicals Limited: process account

	Units	£		Units	£
Materials	20,000	43,200	Completed production	16,000	96,000
Labour		51,300	Work in progress c/f	4,000	12,000
Overhead		13,500			
	20,000	**108,000**		**20,000**	**108,000**

CLOSING WORK IN PROGRESS: VARYING COMPLETION %S OF COSTS

In Example 7.2, the valuation of work in progress was straightforward as all inputs of materials, labour and overhead into the units at the month end were estimated at 50 per cent. What procedure should be followed if there are differing levels of completion for the inputs to work in progress? In many processes, all the materials will be added at the start, but the labour and overhead will be added evenly throughout the entire process. How will these differing levels of completion affect the values calculated for finished goods and work in progress at the end of the accounting period? Again, an example (Example 7.3) will show us the method to follow in valuing finished output and work in progress.

EXAMPLE 7.3

Let's extend Example 7.2. All the costs are the same as in that example, but the completion of the work in progress units is as follows: material input to work in progress is 80 per cent complete, whereas labour and overhead are 50 per cent complete. We shall follow the same steps as in Example 7.2 in order to calculate the value of the completed units and the value of work in progress at the end of September.

Step 1: Calculate the equivalent units of production

As in Example 7.2, the first step will be to work out the equivalent units produced in the month. However, there will be two sets of equivalent units to calculate. The first will be for materials and the second for labour and overhead. Illustration 7.13 presents the calculation of the equivalent units of production during September for both materials and for labour and overhead. 16,000 units are 100 per cent complete and have been transferred to completed production, so this gives a total of 16,000 equivalent units (16,000 × 1.00) for both materials and for labour and overhead. 4,000 units have been started in September, but are not complete by the end of the month. These units are 80 per cent complete with regards to materials, so 4,000 × 80 per cent means that materials in work in progress represent 3,200 equivalent units. Following the same approach for labour and overhead gives us 4,000 × 50 per cent = 2,000 equivalent units of finished product. Adding the equivalent units of output of finished production and work in progress gives us 19,200 equivalent units of materials (16,000 + 3,200) and 18,000 equivalent units of labour and overhead (16,000 + 2,000).

Illustration 7.13 Scary Chemicals Limited: equivalent units of material and labour and overhead for September (Example 7.3)

	Materials			Labour and overhead		
	Total units	× % complete	= Equivalent units	Total units	× % complete	= Equivalent units
Step 1: Output	16,000	100%	16,000	16,000	100%	16,000
Step 1: WIP	4,000	80%	3,200	4,000	50%	2,000
Total units	**20,000**		**19,200**	**20,000**		**18,000**

Step 2: Calculate the cost per equivalent unit of output and work in progress

Where there are varying completion %s for materials and conversion cost, two calculations are required to work out the cost per equivalent unit of material and the cost per equivalent units of labour and overhead.

Materials

The total cost of materials input into the process during the period is £43,200. The cost per unit of completed output and work in progress for 19,200 equivalent units of material is therefore £43,200 ÷ 19,200 = £2.25. The materials in completed production and work in progress will therefore be valued at £2.25 per equivalent unit of material input.

Labour and overhead

The total cost of labour and overhead input into the process during the period is £51,300 (labour) + £13,500 (overhead) = £64,800. The per unit cost of output and work in progress for 18,000 equivalent units of labour and overhead is therefore £64,800 ÷ 18,000 = £3.60. The labour and overhead in completed production and work in progress will be valued at £3.60 per equivalent unit of labour and overhead input.

Step 3: Calculate the total cost of output and work in progress

We now have our costs per equivalent unit for the various inputs into the process, so we can value our finished production and work in progress as follows:

Cost of output of completed production: 16,000 units of material × £2.25 per unit (Step 2) + 16,000 units of labour and overhead × £3.60 per unit (Step 2) = £93,600

Cost of work in progress 3,200 units of material × £2.25 (step 2) + 2,000 units of labour and overhead × £3.60 (step 2) = £14,400

£93,600 + £14,400 = £108,000 so the total cost of production for the period is completely allocated between finished production and work in progress.

Step 4: Complete the process account

Illustration 7.14 presents the completed process account for September. The units of output started in the period in terms of materials are 20,000 of which 16,000 were completed during the month with 4,000 units of work in progress at the end of the month, so both units columns total up to 20,000. Costs of materials, labour and overhead are debited to the process account and add up to £108,000 for the period. The credits to the account are £93,600, the completed production transferred to the production account as calculated in Step 3, together with £14,400 work in progress, inventory carried forward to October. Again, this work in progress will be completed in the next month to produce finished goods ready for transfer to the production account.

Illustration 7.14 Scary Chemicals Limited: process account for September (Example 7.3)

Scary Chemicals Limited: process account					
	Units	£		Units	£
Materials	20,000	43,200	Completed production	16,000	93,600
Labour		51,300	Work In progress c/f	4,000	14,400
Overhead		13,500			
	20,000	**108,000**		**20,000**	**108,000**

WHY IS THIS RELEVANT TO ME?   Valuing work in progress at the end of an accounting period

To enable you as an accounting professional to understand:

• How work in progress and completed production are valued on the basis of equivalent units

• How to account for differing levels of completion for different inputs to a process

MULTIPLE CHOICE QUESTIONS   Are you quite sure that you can calculate equivalent units and the value of work in progress in a process? Go to the **online workbook** and have a go at Multiple choice questions 7.5 to see if you can.

SUMMARY OF KEY CONCEPTS   Can you remember the steps involved in calculating work in progress in a process? Go to the **online workbook** to check your recall of these steps with Summary of key concepts 7.6.

SHOW ME HOW TO DO IT   Do you think you have completely understood how to calculate equivalent units and the value of work in progress in process accounting when there are varying completion percentages for materials and labour and overhead cost? View Video presentation 7.4 in the **online workbook** to see in detail how these calculations are made.

UNIT COSTS WHEN THERE IS OPENING AND CLOSING WORK IN PROGRESS

Closing work in progress in a process at the end of one accounting period becomes the opening work in progress at the start of the next accounting period. Materials, labour and overheads are then added, finished goods are produced and the closing work in progress becomes the next period's opening work in progress. This continuous progression is shown in the process cycle in Figure 7.11. What effect will this opening work in progress have on the valuation of production completed during the accounting period and on the valuation of work in progress at the end of that accounting period? When there is opening work in progress in a process, there are two

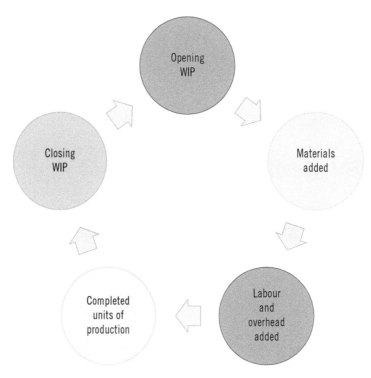

Figure 7.11 The process cycle

options by which to value a process's finished production and closing work in progress: the first in first out method and the average cost method. Let's look at each of these methods in turn to see how they affect the values of finished production and closing work in progress.

VALUING FINISHED PRODUCTION AND WORK IN PROGRESS: THE FIRST IN FIRST OUT METHOD

Figure 7.12 presents the order in which production is completed when valuing finished production and work in progress on the first in first out method. This method assumes that the opening work in progress units in a process are the first to be completed in the next accounting period. Therefore, the first additions of materials, labour and overhead to a process go towards finishing the partially completed units brought forward from the last financial period. Once these opening work in progress units are complete, then new units are started and completed during the accounting period. These units started and completed during the period are 100 per cent complete with respect to materials, labour and overhead. At the end of the month, there will be closing work in progress, units of production that have been started but which are only partially complete at the end of that accounting period. The equivalent units approach is used once more in order to value the units completed during the period and the closing work in progress. Let's continue with the figures from Example 7.3 in Example 7.4.

Figure 7.12 Valuing finished production and work in progress: the first in first out method

EXAMPLE 7.4

In October, Scary Chemicals Limited produced a total of 26,200 units of finished production from its new process. The company incurred materials costs of £59,070 and labour and overheads added to the process totalled up to £91,350. At the end of October, the work in progress (5,000 units) was 40 per cent complete with respect to materials and 16 per cent complete with respect to labour and overhead. Work in progress at the start of October is the closing work in progress detailed in Example 7.3.

Step 1: Calculate the equivalent units of production

Illustration 7.15 presents the equivalent units table for the process for October. Example 7.3 tells us that at the end of September, there were 4,000 units of partially completed production. These units of work in progress are the opening work in progress at the beginning of October. Under the first in first out method of valuing finished production and work in progress, these are the first units to be completed in October. These work in progress units are 80 per cent complete with respect to materials at the end of September: therefore, to complete these units, a further 20 per cent (100 per cent – 80 per cent) of materials will need to be added to the process. The equivalent units of material used in completing this opening work in progress are thus 4,000 × 20 per cent = 800. This makes sense as Illustration 7.13 shows us that the equivalent units of material carried forward in closing work in progress are 3,200. The 3,200 equivalent units of material in work in progress brought forward + the 800 equivalent units of material added to the process in October = 4,000 completed equivalent units of material.

Illustration 7.15 Scary Chemicals Limited: equivalent units table for October using the first in first out method to value finished production and work in progress

Finished output	Materials			Labour and overhead		
	Total units	% to complete	Equivalent units	Total units	% to complete	Equivalent units
Opening WIP completed	4,000	× 20%	800	4,000	× 50%	2,000
Other units started and finished in October	22,200	× 100%	22,200	22,200	× 100%	22,200
Total production in period	26,200		23,000	26,200		24,200
Closing WIP	5,000	× 40%	2,000	5,000	× 16%	800
	31,200		**25,000**	**31,200**		**25,000**

The same approach is used to determine the equivalent units of labour and overhead added to the process in October to complete the units of opening work in progress. Illustration 7.13 tells us that the closing work in progress at the end of September is 50 per cent complete with respect to labour and overhead so a further 50 per cent (100 per cent – 50 per cent) of labour and overhead will need to be added to the process to complete the conversion cost of these units brought forward at the start of October. Fifty per cent × 4,000 means that there are 2,000 equivalent units of labour and overhead used to complete the conversion of the opening work in progress into finished product. Again, we can see that this is correct as Illustration 7.13 shows 2,000 equivalent units of labour and overhead in closing work in progress + 2,000 equivalent units of labour and overhead added in October = 4,000 equivalent units. Once the 800 equivalent units of material and the 2,000 equivalent units of labour and overhead are added to the opening work in progress, then these units of production will be 100 per cent complete.

During October 26,200 units of finished production were produced. These 26,200 units include the completion of the 4,000 units of work in progress brought forward from September. Therefore, the number of equivalent units started and completed during October was 26,200 – 4,000 = 22,200.

The equivalent units of closing work in progress can now be calculated. Five thousand units of production were started but not completed during the month. These units were 40 per cent complete with respect to materials, so this gives equivalent units of material of 5,000 × 40 per cent = 2,000. Likewise, labour and overhead in these 5,000 units is 16 per cent complete so there are 5,000 × 16 per cent = 800 equivalent units of labour and overhead in closing work in progress.

There were 31,200 units of production worked on during October, but these 31,200 units were only equivalent to 25,000 units of material and 25,000 units of labour and overhead.

Step 2: Calculate the cost per equivalent unit of output and work in progress

Under the first in first out method of valuing finished production and work in progress, the costs of opening work in progress are ignored in the cost per equivalent unit calculations. Therefore, the costs incurred in the period are used to determine the cost per equivalent unit of materials and labour and overhead.

Materials

The cost of materials incurred in October was £59,070. The cost per equivalent unit of completed output and closing work in progress for 25,000 equivalent units of material is therefore £59,070 ÷ 25,000 = £2.3628. The materials in completed production and closing work in progress will therefore be valued at £2.3628 per equivalent unit of material input.

Labour and overhead

The total cost of labour and overhead incurred in October was £91,350. The per equivalent unit cost of completed output and closing work in progress for 25,000 equivalent units of labour and overhead is therefore £91,350 ÷ 25,000 = £3.654. The labour and overhead in completed production and closing work in progress will therefore be valued at £3.654 per unit of labour and overhead input.

Step 3: Calculate the total cost of output and work in progress

We now have our cost per equivalent unit for the various inputs into the process, so we can calculate the values for our finished production and work in progress.

The cost of output of completed production is shown below (all figures are rounded to the nearest whole £):

	£
Opening work in progress cost brought forward from September (part of the total cost of production of completed output in October)	14,400
Completion of opening work in progress:	
• 800 equivalent units of material: 800 × £2.3628	1,890
• 2,000 equivalent units of labour and overhead: 2,000 × £3.654	7,308
Production started and finished in October	
• 22,200 equivalent units of material: 22,200 × £2.3628	52,454
• 22,200 equivalent units of labour and overhead: 22,200 × £3.654	81,119
Total cost of completed output during October	**157,171**

The closing work in progress is valued as follows, again rounding to the nearest whole £:

	£
• 2,000 equivalent units of material: 2,000 × £2.3628	4,726
• 800 equivalent units of labour and overhead: 800 × £3.654	2,923
Total cost of work in progress at the end of October	**7,649**

Step 4: Complete the process account

We now have all the relevant numbers with which to complete the process account for October which is presented in Illustration 7.16. Four thousand units of work in progress were brought forward from September at a valuation of £14,400 so this is the first debit to the process account, the asset at the start of the month. Costs incurred during the month are debited to the process account as these are the costs added to the process thereby building up the inventory asset.

Production completed in the month is a credit to the account as the finished production is transferred to the goods for sale account. The remaining credit entry is the closing work in progress, the balance left on the process account of production started but not finished in October which will form the opening balance on the process account for November.

Illustration 7.16 Scary Chemicals Limited: process account for October (Example 7.4) valuing opening work in progress on the first in first out method

Scary Chemicals Limited: process account for October					
	Units	£		Units	£
WIP b/f	4,000	14,400	Completed in month	26,200	157,171
Materials	27,200	59,070	WIP c/f	5,000	7,649
Conversion		91,350			
	31,200	**164,820**		**31,200**	**164,820**

WHY IS THIS RELEVANT TO ME?   Valuing finished production and work in progress: the first in first out method

To enable you as an accounting professional to understand:

- That the first in first out method of valuing finished production and work in progress assumes that the work in progress brought forward is the first production to be completed

- How to calculate the equivalent units for material and conversion cost when finished production and work in progress are valued using the first in first out method

- How to determine the values for finished production and closing work in progress when using the first in first out method

MULTIPLE CHOICE QUESTIONS   Are you certain that you understand and can apply the first in first out method of valuing finished production and work in progress in calculating equivalent units and in the valuation of finished production and closing work in progress? Go to the **online workbook** and have a go at Multiple choice questions 7.6 to check your understanding and abilities in this area.

SUMMARY OF KEY CONCEPTS   Can you recall the steps involved in calculating equivalent units when valuing finished production and work in progress using the first in first out method? Go to the **online workbook** to check your recollection with Summary of key concepts 7.7.

SHOW ME HOW TO DO IT   Did you completely understand how to calculate equivalent units, costs per equivalent unit, the value of finished goods and the value of closing inventory when using the first in first out basis? View Video presentation 7.5 in the **online workbook** to revise in detail how these calculations are made.

VALUING FINISHED PRODUCTION AND WORK IN PROGRESS: THE WEIGHTED AVERAGE COST METHOD

The weighted average cost method involves calculating a weighted average cost for units produced from both opening work in progress and units started in the current period. Figure 7.13 shows that this method of valuing opening work in progress assumes that the opening work in progress units and the new units started in the accounting period are all mixed together. As a result of this mixing together, the resources put into the completion of the opening units and of the units started in the period cannot be identified separately. The new materials, the labour and the overhead added to the process during the month all go towards completing both the opening work in progress and the new units started in the period. Therefore this method does not assume that the opening work in progress units are finished first as the new inputs cannot be separately identified as first completing work in progress and then starting new units. At the end of each financial period, there will still be closing work in progress, units of production that have been started but which are only partially complete at the end of that accounting period. The equivalent units approach is still used to value the units completed during the period and the closing work in progress. To illustrate the weighted average cost method of valuing finished production and work in progress we shall use the same information as given in Example 7.4 and follow the same four steps.

Step 1: Calculate the equivalent units of production

Illustration 7.17 presents the equivalent units table for the process for October. Whereas the first in first out method made a careful set of equivalent unit calculations to determine the material and conversion costs required to complete the units of opening work in progress, the weighted average cost method completely ignores the equivalent units of opening work in progress. The only concern when using the weighted average cost method is the number of units of production completed during the accounting period. In this case, a total of 26,200 units were completed in the month, the 4,000 units of work in progress at the start of the month + the 22,200 units started and completed in the month. These units are 100 per cent complete during the period with respect to both materials and labour and overhead. At the end of the month, 5,000 units of production had been started but not yet finished, being 40 per cent complete with respect to materials and 16 per cent complete with respect to labour and overhead. These unfinished units of work in progress are accounted for in the usual way at the end of the month. As in the case of the first in first out method, there were 2,000 (5,000 units × 40 per cent complete) equivalent units of material and 800 (5,000 units × 16 per cent complete) equivalent units of labour and overhead at the end of October.

Figure 7.13 Valuing finished production and work in progress: the weighted average cost method

Illustration 7.17 Scary Chemicals Limited: equivalent units table for October using the weighted average cost method to value finished production and work in progress

	Materials			Labour and overhead		
	Total units	% complete	Equivalent units	Total units	% complete	Equivalent units
Output completed	26,200	100	26,200	26,200	100	26,200
Work in progress	5,000	40	2,000	5,000	16	800
Total units	**31,200**		**28,200**	**31,200**		**27,000**

Again, there were 31,200 units of production worked on during October, but these 31,200 units were equivalent to 28,200 units of material and 27,000 units of labour and overhead.

Step 2: Calculate the cost per equivalent unit of output and work in progress

Under the weighted average cost method of valuing opening work in progress, the costs of opening work in progress are *not* ignored in the cost per equivalent unit calculations but are added to the material and conversion costs incurred in the period. Therefore, both the costs of opening work in progress and the costs incurred in the period are averaged to determine the cost per equivalent unit of materials and of labour and overhead. This adding together of the costs of opening work in progress and the costs incurred in the period means that completed units of opening WIP are each given a value of one full equivalent unit of production. The weighted average cost method assumes that all the units produced in a given period have the same unit cost and that a unit of part completed opening WIP has, when it has been completed, the same cost as a unit of output started and finished in the period.

Materials

The cost of materials in opening work in progress was £7,200 (Example 7.3). The cost of materials in October was £59,070. The combined material cost for the month was thus £7,200 work in progress + £59,070 cost of materials for October = £66,270. The cost per equivalent unit of completed output and closing work in progress for 28,200 equivalent units of material is therefore £66,270 ÷ 28,200 = £2.35. The materials in completed production and closing work in progress will therefore be valued at £2.35 per equivalent unit of material input.

Labour and overhead

The cost of labour and overhead in opening work in progress was £7,200 (Example 7.3). The cost of labour and overhead in October was £91,350. The combined labour and overhead cost for the month was therefore £7,200 + £91,350 = £98,550. The per equivalent unit cost of completed output and closing work in progress for 27,000 equivalent units of labour and overhead is thus £98,550 ÷ 27,000 = £3.65. The labour and overhead in completed production and closing work in progress will therefore be valued at £3.65 per unit of labour and overhead input.

Step 3: Calculate the total cost of output and work in progress

We now have our cost per equivalent unit for the various inputs into the process, so we can calculate the values for our finished production and work in progress.

	£
Completed production in October	
• 26,200 equivalent units of material: 26,200 × £2.35	61,570
• 26,200 equivalent units of labour and overhead: 26,200 × £3.65	95,630
Total cost of completed output during October	**157,200**

The closing work in progress is valued as follows:

	£
• 2,000 equivalent units of material: 2,000 × £2.35	4,700
• 800 equivalent units of labour and overhead: 800 × £3.65	2,920
Total cost of work in progress at the end of October	**7,620**

Step 4: Complete the process account

The process account for October can now be completed. This process account is presented in Illustration 7.18. Four thousand units of work in progress were brought forward from September at a valuation of £14,400 so this is still the first debit to the account, the asset at the start of the month. Costs incurred during the month are again debited to the process account as these are the costs added to the process as the inventory asset is produced. Production completed in the month is a credit to the account as the finished production is transferred to the goods for sale account. The remaining credit entry is the closing work in progress, the balance left on the process account of production started but not finished in October which will form the opening balance on the process account for November.

Illustration 7.18 Scary Chemicals Limited: process account for October (Example 7.4) valuing finished production and work in progress on the weighted average cost method

Scary Chemicals Limited: process account for October					
	Units	£		Units	£
WIP b/f	4,000	14,400	Output	26,200	157,200
Materials	27,200	59,070	WIP c/f	5,000	7,620
Conversion		91,350			
	31,200	164,820		31,200	164,820

WHY IS THIS RELEVANT TO ME?   Valuing finished production and work in progress: the weighted average cost method

To enable you as an accounting professional to understand:

- That the weighted average cost method of valuing finished production and work in progress pools the values of opening work in progress and costs incurred in a period in determining the weighted average value for units of finished production and closing work in progress

- That only the units completed in the period and the closing work in progress count as equivalent units when using the weighted average cost method of valuing finished production and work in progress

- How to determine the values for finished production and closing work in progress when using the weighted average cost method

MULTIPLE CHOICE QUESTIONS   Are you confident that you understand and can apply the weighted average cost method of valuing finished production and work in progress in calculating equivalent units and in the valuation of finished production and closing work in progress? Go to the **online workbook** and have a go at Multiple choice questions 7.7 to check how well you have understood the techniques applied.

SUMMARY OF KEY CONCEPTS   Are you able to recall how to calculate equivalent units when valuing finished production and work in progress using the weighted average cost method? Go to the **online workbook** to check your recollection with Summary of key concepts 7.8.

SHOW ME HOW TO DO IT   Have you completely understood how to calculate equivalent units, costs per equivalent unit, the value of finished goods and the value of closing inventory when using the weighted average cost basis? View Video presentation 7.6 in the **online workbook** to go over in detail again how these calculations are made.

CHAPTER SUMMARY

You should now have learnt that:

- Process transactions are recorded in a process account

- A process account is a T account with columns for units of input and output and values of inputs and outputs

- Normal losses are never valued in process costing

- Normal losses are expected losses so any costs associated with normal losses are rolled up into the cost of completed production

- Abnormal gains and losses are valued on the basis of the unit cost of expected production from a process

- Abnormal gains and losses are reported separately in the costing statement of profit or loss to focus management's attention on these unexpected costs and revenues

- The disposal cost of normal losses increases the costs of production in the process account

- The disposal cost of abnormal losses increases the expense on the abnormal loss account

- Income received from the disposal of normal losses decreases the costs of production in the process account

- Income received from the disposal of abnormal losses decreases the expense on the abnormal loss account

- In order to value finished goods and closing work in progress in a process equivalent units are calculated for materials and for labour and overhead consumed in each accounting period

- Equivalent units = the number of units in a process × the % completion of those units

- Finished production and work in progress can be valued on either the first in first out method or on the weighted average cost method

- The first in first out method of valuing finished production and work in progress assumes that the first units completed in a period are those units brought forward in closing work in progress from the previous accounting period

- The first in first out method of valuing finished production and work in progress calculates equivalent units in a period as completion of opening work in progress + units started and finished in a period + units in closing work in progress

- The weighted average cost method of valuing finished production and work in progress assumes that the resources used to complete opening work in progress and the units started and finished in the period are indistinguishable

- The weighted average cost method of valuing finished production and work in progress calculates equivalent units in a period as units completed in the period + units in closing work in progress

- The weighted average cost method of valuing finished production and work in progress averages the costs brought forward in opening work in progress and costs incurred in the period to calculate an average cost for each equivalent unit of material and of labour and overhead

QUICK REVISION   Test your knowledge with the online flashcards in Summary of key concepts and attempt the Multiple choice questions, all in the **online workbook**.

END-OF-CHAPTER QUESTIONS

Solutions to these questions can be found in the **online workbook**.

❯ DEVELOP YOUR UNDERSTANDING

❯ Question 7.1

Iron Bar Limited produces soft drinks. A new product, Aloo Brew, has been developed and has just gone into production. During March, 30,000 litres of materials were input to the process at a cost of £7,425. Labour on the production process for the month cost £4,950 and overheads for the product for March totalled up to £2,625. 30,000 litres of Aloo Brew were produced in March and sent to the bottling section. There was no work in progress at the start or the end of the month and the expected normal loss from the Aloo Brew process is 0% of materials input.

Required

For Aloo Brew for March:

- Draw up the process account.
- Calculate the per litre cost of production.

❯ Question 7.2

The Big Bang Chemical Company produces explosives for use in the mining industry. All explosives are produced in chemical processes involving the input of materials, labour and overheads. The following data applies to the product Whimper for October:

- 12,000 kilograms of materials were input to the process at a cost of £51,000.
- Process labour for October cost £27,000.
- Overheads for Whimper for the month were £19,200.
- Normal losses are expected to be 10% of input materials.
- A total of 10,600 kilograms of Whimper were produced in October and transferred to finished goods for sale.
- There was no opening or closing work in progress of Whimper at the beginning or end of the month.

Required

For the production of Whimper in October:

- Calculate the expected normal loss in kilograms.
- Determine whether there is an abnormal loss or abnormal gain during production of the product in the month.
- Calculate the per kilogram cost of production of the product.
- Draw up the process account for the month.

> Question 7.3

The refining process operated by Inedible Oils plc generated 24,000 litres of engine oil during June. Inputs to the process during the month were 25,000 litres of unrefined oil costing £52,875, labour costing £22,325 and overheads of £28,200. Normal losses are expected to be 6% of the quantity of materials input to the process. There was no opening or closing work in progress at the start or end of the month.

Required

For the production of engine oil in June:

* Calculate the expected normal loss in litres.
* Determine whether there is an abnormal loss or abnormal gain during production in the month.
* Calculate the per litre cost of production of the product.
* Draw up the process account for the month.

> Question 7.4

SCT Limited produces moisturising cream. Normal losses are expected to be 12% of the quantity of input materials. The waste products produced as normal and abnormal losses can be sold for 80 pence per litre. Input costs for August were:

* 7,500 litres of material at a cost of £26,500.
* Labour costing £11,880.
* Overheads of £8,540.

Actual production in August was 6,450 litres of moisturising cream. There was no opening or closing work in progress at the start or end of the month. SCT received the cash for all the scrap units sold from the process on 31 August.

Required

For the production of moisturising cream in August:

* Calculate the expected normal loss in litres.
* Determine whether there is an abnormal loss or abnormal gain during production in the month.
* Calculate the per litre cost of production of the product.
* Draw up the process account, the abnormal loss or abnormal gain account and the scrap account for the month.

> Question 7.5

Mr Threshy produces luxury ice cream. The process inputs for April were as follows:

* Materials: 30,000 litres at a cost of £0.66 per litre.
* Labour: 1,000 hours at a cost of £10 per hour.
* Overhead: 1,000 hours at a cost of £5 per hour.

During the process, the materials undergo regular skimming to produce the uniquely creamy Mr Threshy luxury ice cream. The materials skimmed off are disposed of at a cost of 20 pence per litre for both normal and abnormal losses. Normal losses are expected to be 20% of input materials. In April 23,750 litres of ice cream were produced from the process. There was no opening or closing work in progress in the process at the beginning or end of the month. The disposals cost for the month was paid on 30 April.

Required

For the production of ice cream in April:

- Calculate the expected normal loss in litres.
- Determine whether there is an abnormal loss or abnormal gain during production in the month.
- Calculate the per litre cost of production of the product.
- Draw up the process account, the abnormal loss or abnormal gain account and the disposals cost account for the month.

>> TAKE IT FURTHER

>> Question 7.6

Mobo Chemicals Limited operate a refining process to produce cooking oils. At 1 December, the work in progress in the refining process was made up as follows:

- Materials: £26,187.
- Labour and overhead: £18,450.
- 10,000 work in progress units, 80% complete with respect to materials and 50% complete with respect to labour and overhead.

During December, materials costing £105,350 and labour and overhead costing £147,600 were added to the process. Completed output from the process for the month was 40,000 litres of cooking oils.

At 31 December, there were 5,000 units of work in progress, 60% complete with respect to materials and 20% complete with respect to labour and overhead.

Required

Present the two process accounts for Mobo Chemicals Limited on the basis that:

1. Finished production and work in progress are valued using the first in first out method.
2. Finished production and work in progress are valued using the weighted average cost method.

>> Question 7.7

Giant Plant Fertilisers Limited produce liquid fertilisers for industrial agricultural use. At 1 May, the work in progress in the process was made up as follows:

- Materials: £51,660.
- Labour and overhead: £15,213.
- 12,000 work in progress units, 70% complete with respect to materials and 35% complete with respect to labour and overhead.

During May, materials costing £442,800 and labour and overhead costing £304,260 were added to the process. Completed output from the process for the month was 84,800 litres of liquid fertiliser.

At 31 May, there were 20,000 units of work in progress, 68% complete with respect to materials and 37% complete with respect to labour and overhead.

Required

Present the two process accounts for Giant Plant Fertilisers Limited on the basis that:

1. Finished production and work in progress is valued using the first in first out method.

2. Finished production and work in progress is valued using the weighted average cost method.

>> Question 7.8

Acetic Industries Limited operates a two stage process in the production of vinegar. Details of the inputs and outputs to the two processes in July are presented below.

Process 1

Inputs for the month:

- 47,000 litres of material at a cost of £129,250.
- Labour costing £31,300.
- Overheads of £20,870.

Production in July and other details relating to Process 1 are as follows:

- Normal loss is expected to be 5 per cent of the quantity of input materials.
- Actual output from Process 1 to Process 2 in the month was 44,000 litres.
- Normal and abnormal losses from Process 1 can be sold for £1.20 per litre. At 31 July, no cash had yet been received for the scrap value of the losses incurred in the month.
- There was no opening or closing work in progress in Process 1. All output during the month was transferred into Process 2 at cost.

Process 2

There were 6,000 units of work in progress at the start of July. Opening work in progress in Process 2 was made up of £22,800 of materials and £12,960 of labour and overhead. Opening work in progress was 100% complete with respect to materials and 50% complete with respect to labour and overhead.

All input materials in July came from Process 1. There was no other material input to the process. Labour and overhead costs incurred in July totalled up to £207,360. Forty six thousand litres of vinegar were completed in Process 2 during the month and transferred to finished goods. No losses are expected from Process 2 and no losses were incurred during July.

Four thousand litres of vinegar were in progress at 31 July. These work in progress units were 100% complete with respect to materials and 50% complete with respect to labour and overhead.

Required

Write up the process accounts for Processes 1 and 2 for July together with any other accounts relevant to the two processes. Your answer should value the output and work in progress from Process 2 using both the first in first out and weighted average cost methods of valuing finished production and work in progress.

8

CAPITAL INVESTMENT APPRAISAL

LEARNING OUTCOMES

Once you have read this chapter and worked through the questions and examples in both this chapter and the online workbook, you should be able to:

- Understand what is meant by the term capital investment

- Understand why businesses undertake capital investment appraisal when making long-term investment decisions

- Explain how the four main capital investment appraisal techniques work

- Apply the four main capital investment appraisal techniques to capital investment decisions

- Explain the advantages and limitations of each of the four main capital investment appraisal techniques

- Understand the idea of the time value of money

INTRODUCTION

In the last few chapters we have looked at the costing of products and services and the role of cost accounting in various short-term decision-making and planning techniques. These short-term decision-making techniques aim to maximise contribution and profits over periods of a few weeks or months. What techniques should be applied if we want to maximise our value over the long term? This question arises when businesses want to make long-term investment decisions involving the outlay of significant amounts of money and resources (capital investment). What contribution and profits will any new investments make to the business? Will the new investments be valuable in the long run rather than just being profitable over short periods? Will the contribution and profits be higher than the returns we could generate from alternative investment options or from just putting the money into an interest paying bank account? These are important questions to ask when businesses are considering the investment of considerable sums of money in new projects and ventures. Businesses want to know if the contribution generated by these new investments will return their original cost and more. If a long-term investment fails to return the money originally invested, there would be little point undertaking the project in the first place.

WHAT IS CAPITAL INVESTMENT?

Non-current assets and new long term investments require funding in order to maintain or expand a business's operations. Assets wear out or become outdated. Failure to replace and renew assets means that businesses are operating less efficiently and less profitably than they should. Without investment in new assets and new projects, businesses will not survive over the long term. When new investment is undertaken, this gives rise to new non-current assets that will be used to generate revenues, profits and cash over several years. Expenditure on these new non-current assets is termed capital expenditure, spending money now to benefit the future through the acquisition of these long-lasting, long-term assets. Consider Example 8.1.

EXAMPLE 8.1

If you were in charge of a haulage business, every few years you would need to invest in a new fleet of lorries. This fleet of lorries would then be used to generate revenue for several years before they themselves were replaced with a new fleet. Paying for these new vehicles would require long-term investment today. If the company did not currently have the cash on hand with which to pay for these new assets, these long-term funds would be provided by lenders in the form of loans or by shareholders in the form of new share capital subscribed by the shareholders.

Businesses undertake capital investment appraisal to determine whether new investments will be worthwhile and whether they will generate more cash than they originally cost.

To enable you as an accounting professional to:

- Appreciate the need for businesses to invest continually in new long-term assets from which to generate increased revenue, profits and cash
- Reinforce your ability to distinguish between short-term working capital management and long-term capital investment

GO BACK OVER THIS AGAIN!   Are you sure that you can distinguish between short- and long-term investment decisions? Go to the **online workbook** Exercises 8.1 to make sure you can make these distinctions.

WHY IS CAPITAL INVESTMENT APPRAISAL IMPORTANT?

Capital investment appraisal is essential when considering investments in new projects or in new assets. Without this appraisal, we will not be able to decide whether our investment is likely to be worthwhile in financial terms. Think about the points raised in Example 8.2.

EXAMPLE 8.2

When choosing the university at which you wanted to study, you might have weighed up the benefits and drawbacks from your current course compared with the benefits and drawbacks of choosing another programme at another university. Your thoughts will have centred not just on financial considerations: you might have reflected on the nightlife, the sporting facilities and the academic reputation of your chosen university among many other things. But at some point you will have taken into account the costs of studying at a particular college compared with the costs of studying elsewhere and the likely career and salary opportunities that would be open to you upon completion of your chosen course.

In the same way, businesses will want to know whether proposed investments are likely to represent a valuable addition to current operations and whether a positive return will be generated for shareholders. If not, there is no point in undertaking the project. Businesses will want to take on all projects that capital investment appraisal techniques suggest will make a positive return. However, cash for investment purposes, like many other resources, is often in short supply. Therefore, entities will undertake capital investment appraisal to determine which one of the several options competing for funds is the most valuable project in which to invest, given the levels of risk involved. Again, a simple example (Example 8.3) will illustrate these ideas.

If you have spare cash to invest, there are many banks, building societies and other investments competing for your money. You will weigh up each of the available options on the basis of which investment will give you the highest rate of interest, but also consider which investment is likely to be the safest home for your savings. It would be pointless putting your cash into an investment paying a high rate of interest if you were likely to lose all your money when the investment collapsed into liquidation.

Finally, the future is uncertain. What might seem like a good investment now might not look like such a good idea two years down the line. Therefore, managers have to exercise due care and attention when investing shareholders' money into projects in the expectation that they will produce the best outcomes for investors and other stakeholders. Capital investment appraisal is a further example of managers exercising control over an entity's operations as illustrated in Give me an example 8.1.

GIVE ME AN EXAMPLE 8.1   Capital investment appraisal

8

The following extract from the published report of Rio Tinto plc illustrates the rigorous approach adopted by company management to evaluating new investment opportunities.

We have strengthened our investment assessment criteria, our levels of independent review of opportunities and our investment approval processes. We approve investment only in opportunities that, after prudent assessment, offer attractive returns that are well above our cost of capital.

Rio Tinto plc Annual Report and Accounts 2014, Strategic Report, page 11.

Source: www.riotinto.com

WHY IS THIS RELEVANT TO ME?   Capital investment appraisal

As an accounting professional you will be expected to:

- Understand the importance of evaluating long-term investment projects and what they will contribute to an organisation

- Be involved in capital investment decisions and appraise both the financial and non-financial aspects of these decisions

- Undertake the necessary capital investment appraisal of long-term projects you are proposing yourself

GO BACK OVER THIS AGAIN!   Are you confident that you can describe capital investment appraisal and explain why it's needed? Go to the **online workbook** Exercises 8.2 to make sure you appreciate what capital investment appraisal involves.

WHAT FINANCIAL INFORMATION WILL I NEED TO UNDERTAKE CAPITAL INVESTMENT APPRAISAL?

Capital investment appraisal relates to future events, so a substantial amount of estimation is required when undertaking this technique as shown in Figure 8.1. All costs and revenues associated with a proposed project are expressed in terms of cash inflows and cash outflows.

The first piece of information required will be the cost of the new capital investment in £s. This is easily acquired as this cost will be readily available from the supplier of the new assets. In our haulage business example (Example 8.1), the capital investment will be the cost of the new lorries. This could be the list price or the list price less a discount for the purchase of several vehicles, but it is an easily ascertainable cost. If the capital investment involves the construction of a new building, then cost will be the cost of acquiring the land plus the construction costs. Again, the cost of the land will be a verifiable fact from the price the seller requires for the land, while the cost of the building will be the contract price determined by the engineers and designers at the construction company chosen to complete the project.

More difficult will be the estimates of revenue and costs arising from the new investment in each year of the proposed project's life. Demand for the new product or service will have to be determined along with the associated costs of providing the service or producing the product. Current demand and current revenue arising from that demand can be calculated quite easily, but future demand and future revenue will depend upon many uncertainties. Demand might fall to zero very quickly as a result of superior services and products from competitors or it might rise very rapidly as the business becomes the leading provider in the sector. Technology might reduce costs very quickly or costs might rise as a result of demand for particular raw materials that are in short supply. Whatever the revenues and costs, they will be subject to a high degree of estimation and in many ways will just represent a best guess.

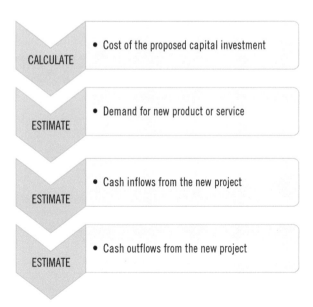

Figure 8.1 Steps in the capital investment appraisal process

CAPITAL INVESTMENT APPRAISAL TECHNIQUES:
COMPREHENSIVE EXAMPLE

To illustrate the capital investment appraisal techniques that are used in practice we will now turn to a comprehensive example.

Anna is looking to expand by diversifying into different areas of business. She currently has £500,000 to invest in acquiring the assets of an existing business from its owners. She has identified a stonemason, a furniture workshop and a garden design and build company as possible targets for her new investment. Market research and costings indicate that the net cash inflows (revenue – expenditure) into the three businesses over the next five years are expected to be those shown in Illustration 8.1.

Illustration 8.1 Anna: cash flows from the three possible capital investment projects

	Stonemason	Furniture workshop	Garden design and build
	£000	£000	£000
Investment cost (an outflow of cash)	(500)	(500)	(500)
Net cash inflows in year 1	160	190	50
Net cash inflows in year 2	160	180	100
Net cash inflows in year 3	160	170	150
Net cash inflows in year 4	160	160	250
Net cash inflows in year 5	160	150	350
Cash inflow from sale of the investment at the end of year 5	200	100	300
Total net cash inflows	1,000	950	1,200
Total net cash inflows – investment cost	500	450	700

All three businesses require the same initial investment, but produce differing total cash inflows after deducting the cost of the original investment. One business is expected to provide a steady income throughout the five years, one produces high initial cash inflows, but these then decline, while the final opportunity starts with very low net cash inflows, which then grow rapidly. How will Anna choose the business in which she should invest? Initially, it would appear that Anna will choose the garden design and build business for her investment as this produces the highest net cash inflow over the five years along with a higher resale value for the assets. However, the majority of the cash inflows from the garden design and build operation occur towards the end of the five years. Later cash inflows are much less certain (and hence riskier) than cash inflows that occur earlier in the other projects' lives. The following capital investment appraisal techniques can be used to help Anna make her decision.

CAPITAL INVESTMENT APPRAISAL TECHNIQUES

There are four commonly used techniques when undertaking capital investment appraisal. These are:

- Payback
- Accounting rate of return (ARR)
- Net present value (NPV)
- Internal rate of return (IRR)

We will look at each of the above techniques in detail to show how each of them works and what each of them tells us about the positive or negative financial returns from each project.

Payback

This method calculates the number of years it will take for the cash inflows from the project to pay back the original cost of the investment. An investment of £1,000 into a deposit account that pays 5 per cent interest per annum would provide you with annual interest of £50 (£1,000 × 5 per cent). To repay your initial investment of £1,000 would take 20 years (£1,000 ÷ £50). In the same way, businesses assess how long the cash inflows from a project would take to repay the initial investment into the project.

> **GO BACK OVER THIS AGAIN!**   Are you certain that you can calculate a simple payback period? Go to the **online workbook** and have a go at Exercises 8.3 to make sure you can undertake these calculations successfully.

Looking at Anna's investment opportunities, let's consider the payback from the first option, the stonemason. To calculate the payback period, a payback table is drawn up to show how long the project will take to pay back the original investment. The first column of the table (see Table 8.1) lists the annual cash inflows and outflows, while the second column presents the initial investment outflow less the cash inflows received each year.

In Table 8.1 the investment of £500,000 is made at the present time and so is shown as the initial outflow of cash from the project. Investments made at the start of a project, the present time, are conventionally referred to as being made in year 0 or at time 0. As cash flows into the project, so the initial investment is paid back and the investment in the project not yet paid back falls.

At the end of year 1, after deducting the first year's cash inflows of £160,000, there is £500,000 − £160,000 = £340,000 still to be recovered from the project before the full £500,000 is paid back. In year 2, the project generates another £160,000, so at the end of year 2 there is still £340,000 − £160,000 = £180,000 required from the project before the initial investment is repaid in full. This process is repeated until the cumulative cash flows show £Nil or a positive number. At this point, the initial investment has been paid back by cash inflows into the project.

Table 8.1 shows that the stonemason project would repay the initial investment of £500,000 at some time between the end of years 3 and 4 as the cumulative cash flows (original investment − net cash inflows) turn positive by the end of year 4.

However, we can be more precise. Only £20,000 out of the £160,000 cash inflow in year 4 is required to repay the investment in the project that has not yet been repaid by the cash inflows

	Cash flows £000	Cumulative £000
Initial investment year 0	(500)	(500)
Net cash inflows year 1	160	(340)
Net cash inflows year 2	160	(180)
Net cash inflows year 3	160	(20)
Net cash inflows year 4	160	140
Net cash inflows year 5	160	300
Cash inflow from sale of the investment at the end of year 5	200	500

in years 1, 2 and 3. Therefore, the exact payback period for an investment in the stonemason business would be:

$$3\,\text{years} + \frac{\pounds 20,000}{\pounds 160,000} = 3.125\,\text{years}$$

As 0.125 years is roughly equivalent to 1½ months (12 × 0.125), the initial investment of £500,000 at time 0 is fully repaid after 3 years and 1½ months.

NUMERICAL EXERCISES   Do you think you can calculate a payback period for a project? Work your way through the above example again to confirm your understanding of how we arrived at the payback period for the stonemason project and then go to the **online workbook** and attempt Numerical exercises 8.1 and 8.2 to make sure you can apply this investment appraisal technique to the other two investments that Anna is considering.

Payback: the decision criteria

When using the payback method of capital investment appraisal, the project chosen is always the investment that pays back its initial cash outlay most quickly. In Anna's case, on the basis of payback, she would choose to invest in the furniture workshop as this repays the initial outlay of £500,000 in less than three years while the other two projects repay the same initial investment in more than three years, as shown in Figure 8.2.

Would this be a good decision? If Anna is concerned with just the speed of her cash recovery, then the furniture workshop would be the correct choice as her initial investment is returned to her in the shortest possible time. The payback calculation is easy to make and easy to understand, but it does not consider the time value of money (see this chapter, The time value of money). It also ignores the cash flows after the payback period is complete. In the case of the furniture workshop, a further £450,000 is generated from this project after the initial investment is paid back,

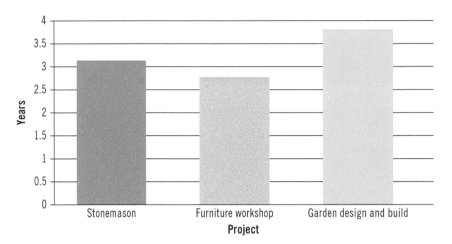

Figure 8.2 Payback periods in years of the three investment opportunities available to Anna

whereas the garden design and build project yields a further £700,000 after payback, £250,000 more than the cash inflows from the preferred investment on the basis of the payback period.

Should the payback period be the sole criterion upon which to base an investment decision? The answer to this question is 'no'. Payback will be just one of the criteria upon which any investment decision is based. Further decisions have to be made about the long-term revenue generation prospects of the investment. You probably noticed that the cash inflows from the furniture workshop are reducing year by year and that the resale value of the assets of this business is significantly lower than the resale value of the assets in the other two projects under consideration. Any further investment in this business after the five-year period will probably generate lower cash inflows than the other two options, so, from a longer-term point of view, an investment in the furniture workshop is probably not the best use of Anna's money if she wants to maximise the potential returns on her investment.

Looking at the other investment options, the garden design and build, while presenting the longest payback period, shows rising cash inflows each year that accelerate towards the end of the five-year period. Therefore, this might well be a better investment for the longer term as demand for this business's services seems to be rising sharply and might be expected to increase even further after the end of year 5. The stonemason business shows steady inflows of cash each year, but no increase or decrease in demand. This would seem to be the safest investment, but it is not one that will perform beyond expectations.

WHY IS THIS RELEVANT TO ME?   Payback method of capital investment appraisal

To enable you as an accounting professional to:
- Calculate a payback period for a proposed investment
- Understand the criteria on which to take an investment decision based on payback
- Understand the advantages and limitations of the payback method
- Appreciate that capital investment decisions have to be based on not just one but several criteria

Accounting rate of return (ARR)

This investment appraisal method averages the projections of accounting profit to calculate the expected rate of return on the average capital invested, as summarised in Figure 8.3. Accounting profit is represented by the net cash inflows of the project over its life, less the total depreciation (remember that depreciation is not a cash flow, but is treated as an expense in arriving at accounting profit). The total accounting profit projections are divided by the number of years the project will last to give the average profit over the life of the investment. This is then divided by the average capital employed over the life of the project to determine the ARR.

Let's see how the ARR would be calculated for the stonemason business and then you can practise this technique on the other two potential investment opportunities.

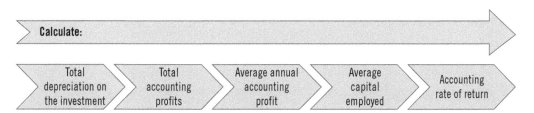

Figure 8.3 Steps in calculating the accounting rate of return (ARR) on an investment

ARR Step 1 Calculate the total depreciation on the investment

First, we will need to calculate the total depreciation on the investment in the stonemason project. Remember that the total depreciation provided on non-current assets is given by the assets' cost − the residual value of those assets.

From Illustration 8.1:

- The cost of the assets is £500,000

- The residual value is the cash inflow from the sale of the investment at the end of year 5 of £200,000

Therefore, total depreciation over the five years of the project's life is:

£500,000 (cost) − £200,000 (residual value) = £300,000

ARR Step 2 Calculate the total accounting profits

Total accounting profits are the total net cash inflows – the total depreciation. Total net cash inflows into the stonemason project are £160,000 for five years, a total of £800,000. The resale value of the assets is not included in the net cash inflows as this figure is used to calculate both the total depreciation on the project's assets and the average capital investment over the project's life.

Total accounting profits are thus £800,000 (net cash inflows) – £300,000 (depreciation) = £500,000.

ARR Step 3 Calculate the average annual accounting profit

The average annual accounting profit is then £500,000 ÷ 5 years = £100,000 per annum.

ARR Step 4 Calculate the average capital employed

The average capital employed in the stonemason project is found by adding together the original cost of the investment and the resale value of the assets at the end of the project and dividing this total figure by 2.

From Illustration 8.1:

- The cost of the assets is £500,000

- The residual value is the cash inflow from the sale of the investment at the end of year 5 of £200,000

Therefore, average capital employed in the stonemason business over the five years is:

(£500,000 (cost) + £200,000 (residual value)) ÷ 2 = £350,000

ARR Step 5 Calculate the accounting rate of return

The ARR is then the average annual accounting profit divided by the average capital employed in the project:

$$\frac{£100{,}000 \text{ (average annual profit)}}{£350{,}000 \text{ (average capital employed over the five years)}} \times 100\% = 28.57\%$$

NUMERICAL EXERCISES   How confident are you that you can calculate an accounting rate of return for a project? Work your way through the above example again to confirm your understanding of how we arrived at the accounting rate of return for the stonemason project and then go to the **online workbook** and attempt Numerical exercises 8.3 and 8.4 to make sure you can apply this investment appraisal technique to the other two investments that Anna is considering.

Accounting rate of return: the decision criteria

The investment decision based on the ARR requires us to choose the proposed investment with the highest ARR, provided that this meets or exceeds the required ARR of the business. Assuming that the ARR meets Anna's target rate of return, the project that she will choose will be the garden design and build project as it produces an accounting rate of return of 35 per cent compared with the furniture workshop, which has an accounting rate of return of 30 per cent, as shown in Figure 8.4. This approach produces a quite different decision when compared to the payback method of investment appraisal.

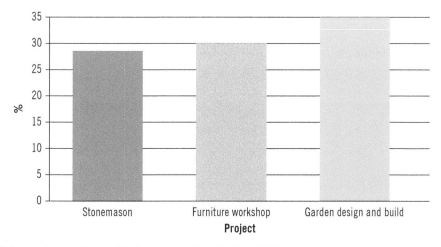

Figure 8.4 Accounting rate of return of the three investment opportunities available to Anna

While the ARR is easy to calculate and is based on accounting profits, it does suffer from some serious limitations:

- As with the payback method of investment appraisal, the ARR ignores the time value of money.

- The ARR is a percentage rather than the total profits generated by an investment, so projects with the same ARR could have hugely different cash flows, one with very low net cash inflows and one with very large net cash inflows. Managers will always prefer larger cash flows to smaller ones, but reliance on the relative measure of ARR might lead to the selection of a project with a higher rate of return but lower net cash inflows. In Anna's case the project with the highest accounting rate of return and the highest cash inflows are the same, but this may not always be the case.

- ARR does not differentiate between projects (as payback does) that have the majority of the net cash inflows in the early stages of the project's life. As we have already noted, early cash inflows can be predicted with more accuracy and so are preferred by businesses as the money is in the bank rather than just being a potential future inflow of cash.

Companies' use of the payback and accounting-based measures of investment appraisal is illustrated in Give me an example 8.2.

GIVE ME AN EXAMPLE 8.2   Companies' use of payback and accounting measures in evaluating investment opportunities

Do companies use payback and accounting based measures in practice to evaluate investment opportunities? The following extract from Next plc's Annual Report and Accounts for the 52 weeks to 28 January 2017 shows that they do.

The profitability of the portfolio of stores opened or extended in the last 12 months is forecast to be 23% of VAT inclusive sales and payback on the net capital invested is expected to be 24 months. Both measures meet our Company investment hurdles of 15% profitability and 24 months payback.

Source: *Next plc Annual Report and Accounts 2017*, page 8.

The time value of money

Before we consider the final two investment appraisal techniques, net present value (NPV) and the internal rate of return (IRR), we need to think about the time value of money. We noted earlier that both the payback and ARR methods of capital investment appraisal ignore this aspect of the investment decision. So why is the time value of money so important? And what do we mean when we talk about the time value of money? This approach to investment appraisal recognises that £1 received today is worth more than £1 received tomorrow. There are various reasons why today's money is more valuable than tomorrow's.

Firstly, inflation will reduce the value of our cash: £1 will buy more today than it will buy this time next year. For example, if a litre of petrol costs £1.40 today, we can buy 30 litres of petrol for £42 (30 × £1.40 = £42). However, if the inflation rate is 5 per cent per annum, this means that in one year's time, one litre of petrol will cost £1.47 (£1.40 × 1.05). Our £42 will now only buy us 28.57 litres of petrol (£42 ÷ £1.47), as the purchasing power of our £42 has fallen as a result of inflation. Therefore, given that inflation reduces the value of our money and what we can buy with it, it makes sense to receive cash today rather than receiving cash tomorrow.

We can combat the effects of inflation by investing our money to generate interest to maintain our purchasing power. £1 invested today at an annual interest rate of 5 per cent will give us £1.05 in a year's time, our original £1 plus 5 per cent interest. If the inflation rate over the same period has been 5 per cent, we will be no worse off and our purchasing power will have remained the same. In our example above, £42 today invested at a rate of 5 per cent would give us £44.10 (£42 × 1.05) in one year's time. With this £44.10 we could buy £44.10 ÷ £1.47 = 30 litres of petrol so the purchasing power of our money has been maintained.

However, if we can invest our £1 for a year at an interest rate of 5 per cent while inflation is only 3 per cent, at the end of the year we would need our original £1 plus a further 3p to buy the same goods in a year's time that £1 will buy today. We will thus be 2p better off as our £1.05 is more than the £1.03 we need for consumption in one year's time. If we cannot have our money today, we will demand something in return to compensate us for waiting for cash that is receivable in the future. By investing our money in the bank or in a project, we are missing out on using the cash today so there is an opportunity cost element to this investment. A higher return on the cash is the compensation we expect for forgoing consumption today.

Finally, money that we will receive in the future is more risky than money we receive today because of the uncertainty that surrounds future income. Investing money carries the risk that we will not receive any interest as well as the risk that our original investment will not be repaid in full. Therefore, investors require a particular level of return to compensate them for the risk they are taking by investing their money. In the same way, businesses require a rate of return to compensate them for risking their capital in a particular venture. The riskier the venture is, the higher the rate of return that will be required to invest in that venture, as shown in Give me an example 8.3.

GIVE ME AN EXAMPLE 8.3   Higher risk = higher return

Two bailout packages totalling €240 billion were advanced to the Greek government in May 2010 and October 2011. In April 2015 growing fears that Greece would fail to repay what it owed to its international creditors, thereby forcing the country out of the European single currency, caused the value of Greek bonds to fall dramatically. As a result, anyone investing their money in Greek two-year bonds on 15 April 2015 would have seen the returns on these bonds rise to 27 per cent. This very high return is due to the risk that the Greek government will be unable either to pay the interest or to repay the capital value of those bonds. Clearly, the higher the risk, the higher the return that investors will demand for taking on that risk. By contrast, the price that investors were paying for German 10-year government bonds (which are considered an ultra-safe investment) on the same day meant that their returns from their investment in these bonds were close to zero.

Source: www.wsj.com/articles/greek-government-bonds-plunge-on-ratings-downgrade-1429180492

To enable you as an accounting professional to:

- Understand that inflation erodes the value of today's money and reduces its future purchasing power
- Appreciate that money received today has more purchasing power than money received tomorrow
- Appreciate that cash expected in the future is less certain and so riskier
- Understand that investors will require a certain rate of return on money invested in order to compensate them for the risks they are taking in investing their money
- Appreciate that investing money in a project involves an opportunity cost as that money cannot be used for something else while it is invested in the project

GO BACK OVER THIS AGAIN!   Are you certain that you have grasped the concept of the time value of money? Go to the **online workbook** and have a look at Exercises 8.4 to make sure you understand this concept and then have a go at Exercises 8.5 to check your grasp of this subject.

MULTIPLE CHOICE QUESTIONS   Are you sure that you understand the time value of money? Go to the **online workbook** and have a go at Multiple choice questions 8.1 to test your understanding.

Business investment and the time value of money

In the same way, businesses invest money with the expectation that their investments will earn them a return in the future. Businesses will determine the acceptable level of return to compensate them for the risks involved in investing and use this level of return to discount expected future cash inflows and outflows to a present value. Present value expresses expected future inflows and outflows of cash in terms of today's monetary values. Discounting to present value thus expresses all a project's cash inflows and outflows in the common currency of today, thereby facilitating a fair comparison of projected cash inflows and outflows for different investment proposals.

The acceptable level of return is referred to as the business's cost of capital and is sometimes known as the hurdle rate of return. If an investment clears the hurdle—that is, the NPV is greater than or equal to £Nil—then it means that the project will deliver a positive return and generate more profit for the business over time than has to be invested at the beginning of the project.

Net present value

Anna estimates that her expected rate of return is 15 per cent. This is the rate of return that she feels will compensate her for the risk she is taking in investing in a new business of which she has no experience. Applying this rate of return to the stonemason project produces the NPV results shown in Illustration 8.2.

Illustration 8.2 Anna: net present value of the investment in the stonemason business discounted at a rate of 15 per cent

	Cash flows	× Discount factor	= Net present value
	£000	15%	£000
Cash outflow year 0	(500)	1.0000	(500.00)
Net cash inflows year 1	160	0.8696	139.14
Net cash inflows year 2	160	0.7561	120.98
Net cash inflows year 3	160	0.6575	105.20
Net cash inflows year 4	160	0.5718	91.49
Net cash inflows year 5	160	0.4972	79.55
Cash inflow from sale of the investment at the end of year 5	200	0.4972	99.44
Stonemason investment: net present value of the project discounted at a rate of 15%			**135.80**

How did we arrive at these figures?

The initial investment is always made at the start of the project, time 0, and so is already expressed in terms of today's money. Therefore, there is no need to discount this figure to present value as today's money is already stated at its present value. This figure is thus multiplied by a discount rate of 1.0000.

All cash inflows are assumed to be received at the end of each year of the project and so are discounted to present value as though they are received at the end of year 1, at the end of year 2, at the end of year 3 and so on, right up to the last expected cash inflow or outflow associated with the project. This is an important convention of the NPV and IRR capital investment appraisal techniques, but is obviously unrealistic as, in reality, cash will flow into and out of projects throughout the year. However, it is an assumption you need to be aware of and this assumption is made to keep the models as simple as possible.

Discount factors are presented in Table 1 in the Appendix. Check that the figures given in Illustration 8.2 are the discount rates for time intervals 1, 2, 3, 4 and 5 for a 15 per cent discount rate. If you ever need to derive your own discount rates, you would divide 1 by $(1 +$ the interest rate being used$)^n$ where n is the number of years into the project. In Anna's case, this is 1 divided by $(1 + 0.15)$ for year 1, 1 divided by $(1 + 0.15)^2$ for year 2, 1 divided by $(1 + 0.15)^3$ for year 3 and so on. Check that these calculations do give you the discount factors shown in Illustration 8.2 by working out these figures on your calculator now. Keep Table 1 in the Appendix handy for the remaining examples in this chapter and when you attempt the various activities in the online workbook.

When calculating NPVs, cash outflows are shown in brackets while cash inflows are shown without brackets. Thus the initial investment, which is an outflow of cash, is shown in brackets while the inflows of cash are shown without brackets. Totalling up the NPV of the outflow and the NPVs of all the inflows gives us a positive NPV of £135,800 for the stonemason project.

NUMERICAL EXERCISES   Are you confident that you can calculate a net present value for a project? Work your way through the above example again to confirm your understanding of how we arrived at the net present value for the stonemason project and then go to the **online workbook** and attempt Numerical exercises 8.5 and 8.6 to make sure you can apply this investment appraisal technique to the other two investments that Anna is considering.

SHOW ME HOW TO DO IT   How clearly did you understand the calculation of a proposed project's net present value? View Video presentation 8.1 in the **online workbook** to see a practical demonstration of how the net present value calculation is carried out.

Net present value: the decision criteria

Projects discounted at the business's cost of capital resulting in either an NPV of £Nil or a positive NPV are accepted. If a company has several projects under consideration, then all projects with a positive or £Nil NPV are taken on. Where more than one project is competing for investment capital, then the project with the highest NPV is accepted first. If investment capital is available to undertake a further project, then the project with the second highest NPV is accepted and so on until all the available capital for investment has been allocated to projects. Proposed projects with a negative NPV are rejected and are not developed beyond the evaluation stage.

In Anna's case, she can only invest in one of the three projects as her capital for investment is limited to £500,000. Figure 8.5 shows that the garden design and build project gives the highest NPV of £183,850, well above the project with the second highest NPV, the stonemason business. The furniture workshop, which was ranked first on the basis of payback and second on the basis of ARR, is now the worst performing project on the basis of NPV. Therefore, Anna will accept the garden design and build project on the basis of the evaluation provided by the NPV method of investment appraisal.

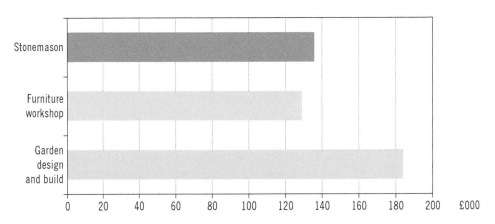

Figure 8.5 Net present value of the three investment opportunities available to Anna

Net present value: advantages

The NPV technique has the following advantages:

- Unlike the payback and ARR investment appraisal techniques, NPV does take into account the time value of money. This makes it a superior method of evaluating and differentiating between several projects.

- NPV discounts all cash inflows and outflows from a project into today's money to enable a fair comparison between projects to be made.

- NPV accounts for all the cash inflows and outflows from a project.

- Cash inflows that arise later in the project's life are riskier than cash inflows that arise earlier. The use of discount factors enables users of this technique to reflect this increased risk arising from later cash inflows as these cash inflows are worth less in current money terms.

- The NPV technique can be used in conjunction with the payback approach to determine when NPVs become positive (see this chapter, Discounted payback and Table 8.2). The further into the future this happens, the riskier the project is.

Net present value: limitations

However, as with all investment appraisal techniques, the NPV approach also suffers from the following disadvantages:

- This method is more difficult to understand than the simpler payback method.

- The technique makes the very large assumption that cash inflows and outflows and discount rates can be predicted with the required level of accuracy.

8

WHY IS THIS RELEVANT TO ME?   Net present value method of capital investment appraisal

To enable you as an accounting professional to:

- Calculate a net present value for a proposed investment project
- Appreciate the criteria on which to make an investment decision based on the net present value method
- Understand the advantages and limitations of the net present value method

---

SUMMARY OF KEY CONCEPTS   Can you remember how net present value is calculated and what its advantages and limitations are? Go to the **online workbook** to revise these with Summary of key concepts 8.3.

Discounted payback

Before we move on to consider the internal rate of return investment appraisal method, it is worth noting that the net present value and payback methods of investment appraisal can be combined to calculate the discounted payback period. This method takes the discounted cash flows under the net present value approach and then determines when those discounted cash flows will turn positive after taking into account the original investment in a project. Table 8.2 presents the discounted payback for the stonemason project.

Table 8.2 Anna: discounted payback table for the investment in the stonemason business

	Cash flows	Cumulative
	£000	£000
Initial investment year 0	(500.00)	(500.00)
Discounted cash inflows year 1	139.14	(360.86)
Discounted cash inflows year 2	120.98	(239.88)
Discounted cash inflows year 3	105.20	(134.68)
Discounted cash inflows year 4	91.49	(43.19)
Discounted cash inflows year 5	79.55	36.36
Discounted cash inflow from sale of the investment at the end of year 5	99.44	135.80

Table 8.2 tells us that the discounted payback period is between 4 and 5 years. Only £43,190 out of the £79,550 discounted cash inflow in year 5 is required to repay the investment in the project that has not yet been repaid by the discounted cash inflows in years 1 to 4. Therefore, the exact discounted payback period for the investment in the stonemason business would be:

$$4 \text{ years} + \frac{43.19}{79.55} \times 12 = 4.543 \text{ years}$$

0.543 years is equivalent to 6½ months (12 × 0.543), so the initial investment of £500,000 at time 0 is fully repaid after 4 years and 6½ months under the discounted payback approach to investment appraisal.

NUMERICAL EXERCISES   Are you sure that you can calculate a discounted payback period for a project? Work your way through the above example again to confirm your understanding of how we arrived at the discounted payback period for the stonemason project and then go to the **online workbook** and attempt Numerical exercises 8.7 and 8.8 to make sure you can apply this investment appraisal technique to the other two investments that Anna is considering.

WHY IS THIS RELEVANT TO ME?   Discounted payback method of capital investment appraisal

To enable you as an accounting professional to:

• Calculate the discounted payback period for a proposed investment project

• Understand how the net present value and payback methods of investment appraisal are combined to determine the discounted payback period for a proposed investment project

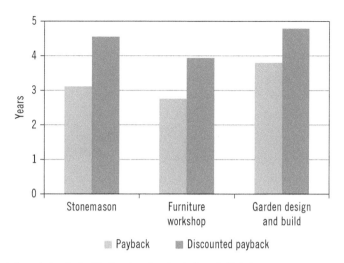

Figure 8.6 Payback and discounted payback of the three investment projects available to Anna

The discounted payback results are shown in Figure 8.6 together with the original payback results (Figure 8.2). The discounted payback decision would be the same as the payback decision with the furniture workshop paying back the initial investment more quickly than the other two investment opportunities. However, the decision to choose the furniture workshop investment on the basis of the discounted payback period would still suffer from the same limitations as outlined earlier (this chapter, Payback: the decision criteria) so Anna has not gained much additional information as a result of these additional calculations.

Internal rate of return (IRR)

The IRR is linked to the NPV technique and is the discount rate at which the NPV of the project is £Nil. The IRR is thus the discount rate at which a project breaks even, the discount rate at which the present value of the cash outflows is equal to the present value of the cash inflows.

To calculate the IRR, a process of trial and error is used. Project cash flows are discounted at successively higher rates until a negative NPV is given for that project. The IRR is then estimated using a mathematical technique called interpolation. This technique is illustrated later.

Figure 8.7 illustrates the IRR, the discount rate which gives an NPV of £Nil. The NPV of a project at various discount rates is determined and plotted on the graph. As the discount rate increases, the NPV of the project falls. The point at which the NPV line crosses the x axis on the graph is the point at which the NPV is £Nil and this is the IRR.

All this may sound very complicated, so let's see how the IRR is calculated using the proposed investment in the stonemason business. We saw in Illustration 8.2 that a discount rate of 15 per cent gave a positive NPV of £135,800 for this project. Using a discount rate of 26 per cent to discount the stonemason project will give us the NPV shown in Illustration 8.3.

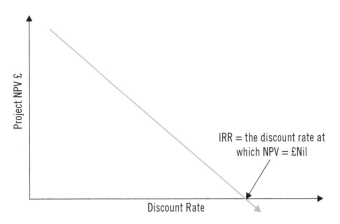

Figure 8.7 Graphical presentation showing the internal rate of return, the point at which the NPV of a project is £Nil

Illustration 8.3 Anna: net present value of the investment in the stonemason business discounted at a rate of 26 per cent

	Cash flows	× Discount factor	= Net present value
	£000	26%	£000
Cash outflow year 0	(500)	1.0000	(500.00)
Net cash inflows year 1	160	0.7937	126.99
Net cash inflows year 2	160	0.6299	100.78
Net cash inflows year 3	160	0.4999	79.98
Net cash inflows year 4	160	0.3968	63.49
Net cash inflows year 5	160	0.3149	50.38
Cash inflow from sale of the investment at the end of year 5	200	0.3149	62.98
Stonemason investment: net present value of the project discounted at a rate of 26%			**(15.40)**

We now know the following facts:

• A discount rate of 15 per cent gives us a positive NPV of £135,800 (Illustration 8.2).

• A discount rate of 26 per cent gives us a negative NPV of £15,400 (Illustration 8.3).

• Therefore, the discount rate that will give us a £Nil NPV lies somewhere between 15 per cent and 26 per cent.

Calculating the internal rate of return

This discount rate is given by the following calculation:

$$15\% + \frac{135.80}{(135.80+15.40)} \times (26\% - 15\%) = 24.88\%$$

How did we arrive at this IRR of 24.88 per cent?

- We know that a discount rate of 15 per cent gives a positive return, so this will be our starting point.
- What we don't know is where the NPV line crosses the x axis on the graph, the point at which the NPV of the project is equal to £Nil (Figure 8.7).
- Therefore, we have to estimate the discount rate at which the NPV is £Nil.
- Our NPV has to fall by £135,800 before we reach the discount rate that gives an NPV of £Nil.
- The total difference between the two results is £135,800 + £15,400 = £151,200 whereas we only need our NPV to fall by £135,800 before a net present value of £Nil is reached.
- Therefore, if we divide £135,800 by £151,200 and then multiply this fraction by the difference between the positive (15 per cent) and negative (26 per cent) discount rates, this will tell us how far along the line between 15 per cent and 26 per cent the IRR is.
- Adding the 15 per cent to this result gives us an IRR of 24.88 per cent.

NUMERICAL EXERCISES   Are you confident that you can calculate an internal rate of return for a project? Work your way through the above example again to confirm your understanding of how internal rates of return are calculated and then go to the **online workbook** and attempt Numerical exercises 8.9 and 8.10 to make sure you can apply this investment appraisal technique to the other two investments that Anna is considering.

SHOW ME HOW TO DO IT   How easily did you follow the calculation of a proposed project's internal rate of return? View Video presentation 8.2 in the **online workbook** to see a practical demonstration of how the internal rate of return calculation is carried out.

Internal rate of return: the decision criteria

Where a project has an IRR higher than an entity's required rate of return on investment projects, then the project should be accepted. Where projects are competing for resources, then the project with the highest IRR would be selected for implementation. In Anna's case, Figure 8.8 shows that the furniture workshop now comes out on top again with an internal rate of return of 25.31 per cent compared with the garden design and build's IRR of 25.00 per cent and 24.88 per cent on the investment in the stonemason. However, the IRR evaluation requires the project originally selected under the net present value technique to be preferred where the decision under the IRR investment appraisal technique differs from the original NPV outcome. This makes sense as the NPV of the garden design and build investment discounted at a rate of 15 per cent was £183,850 compared with a NPV of £128,890 for the furniture workshop investment discounted at the same rate. As we noted earlier, managers will always prefer a higher cash inflow to a lower one.

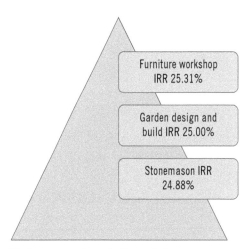

Figure 8.8 Internal rate of return of the three investment opportunities available to Anna

Internal rate of return: advantages

The IRR has the following advantages:

- As with the NPV technique, the time value of money is taken into account. This gives the IRR the same advantages as the NPV technique when compared with the ARR and payback investment appraisal methods.

- In the same way as NPV, the IRR method accounts for all the cash inflows and outflows from a project and discounts all these figures into today's money.

- Similarly, cash inflows that arise later in the project are riskier than cash inflows that arise earlier in the project. The use of discount factors enables users of this technique to reflect this increased risk arising from later cash inflows as these cash inflows are worth less in current money terms.

- The IRR technique tells us what the percentage discount rate is that will give an NPV of £Nil, the break-even NPV for a project. Thus, the technique does not require entities to specify in advance what their cost of capital is, but allows users to determine whether the rate of return is acceptable or not.

- The IRR provides more information than the NPV technique in that it tells users which project gives the highest rate of return where all projects have a positive NPV when discounted at the entity's cost of capital.

Internal rate of return: limitations

- Just as you found with the NPV technique, the IRR is difficult to understand! However, with practice and thought you will become familiar with this technique and be able to apply it in practice.

- The IRR, like the ARR, is a percentage rather than an absolute figure, so there is a risk that projects with a higher internal rate of return will be accepted even when the net present value of the cash flows from other projects discounted at the entity's cost of capital is higher. Hence the requirement that the IRR does not overrule the original decision under the NPV technique. The absolute magnitude of the figures must be considered alongside any ratios or percentages calculated when making decisions.

- The IRR cannot be used if cash flows are irregular. Where cash flows turn from being inflows to outflows and back again, a project will have two or more internal rates of return as the NPV line will cross the x axis in two or more places (illustration of this is beyond the scope of the present book).

WHY IS THIS RELEVANT TO ME?   Internal rate of return method of capital investment appraisal

To enable you as an accounting professional to:

- Calculate an IRR for an investment project
- Appreciate the criteria on which to make an investment decision based on the IRR
- Understand the advantages and limitations of the IRR method

8

SUMMARY OF KEY CONCEPTS   Can you remember the formula to calculate the internal rate of return and what its advantages and limitations are? Go to the **online workbook** to revise these with Summary of key concepts 8.4.

What use do companies make of discounted cash flow measures in practice? Have a look at Give me an example 8.4 to see the ways in which GlaxoSmithKline plc uses discounted cash flow techniques to evaluate investment projects.

MAKING A FINAL DECISION

Which project should Anna choose to invest in? Based on our earlier results and the results from the Numerical exercises, we can draw up a table to show us the rankings of the projects based on the results of each of the four capital investment appraisal techniques we have applied to the three proposals. These results are shown in Table 8.3.

The investment in the stonemason fails to come out on top on any of the investment appraisal criteria. Therefore, on purely financial grounds, investment in this project would be rejected. The other two projects are ranked first on the basis of two techniques, second once and third once. However, as already noted under Internal rate of return, where the IRR technique gives a different result from the NPV technique, then the original choice under the NPV technique should

GIVE ME AN EXAMPLE 8.4 **Companies' use of discounted cash flow measures in evaluating investment opportunities**

The following extracts from the annual report of GlaxoSmithKline plc illustrate the use of both the NPV and the IRR methods of investment apprais-al used in evaluating investment opportunities (R&D = Research and Development):

> In 2010, we calculated that our estimated R&D internal rate of return (IRR) was 11% and stated a long-term aim of increasing this to 14%. We continue to improve the finan-cial efficiency of our R&D and in February 2014 announced an estimated IRR of 13%. We continue to target 14% on a longer-term basis. Our estimated IRR is an important measure of our financial discipline and our strategic progress to improve the economics of R&D. It also underpins our strategy to

create more flexibility around the pricing of our new medicines.

> Source: *GlaxoSmithKline plc, Annual Report 2014*, page 27

> We have a formal process for assessing potential investment proposals in order to ensure decisions are aligned with our over-all strategy. This process includes an assess-ment of the cash flow return on investment (CFROI), as well as its net present value (NPV) and internal rate of return (IRR) where the timeline for the project is very long term. We also consider the impact on earnings and credit profile where relevant.

> Source: *GlaxoSmithKline plc, Annual Report 2014*, page 68

be the project selected. In this case, the garden design and build will be accepted by Anna on the basis of the capital investment appraisal techniques applied to the three proposals. The garden design and build has the highest NPV and the highest ARR, as well as seeming to offer the high-est net cash inflows and the highest growth potential among the projects on offer.

Table 8.3 Anna: summary of rankings based on the results of each of the four capital investment appraisal techniques applied to the three proposed investments

Capital investment appraisal technique	Stonemason	Furniture workshop	Garden design and build
	Ranking	Ranking	Ranking
Payback and discounted payback	2	1	3
Accounting rate of return	3	2	1
Net present value	2	3	1
Internal rate of return	3	1	2

POST INVESTMENT AUDIT

In previous chapters we have placed emphasis on the need to compare actual outcomes to expectations. Capital investment decisions are no exception to this approach. Once the investment in new non-current assets has been made and cash is flowing in from each new project, then managers will gather relevant information to evaluate how precise or how inaccurate their expectations and forecasts were. A post investment audit will be conducted to compare actual and forecast cash inflows and outflows. The aim of this comparison is to improve the accuracy of future capital investment appraisal proposals in order to minimise unfavourable outcomes. At the end of each project's life, the post investment audit will consider all aspects of the project and compare these with the expectations in the original proposal. Recommendations for improving the capital investment appraisal process will then be made and submitted to management for consideration and implementation.

SENSITIVITY ANALYSIS

In Chapter 6 sensitivity analysis was applied to budgets to determine the extent to which the outcome would change if the assumptions on which the budget was based were relaxed. In the same way, capital investment appraisal can be subjected to sensitivity analysis to see what the result would be if the cash inflows were reduced or increased by 10 per cent or 20 per cent, if the cost of the investment were increased by 10 per cent or 20 per cent and if the cost of capital were increased or decreased. By undertaking these additional calculations, a more informed investment decision can be made.

CHAPTER SUMMARY

You should now have learnt that:

- Capital investment involves the acquisition of new non-current assets or the investment in projects with the aim of increasing sales, profits and cash flows to the long-term benefit of a business.
- Capital investment appraisal is undertaken to evaluate the long-term cash generating potential of investment projects.
- Capital investment appraisal of new projects is important in assisting decision makers in allocating scarce investment capital resources to projects that will maximise the profits of the entity in the long run.
- Payback, accounting rate of return, net present value and internal rate of return calculations assist in the appraisal of capital investment projects.
- All four capital investment appraisal techniques offer both advantages and limitations when used in capital investment decisions.
- Money received tomorrow is less valuable than money received today.

END-OF-CHAPTER QUESTIONS

Solutions to these questions can be found in the **online workbook**

❯ DEVELOP YOUR UNDERSTANDING

Note to Questions 8.1–8.5: don't forget to use Table 1 in the Appendix when calculating the NPV and IRR of an investment project.

❯ Question 8.1

Podcaster University Press is evaluating two book proposals, one in accounting and one in economics. The directors are keen on both books but have funding for only one and they cannot decide which book to publish. Details of the two books are as follows:

Accounting book

The accounting book requires an investment of £450,000 to be made immediately. The book will produce net cash inflows of £160,000 in years 1 to 3 and £100,000 in years 4 and 5. The non-current assets involved in the book's production are expected to have a resale value of £50,000 after five years. It is the directors' intention to sell the non-current assets from this project at the end of year 5 to realise the £50,000 cash inflow.

Economics book

The economics book requires an immediate investment of £600,000. The book will produce net cash inflows of £240,000 in year 1, £200,000 in year 2, £160,000 in year 3 and £105,000 in years 4 and 5. The non-current assets bought to print this book are expected to have a resale value of £100,000 at the end of the project. It is the directors' intention to sell the non-current assets from this project at the end of year 5 to realise the £100,000 cash inflow.

Podcaster University Press has a cost of capital of 10 per cent.

You should use a discount rate of 20 per cent when calculating the IRR of the two book projects.

Required

Evaluate the two book projects using the payback, ARR, NPV and IRR methods of investment appraisal. Which project will you recommend and why will you recommend this project?

❯ Question 8.2

Zippo Drinks Limited is considering an investment into its computerised supply chain with a view to generating cash savings from using the benefits of currently available technology. Two options are under consideration. Option 1 will cost £200,000 and operate for five years, while Option 2 will cost £245,000 and remain operational for seven years. Given the longer implementation period, Option 2 will not realise any cash savings until the end of year 2. Neither investment will have any resale value at the end of its life. Because of the scarcity of investment capital, Zippo Drinks Limited can only undertake one of the supply chain projects. The directors of the company are asking for your help in evaluating the two proposals. The cash savings from any new investment in the years of operation are expected to be as follows:

	Option 1 £000	Option 2 £000
Year 1	50	–
Year 2	70	80
Year 3	80	85
Year 4	70	86
Year 5	60	101
Year 6	–	81
Year 7	–	71

Zippo Drinks Limited has a cost of capital of 15 per cent.
For your IRR calculations, you should discount the two projects using a 19 per cent discount rate.

Required
Calculate the payback periods, ARRs, NPVs and IRRs of the two supply chain investment proposals. On the basis of your calculations, advise the directors which of the two investments they should undertake. You should also advise them of any additional considerations they should take into account when deciding which project to adopt.

> Question 8.3

You are considering a five-year lease on a small restaurant serving light meals, snacks and drinks. The five-year lease will cost £80,000 and the lease will have no value at the end of the five years. The costs of fitting out the restaurant will be £30,000. After five years, you expect the restaurant fittings to have a scrap value of £2,000. You anticipate that net cash inflows from the restaurant will be £35,000 in the first year, £45,000 in the second year, £60,000 in the third year, £65,000 in the fourth year and £55,000 in the final year of operation. You have been approached by a fellow entrepreneur who is also very interested in the restaurant. She has proposed that you pay the £80,000 to take on the lease while she will fit out the restaurant at her own expense and pay you £40,000 per annum as rent and profit share. You expect a return of 12 per cent per annum on any capital that you invest.

You are now uncertain whether you should fit out and run the restaurant yourself or sub-let the restaurant to your fellow entrepreneur. Running the restaurant yourself results in an IRR of 33.84 per cent while allowing your fellow entrepreneur to run the restaurant and pay you rent and a share of the profits generates an IRR of 41.10 per cent.

Required
Evaluate the above alternatives using the payback, ARR and NPV capital investment appraisal techniques. Which of the two options will you choose? In making your decision, you should also consider any other factors that you would take into account in addition to the purely financial considerations.

>> **TAKE IT FURTHER**

>> Question 8.4

Ambulators Limited makes prams and pushchairs. The company is currently evaluating two projects that are competing for investment funds.

The first project is the introduction to the market of a new pram. The new pram will require an initial investment of £3,300,000 in marketing and enhanced production facilities and each new pram will sell for £450 over the life of the product. Market research has shown that demand for the new pram is expected to be 5,000 units in the first year of production, with demand rising by 20 per cent per annum on the previous year's sales in years 2 to 5. At the end of year 5, a new improved pram will have entered production and the investment in the new pram will have a residual value of £Nil.

The second project is a new pushchair. This will require an initial outlay on marketing and enhanced production facilities of £2,200,000. Each new pushchair will sell initially in the first year of production and sales for £220, but the directors expect the price to rise by £10 each year in each of years 2 to 5. Market research has projected that initial demand will be for 6,000 pushchairs in year 1 and that demand will rise by 10 per cent per annum on the previous year's sales in years 2 to 5. At the end of year 5, the production facilities will be used to produce a new pushchair and will be transferred to the new project at a valuation of £500,000.

Both projects are competing for the same capital resources and only one of the projects can be undertaken by the company.

The cost cards for the new pram and the new pushchair are as follows:

	Pram	Pushchair
	£	£
Direct materials	150.00	80.00
Direct labour	75.00	40.00
Variable overhead	25.00	10.00
Fixed overhead	50.00	20.00
Total cost	**300.00**	**150.00**

Fixed production overhead allocated to the cost of each product is based on 5,000 units of production for prams and 6,000 units of production for pushchairs. Fixed costs do not include depreciation of the new investment in each project.

Ambulators Limited has a cost of capital of 11 per cent.

Required

For the proposed investment in the new pram or pushchair, calculate for each project:

• The payback period.

• The ARR.

• The NPV.

• The IRR.

You should round your sales projections to the nearest whole unit of sales.

The directors would like to hear your views on which project they should accept. Your advice should take into account both the financial aspects of the decision and any other factors that the directors of Ambulators Limited should consider when deciding which project to invest in.

>> Question 8.5

Chillers plc manufactures fridges and freezers. The company is considering the production of a new deluxe fridge-freezer. The fridge-freezer will sell for £600 and the company's marketing department has produced a forecast for sales for the next seven years as follows:

Year	Units sold
2020	3,500
2021	4,000
2022	4,500
2023	5,250
2024	5,750
2025	5,500
2026	5,250

Variable costs are budgeted to be 40 per cent of selling price. Fixed costs arising from the sale and production of the new deluxe fridge-freezer are expected to be £1,200,000 per annum. Fixed costs exclude depreciation of the new investment.

As a result of the introduction of the new deluxe fridge-freezer, the company expects to lose sales of 2,000 standard fridge-freezers each year over the next seven years. These standard fridge-freezers sell for £350 each with variable costs of 35 per cent of selling price. The reduction in sales of standard fridge-freezers will save cash expenditure on fixed costs of £395,000 per annum.

The initial expenditure on the production line for the new deluxe fridge-freezer has been estimated at £2,000,000. At the end of seven years, this production line will have a scrap value of £100,000.

Chillers plc has a required rate of return on new investment of 13 per cent.

Required

For the proposed investment in the new deluxe fridge-freezer, calculate:

- The payback period.
- The ARR.
- The NPV.
- The IRR.

Advise the directors of Chillers plc whether the project should go ahead or not.

9

CORPORATE GOVERNANCE AND SUSTAINABILITY

LEARNING OUTCOMES

Once you have read this chapter and worked through the questions and examples in both this chapter and the online workbook, you should be able to:

- Understand the control problems that arise within limited liability companies as a result of shareholders appointing directors to run the companies in which they invest

- Describe how the agency problem arises whenever a task is delegated to another party

- Define what is meant by the term corporate governance

- Describe the roles and responsibilities of the various participants in the corporate governance process

- Outline how corporate governance is used to monitor and control directors' actions and decisions to focus on the long term success of a business

- Describe how the Corporate Governance Code and other regulations work together to assure the integrity of the financial reporting process

- Appreciate that the modern corporation has responsibilities beyond just generating a profit for shareholders

- Describe corporate social responsibility reporting and what it involves

- Define the term sustainability

- Appreciate that the modern business entity is expected to present more than just financial information about its operations and activities
- Discuss how information about a range of performance measures beyond mere financial measures is beneficial to an organisation and its long-term survival

INTRODUCTION

Directors are appointed by shareholders to run companies on their behalf (Chapter 1, Control, accounting and accountability) (Figure 9.1). Shareholders firstly want to know that the resources entrusted to the directors are being used effectively and efficiently to generate profits and dividends. As shareholders are not involved in the day-to-day running of the company, their only source of financial information about their company is the annual report and accounts. The annual report and accounts are prepared by the directors. Shareholders thus have an information asymmetry problem: the directors know all about the company but shareholders know only what they are told (Figure 9.1). As a result of this information asymmetry, various other questions arise for shareholders. How can they be sure that what the directors are telling them in the annual financial statements is a fair representation of what has actually happened during the past 12 months? Are the directors hiding anything? Do the annual financial statements tell them everything they need to know for decision making purposes? Apart from the financial results, how can shareholders be sure that the directors are running the business honestly, ethically and in accordance with the law? Is their company a good corporate citizen or are the directors engaging in illegal or morally suspect behaviour? What controls are there on the directors to make sure that they always take the right decisions and always act in the best interests of the shareholders?

These questions also arise as a result of the agency problem. In these situations, someone (the agent) is entrusted to undertake a task by someone else (the principal). In the case of limited companies, the shareholders are the principals who appoint the directors as their agents (Figure 9.1).

Figure 9.1 Information asymmetry between directors and shareholders

In an ideal world, the aims and objectives of the shareholders and of the directors would be exactly the same. However, the agency problem means that agents will always act in their own best interests and not in those of their principals. Directors will therefore seek to maximise the short-term profits of the company and thereby their own remuneration rather than taking decisions now that will generate long-term benefits for the shareholders. This is not a problem in small companies in which shareholders and directors are the same persons. But in listed companies (public limited companies, plcs), directors do not remain in their posts for lengthy periods of time, so, by the time today's investments pay off in say 5 or 10 years' time, the directors may no longer be employed by the company and so they will gain no benefit from considering the long-term interests of shareholders at the expense of their own short-term advantage.

Happily, help is at hand. The Companies Act 2006 together with Corporate Governance as enshrined in the Corporate Governance Code provides rules and guidance on many aspects of organisational management with a view to ensuring that entities are fully under control, that directors are not exceeding their powers and that business entities are run for the long-term benefit of stakeholders and not just to satisfy the short-term interests of directors. This chapter will consider in outline how these legal and governance rules work in order to limit shareholders' concerns over the running of their companies.

WHY IS THIS RELEVANT TO ME?   The information asymmetry and agency problems

To enable you as an accounting professional to understand:

- What is meant by the terms agency problem and information asymmetry
- The control problems that arise when shareholders delegate the running of companies to directors
- The causes of the problems that may arise from information asymmetry and the agency problem

GO BACK OVER THIS AGAIN!   Do you fully appreciate the control problems that arise in limited liability companies as a result of the agency problem and information asymmetry? Go to the **online workbook** and have a go at Exercises 9.1 to check your understanding.

CORPORATE GOVERNANCE: A BRIEF HISTORY

Following a series of financial scandals and corporate collapses in the late 1980s and early 1990s which had undermined the credibility of reported financial information and eroded trust in business, the Financial Reporting Council, the London Stock Exchange and the accountancy profession established the Committee on the Financial Aspects of Corporate Governance with Sir Adrian Cadbury as its chair. The aim of the committee was to consider the ways in which investor confidence in the honesty and accountability of listed companies should be restored. The Committee's report in 1992 was named after its chair and is always known as the Cadbury Report. All the proposals in the Cadbury Report were built on existing good practice, but the report gave them much more formal recognition and established the basis on which all publicly listed and public interest companies would henceforth be governed.

CORPORATE GOVERNANCE: A DEFINITION

What is meant by the term corporate governance? Section 2.5 of the Cadbury Report provides the following definition:

> Corporate governance is the system by which companies are directed and controlled. Boards of directors are responsible for the governance of their companies. The shareholders' role in governance is to appoint the directors and the auditors and to satisfy themselves that an appropriate governance structure is in place. The responsibilities of the board include setting the company's strategic aims, providing the leadership to put them into effect, supervising the management of the business and reporting to shareholders on their stewardship. The board's actions are subject to laws, regulations and the shareholders in general meeting.

The original report produced by the Cadbury Committee has been updated over the intervening years to embrace additional aspects in Corporate Governance. However, the main features are clear from the above quotation. The current Corporate Governance Code is built up of the main principles, supporting principles and code provisions. The aim of the Corporate Governance Code is to ensure that shareholders and boards of directors interact and work together to ensure that their company is effectively directed and controlled. Before we consider how the Code shows how effective direction and control can be achieved, let's look at the different parties who play a role in the corporate governance process.

SUMMARY OF KEY CONCEPTS   Can you remember the definition of corporate governance? Go to the **online workbook** to revise this definition with summary of key concepts 9.1.

CORPORATE GOVERNANCE: THE PARTIES INVOLVED

Figure 9.2 sets out the key participants in the corporate governance process. These participants and their corporate governance roles and responsibilities will each be considered in turn. Once these roles and responsibilities are clear, we can then determine how the interaction of the various parties aims to ensure that publicly listed and public interest companies are effectively directed and controlled in order to address the concerns that shareholders have.

The board of directors: executive and non-executive directors

All companies have a board of directors who are responsible for running the company. The board of directors is made up of two categories of director: executive and non-executive. Both executive and non-executive directors are elected by the shareholders. The executive directors are responsible for the day-to-day running and management of the company, implementing policies and dealing with all the operational issues that arise on a daily basis. Executive directors are employees of the company and are remunerated on the basis of their employment contracts with the company.

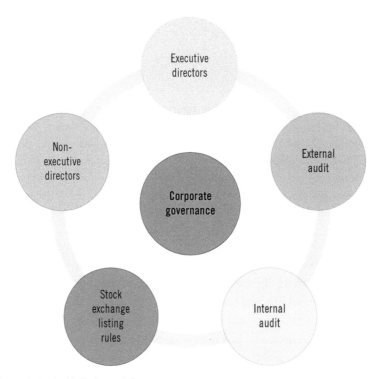

Figure 9.2 The key parties involved in the Corporate Governance process

9

Non-executive directors, on the other hand, do not perform any executive management functions. They are thus not involved in any day-to-day running of the business. Despite being members of the board of directors, non-executive directors are not employees of the company but charge fees for their services rather than receiving a salary.

Non-executive directors attend monthly board meetings and also set up and run various board committees. These board committees are composed of non-executive directors only and they fulfil critical functions in relation to financial reporting (the audit committee), directors' remuneration and the nomination of new board members. Figure 9.3 summarises the roles and responsibilities of both the executive and the non-executive directors.

WHY IS THIS RELEVANT TO ME?   Board of directors: executive and non-executive directors

To enable you as an accounting professional to understand:

- The different roles of the executive and non-executive directors in the running of listed and public interest companies
- That executive directors are excluded from the financial reporting, directors' remuneration and nomination committees

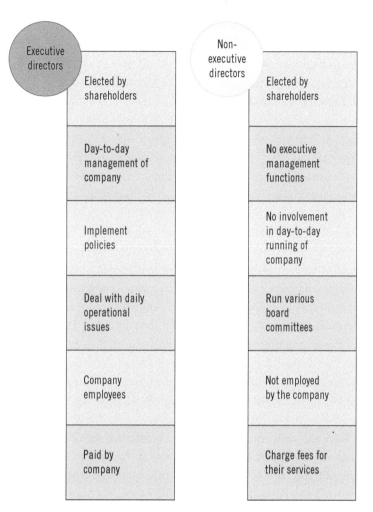

Figure 9.3 The roles and responsibilities of the executive and the non-executive directors

---

SUMMARY OF KEY CONCEPTS   Are you certain you can describe the different duties and roles of executive and non-executive directors? Go to the **online workbook** to check your recollection with summary of key concepts 9.2.

GO BACK OVER THIS AGAIN!   Are you confident that you can distinguish between the roles of the executive and non-executive directors? Go to the **online workbook** and have a go at Exercises 9.2 to check your ability in this area.

External audit

The directors prepare the financial statements for their company on an annual basis. As we noted earlier (this chapter, Introduction: the information asymmetry and agency problems) accounting results for the year might not reflect all the relevant facts and figures. Alternatively, because directors control the financial reporting process and content, the annual report and accounts might be presented in a more favourable way than is warranted in order to secure greater financial rewards and continued employment for the directors. Therefore, shareholders require reasonable assurance that the figures in the annual report and accounts present a true and fair view of the results for the year together with all the relevant disclosures and details required by both the Companies Act 2006 and by the financial reporting standards issued by the International Accounting Standards Board.

In order to gain this assurance, shareholders (not directors) appoint auditors annually at the annual general meeting. Auditors are qualified accountants who are completely independent of the company they are auditing. They review the financial statements presented by the directors, undertake testing of balances and transactions on a sample basis in order to verify that the financial statements present a true and fair view of the financial position of the company at the year end and of the profit or loss and the cash flows for the year. In addition, auditors use their expert knowledge and experience to ensure that all the disclosures required by the Companies Act 2006 and by International Financial Reporting Standards have been made in full and that no material information is omitted. All audit procedures are carried out in accordance with International Standards on Auditing (ISAs) issued by the International Auditing and Assurance Standards Board (IAASB).

Auditors report directly to shareholders without any interference from the directors in order to safeguard the independence of their report and their findings. The audit report comments on the financial statements prepared by the directors (note that the auditors do not prepare the financial statements—this is a common misunderstanding of the auditors' role). Where the financial statements do not make all the relevant disclosures or where directors have obstructed the auditors in the performance of their duties, then the auditors can inform the shareholders of their concerns in their report or in person at the annual general meeting.

The auditors' work and their reports enable users of financial statements to place a high degree of confidence in the audited financial information and in the audit reports attached to them. The auditor and the audit process also facilitate the workings of the capital markets which require assurance on the truth and fairness of financial information as a basis for the buying and selling of shares. Audited information is also used as a reliable basis for both investment in and lending to limited liability companies.

WHY IS THIS RELEVANT TO ME?   External audit

To provide you with:

- A brief overview of the role of external auditors in the financial reporting regime
- A foundation for your later studies in auditing

SUMMARY OF KEY CONCEPTS   Do you think you can describe the roles and responsibilities of external audit? Go to the **online workbook** to check your abilities in this area with summary of key concepts 9.3.

GO BACK OVER THIS AGAIN!   Are you certain you understand the role and activities of external auditors? Go to the **online workbook** and have a go at Exercises 9.3 to check your understanding.

Internal audit

The internal audit function on the other hand is set up by the board of directors. As the name indicates, internal audit activities are undertaken by individuals working within the organisation. Whereas external audit is narrowly focused on the truth and fairness of the annual financial report and accounts and their compliance with the relevant legislation and international financial reporting standards, internal audit is given a very much wider ranging remit. While external audit aims to verify past results, internal audit is focused on not just past but also current operations as well as being forward looking and proactive. Internal audit concentrates attention upon the entire range of organisational operations involving an assessment of the effectiveness of the risk management, control and governance procedures alongside an evaluation of the integrity and accuracy of the reporting and internal control systems. Internal audit reports provide evaluations of every aspect of a business's activity with a view to improving and enhancing those activities to further the business's objectives and to help it achieve its aims. The aim of internal audit is always to add value to an organisation and its activities.

In the same way as external audit, internal audit, despite being staffed by employees of the business, aims to provide independent reports of its findings. This independence is enhanced by reporting not to the executive directors (who might be criticised by internal audit or seek to limit the internal auditors' range of activities) but to the independent non-executive directors on the audit committee. Internal auditors are not involved in the day-to-day operations of a business (you cannot be independent when you are evaluating your own work) but stand back from daily operational activities to present an objective overview of operations and activities, their effectiveness and their compliance with the legal and ethical obligations of the entity. This organisational independence from management enables unrestricted evaluation of management activities and personnel. Figure 9.4 presents a comparison of internal and external audit.

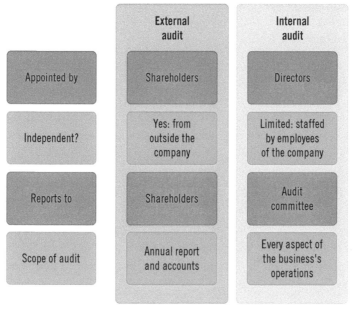

Figure 9.4 A comparison of external and internal audit

Directors have a responsibility to ensure that organisational operations and activities are fully under control and that assets are adequately safeguarded (for example, how easily could cash be stolen from a business?). To fulfil these responsibilities, the board of directors will set up an internal control system which puts in place checks and balances whose aim is both to prevent fraud and errors occurring and to result in their discovery if they do. Internal audit will assess and evaluate these internal control systems to determine their effectiveness and their ability to prevent the theft of assets and the occurrence of errors. In addition, a rigorous review of the internal controls will enable internal auditors to assess the reliability of information used in the financial and management reporting systems as well as evaluating an organisation's full compliance with laws and regulations.

WHY IS THIS RELEVANT TO ME?   Internal audit

To enable you as an accounting professional to appreciate:

- The extensive and wide ranging role of internal auditors within organisations
- The differences in the roles and responsibilities of both internal and external auditors
- How internal auditors continually monitor management and operations in shareholders' best interests

---

SUMMARY OF KEY CONCEPTS   Are you sure that you can describe the roles and responsibilities of internal audit? Go to the **online workbook** to check your abilities in this area with Summary of key concepts 9.4.

GO BACK OVER THIS AGAIN!   Are you confident that you understand what internal auditors do? Go to the **online workbook** and have a go at Exercises 9.4 to check your understanding.

GO BACK OVER THIS AGAIN!   Are you able to distinguish between the roles and responsibilities of internal and external auditors? Go to the **online workbook** and have a go at Exercises 9.5 to check your abilities in this area.

Stock exchange rules

Public limited companies can apply to have their shares listed on a recognised stock exchange. All companies accepted and listing their shares on the London Stock Exchange must ensure that they comply with the mandatory listing rules. The aim of these listing rules is to protect investors and to uphold the highest standards of conduct in those companies listing their shares. The listing rules guarantee the efficiency and regulation of the stock market, providing, in the same way as auditors do for company financial statements, a high degree of confidence in the operations and integrity of the market. One of the listing rules requires that all companies listing on the Stock Exchange should abide by the Corporate Governance Code. The rules dictate that listed companies provide a statement in their annual report and accounts stating how the principles in the Corporate Governance Code have been applied. Confirmation of compliance with the Code's provisions is also required. In situations where listed companies have not complied with the Code's principles, they must provide an explanation of their non-compliance. This regime is referred to as 'comply or explain'. This oversight by the Stock Exchange provides an additional safeguard for investors. Compliance with the listing rules ensures that boards of directors study the Code to make sure that they do comply. Studying the Code in this way will help the directors to determine whether their company is complying or not. Where they are not complying, they can take steps to make sure that their procedures and operations are in full compliance.

WHY IS THIS RELEVANT TO ME?   Stock exchange rules

To enable you as an accounting professional to appreciate:

- The role of the stock exchange rules and oversight in corporate governance
- The disclosures companies have to make in their annual reports and accounts to certify compliance with the stock exchange rules

---

SUMMARY OF KEY CONCEPTS   Are you quite sure you understand the role of the stock exchange rules in corporate governance? Go to the **online workbook** to check your understanding with summary of key concepts 9.5.

ADDRESSING SHAREHOLDER CONCERNS

Now that the participants in the corporate governance process are clear, we can consider the ways in which these participants and the Corporate Governance Code itself work together to meet shareholders' concerns. These concerns fall under various headings, so we shall consider each issue in turn under a separate heading.

Long-term success v. short-term profits

Firstly, let's consider how the Corporate Governance Code addresses the issue of whether the directors' focus should be on long-term success or short-term profits. Shareholders invest for the long term, whereas directors aim to achieve the highest short-term profits possible in order to maximise their remuneration. These opposing aims pull in opposite directions as shown in Figure 9.5.

Figure 9.5 The opposing aims of directors and shareholders

Given this tension between the two opposing interests, shareholders will want reassurance that it is their long-term interests that are at the centre of directors' decision making. Both the Companies Act 2006 and the Corporate Governance Code recognise this conflict and give shareholders' interests priority. The Companies Act 2006 and the Corporate Governance Code together emphasise that it is the long-term success of the company that counts. Section 172(1) of the Companies Act 2006 imposes a duty on directors to promote the success of the company and requires directors to consider the likely consequences of any decision in the long term. This long-term focus is given further emphasis in the Corporate Governance Code which stresses as a main principle that '[e]very company should be headed by an effective board which is collectively responsible for the *long-term success* of the company' (Corporate Governance Code, Section A Leadership, emphasis added). This aim of long-term success is a recurring theme in the Corporate Governance Code, with this objective being stated once in the preface (paragraph 4) and twice in the introductory section on Governance and the Code (paragraphs 1 and 4).

Company decision making

Directors should work together as a board, to make decisions as a body not as individuals. However, shareholders will worry that the board of directors might not be acting in the best interests of the business, might be taking unnecessary risks or might include directors who are acting on their own initiative without consulting the other directors about the decisions they are taking. Section A of the Corporate Governance Code deals with the leadership of a company and states the main principle that 'every company should be headed by an effective board which is *collectively* responsible for the long-term success of the company' (emphasis added). The board is thus required to work as a unit and to take decisions together rather than individual directors making decisions without consulting the board as a whole. How does this work in practice? Give me an example 9.1 presents Ted Baker's statement relating to board operations in the company's Corporate Governance report. This example illustrates the directors' collective responsibility for decision making exercised by the board working together as a complete unit as a means of preventing risky individual actions in key strategic and operational decisions.

> **GIVE ME AN EXAMPLE 9.1   Collective decision making by the board**
>
> 'BOARD OPERATION
>
> The Board meets regularly throughout the year. It considers, with the support of the Board Committees and the Executive Committee, all issues relating to the strategy, direction and future development of the Group. The Board has a schedule of matters reserved to it for decision that is regularly updated. These include decisions on the Group's strategy, financial budgets, major capital expenditure and transactions, appointment of territorial and product licence partners, store openings, dividend policy, Group bonus and risk profile. The requirement for Board approval on these matters is understood and communicated widely throughout the Group.'
>
> Source: *Ted Baker Annual report and accounts 2017/2018,* http://www.tedbakerplc.com

As well as collective responsibility for decisions, the Code emphasises that a clear division of responsibilities should exist within the board of directors. The executive directors are responsible for running the business on a day-to-day basis while the non-executive directors' role is to run the board and its associated committees. Section A of the Code sets out the main principle that '[t]here should be a clear division of responsibilities at the head of the company between the running of the board and the executive responsibility for the running of the company's business. No one individual should have unfettered powers of decision' (Section A Leadership, Supporting principles) so that every board member participates in the decision making process as illustrated by the wording presented in Give me an example 9.1. In order to ensure that there is a clear division of duties, the Code requires that 'the roles of chairperson and chief executive should not be exercised by the same individual' (Section A, Leadership, Code provision 2.1). This clear division of duties ensures that no one person has unrestricted decision-making responsibility. In situations in which one individual makes all the decisions, then risks are increased as opposing views and counsels are ignored and there is no restraining hand to rein in dominant personalities. Splitting the leadership of the company and requiring key decisions to be taken by the board of directors as a whole will reassure shareholders that the direction of the business is fully under control and extreme or excessively risky actions are being avoided.

This all sounds like a very good control mechanism on the executive directors but what is to prevent the executive directors simply overwhelming the non-executive directors through sheer force of numbers and forcing their policies through? This problem is addressed in a supporting principle to Section B of the Code which requires that each company board should comprise of a suitable combination of executive and non-executive directors. Code provision B1.2 takes this further and dictates that half the board, excluding the chair (who should always be a non-executive director), should be made up of non-executive directors. This provision thus aims to ensure that the non-executive directors cannot be dominated by the executive directors to enable effective enforcement of corporate governance in each and every company. Give me an example 9.2 presents an example of how this works in practice.

9

GIVE ME AN EXAMPLE 9.2   Non-executive and executive director numbers

The board of Ted Baker plc is made up of 2 executive directors, one non-executive chair and 3 non-executive directors. The three non-executive directors have lengthy experience in e-commerce, digital transformation and brand marketing, banking and international retail and are all considered to be independent. Through this structure, the board has a balance of skills, experience and independence in combination with the executive directors' knowledge and experience in both the fashion industry and finance. The number of non-executive directors comfortably exceeds the number of the executive directors so that the non-executive directors can fulfil their oversight and advisory roles effectively.

Source: *Ted Baker Annual report and accounts 2017/2018*, http://www.tedbakerplc.com

To enable you as an accounting professional to appreciate that:

- The executive directors run the business on a day-to-day basis
- The non-executive directors run the board and its associated committees
- The Corporate Governance Code requires that no one individual should have unfettered powers of decision making and control
- All board members both executive and non-executive participate in the decision making process
- The chair and chief executive roles are exercised by different individuals

GO BACK OVER THIS AGAIN!   Are you sure you understand the roles of the various parties in the decision-making process in companies? Go to the **online workbook** and have a go at Exercises 9.6 to check your appreciation of the Corporate Governance Code requirements in this area.

Board effectiveness

As we have seen, the Corporate Governance Code requires companies to be headed by an effective board. But how is this effectiveness achieved and what steps should directors be taking to ensure that they are effective? Directors should avoid complacency and just following the same approaches as in the past. They should question and test the strategy and direction of the company to make sure that the strategy adopted by the company is the most effective means of achieving the company's long-term goals. There should be procedures in place to ensure that directors are fulfilling their roles and responsibilities effectively and they should actively question their own effectiveness and review what they have achieved to determine what they might have done better. What does the Corporate Governance Code have to say about these aspects of board effectiveness?

Section B of the Code deals with effectiveness and states the main principle that '[t]he board and its committees should have the appropriate balance of skills, experience, independence and knowledge of the company to enable them to discharge their respective duties and responsibilities effectively'. The other main principles outlined in Section B are presented in Figure 9.6. These are the factors essential in promoting the effectiveness of the board and of the individual board members. To be effective, directors must have sufficient time in which to fulfil their duties, they need induction on starting in their roles and they should update their skills and knowledge on a regular basis. Timely information is essential to enable them to fulfil their roles together with periodic assessment of their performance by their fellow directors and feedback on whether they are meeting the requirements of the role. Shareholders are also involved in the assessment process as they are given a regular say on their directors' performance through the opportunity to re-elect the directors or to reject their re-appointment. A continuous flow of new blood onto boards to replace those retiring and to reinforce and strengthen the directors as a body is also required. Diversity on the board will encourage a

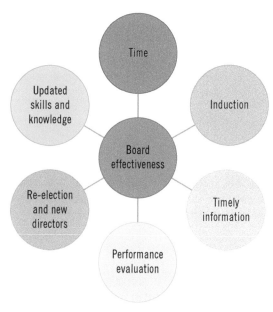

Figure 9.6 The main principles of board effectiveness in the Corporate Governance Code Section B

range of opinions and ideas to be put forward and a board with a suitable balance of skills will enable the shareholders to be confident that all the different aspects of controlling and directing the company are covered.

Non-executive directors have considerable knowledge, skills and experience gained in running other businesses as they are recruited from other publicly listed companies or other senior positions. This prior experience brings valuable insights and knowledge to boards of directors to ensure that these boards are effective in directing and controlling their companies. The non-executive directors provide an advisory and oversight function on the board. In this role, a main principle in Section A of the Code states that they should constructively challenge the executive directors and help to develop proposals on strategy. The non-executive directors' role is to take an independent, broad overview of the business and its progress to ensure that it is moving in the right direction and adopting the correct strategies through which to achieve its aims. As they are not employees of the company, non-executive directors are able to adopt a much more objective overview of the business which executive directors, due to their close involvement in the day-to-day affairs of the company, cannot take.

As a further control on the executive directors, the non-executive directors are required to meet as a body (without the executive directors being present) to discuss the company's affairs and to appraise the performance of the executive directors in meeting the objectives of the business. One of the main principles in Section B of the Code requires the board to 'undertake a formal and rigorous annual evaluation of its own performance and that of its committees and individual directors'. Appraisal of this kind ensures that directors are fulfilling their responsibilities effectively and act as a timely corrective to any shortcomings in this respect.

Ensuring the integrity of financial statements

One of the most important duties of the board of directors is to prepare and present the annual financial statements. As we have seen earlier in this chapter, the shareholders' main concern relates to the completeness of the annual report and financial statements and whether they present a true and fair view of the profits, cash flows and financial position of the company in compliance with the reporting requirements of both the Companies Act 2006 and of International Financial Reporting Standards.

What provisions are there in the Corporate Governance Code to ensure that the information presented in the annual report and financial statements shows a true and fair view of profits, cash flows and the statement of financial position and that all the information presented is complete and unbiased?

As the financial statements are audited by independent auditors from outside the company, the auditor's report already adds credibility to the financial information presented (this chapter, External audit). However, there is a risk that the directors may bully the auditor into accepting a reduction in the disclosures made or to agree to accounting treatments that are biased, reflecting the concerns of the directors rather than the true and fair view required by the Companies Act 2006. What guiding principles does the Corporate Governance Code provide with a view to preventing such misleading financial statements?

The Corporate Governance Code (Section C) requires that 'the board should present a fair, balanced and understandable assessment of the company's position and prospects'. This duty is imposed on the board as a whole, so all the members of the board of directors, both executive and non-executive, have to read, review and consider the financial statements to ensure that they adhere to these requirements. Further safeguards are added in the Code's supporting principles. As noted earlier (this chapter, The board of directors: executive and non-executive directors), the audit committee is made up of non-executive directors. There should be at least three independent non-executive directors on the audit committee, at least one of whom should have recent, relevant financial experience (Corporate Governance Code, Code Provision 3.1). This recent relevant financial experience will enable the audit committee to assess whether the report and financial statements present a fair, balanced and understandable assessment of the company's position and prospects as mandated by the Corporate Governance Code. This supporting principle also requires the audit committee members to have competence relevant to the sector in which the company operates. This competence gives the audit committee a benchmark against which to evaluate the report and financial statements of an organisation and will enable the audit committee members to see potential gaps or potentially misleading information due to their in-depth sector knowledge and experience.

Code Provisions 3.2 and 3.4 also emphasise the audit committee's role in meeting the requirements of the code with respect to the financial statements. The audit committee's main role and responsibilities set out in written terms of reference should include:

- 'To monitor the integrity of the financial statements of the company and any formal announcements relating to the company's financial performance, reviewing significant financial reporting judgements contained in them (3.2).
- Where requested by the board, the audit committee should provide advice on whether the annual report and accounts, taken as a whole, is fair, balanced and understandable and provides the information necessary for shareholders to assess the company's position and performance, business model and strategy (3.4).'

As well as reviewing the final report and financial statements to ensure that they meet the requirements of the code, the audit committee is also charged with various duties that relate to ensuring the integrity of the financial records upon which the report and accounts are based. Thus Section 3.2 of the supporting principles also requires the audit committee to review the company's internal financial controls and internal control and risk management systems. Alongside this duty, the audit committee is tasked with monitoring and reviewing the effectiveness of the company's internal audit function and assessing the effectiveness and independence of the external auditors. The audit committee makes recommendations on the appointment and reappointment of the external auditor for the shareholders' consideration. Where the external auditor's independence appears to have been compromised, the audit committee can recommend the removal of the external auditor to the shareholders.

In addition to overseeing the external audit process, the audit committee and the external auditors meet on a regular basis to discuss the financial statements and any issues arising. These meetings between the members of the audit committee and the external auditors help to maintain auditor independence and the integrity of the external audit process: there are no executive directors on the audit committee who might pressure the external auditors in the ways suggested earlier, so the external auditors are free to express their opinions on the financial statements and any shortcomings they have identified. As the audit committee members are non-executive directors with a purely oversight role and whose fees are not affected by the financial results, there is no incentive for the audit committee members to pressurise the external auditors into accepting less than complete or misleading disclosures. Give me an example 9.3 provides extracts from the audit committee report of Ted Baker plc to illustrate the issues we have been considering in this section to show you how these provisions of the Code work in practice.

'AUDIT COMMITTEE REPORT

Dear Shareholder,

The role of the Audit Committee is to monitor the integrity of the Group's financial statements and reporting responsibilities and to maintain its internal control and compliance procedures.

This year, the Audit Committee met four times. In its meetings it focused on the Group's risk management, internal controls, tax, and external risk factors …

This Audit Committee Report has been prepared in accordance with the Code and includes:

- a description of the significant issues that the Audit Committee considered in relation to the financial statements, and how these issues were addressed;
- an explanation of how the Audit Committee

has assessed the effectiveness of the external audit process and the approach taken to the reappointment of the external auditor, and information on the length of tenure of the current audit firm and when a tender was last conducted; and

- an explanation of how the Group's auditors' objectivity and independence are safeguarded when providing non-audit services.

Meetings with senior management, internal audit and the external auditor, together with the regular circulation and review of board papers and financial information, have enabled the Audit Committee to discharge its duties and responsibilities effectively.'

Source: *Ted Baker Annual report and accounts 2017/2018*, http://www.tedbakerplc.com

To enable you as an accounting professional to understand:

- How the Corporate Governance Code requires the board of directors as a whole to present a fair, balanced and understandable assessment of the company's position and prospects
- The ways in which the audit committee monitors the integrity of the financial statements
- That the audit committee is responsible for monitoring and reviewing the internal control and risk management systems of a company
- That the audit committee monitors the performance of the internal and external auditors
- The way in which the audit committee helps to maintain the independence and integrity of the external audit process

GO BACK OVER THIS AGAIN!   Do you think you understand how the integrity of the financial statements is assured? Go to the **online workbook** and have a go at Exercises 9.8 to check your understanding.

Directors' remuneration

As the directors run the company, what is to stop them deciding their own remuneration and paying themselves excessive amounts at the shareholders' expense? What restraints are there on the directors to prevent them abusing their position in this way?

The main principles stated in Section D of the Corporate Governance Code require that 'executive directors' remuneration should be designed to promote the long-term success of the company. Performance-related elements should be transparent, stretching and rigorously applied. There should be a formal and transparent procedure for developing policy on executive remuneration and for fixing the remuneration packages of individual directors. No director should be involved in deciding his or her own remuneration.' As a result of these clear principles, directors are unable to set their own remuneration. The remuneration of the executive directors is decided by the remuneration committee which is staffed entirely by non-executive directors. As the non-executive directors are responsible for evaluating the executive directors' performance (this chapter, Board effectiveness), they are in a very good position to determine the executive directors' remuneration. In this way, the Corporate Governance Code seeks to ensure that directors' remuneration is not excessive for the levels of profits and performance achieved.

Shareholder communications

The final shareholder concern relates to communications from their directors and how effective these are. Section E of the Corporate Governance Code presents the main principles in this area: 'There should be a dialogue with shareholders based on the mutual understanding of objectives. The board as a whole has responsibility for ensuring that a satisfactory dialogue with shareholders takes place. The board should use general meetings to communicate with investors and to encourage their participation.' Communications take place through the annual report and accounts and through the annual general meeting. Other communication opportunities are afforded to shareholders by the directors as illustrated in Give me an example 9.4.

9

GIVE ME AN EXAMPLE 9.4   Shareholder communications

'COMMUNICATION WITH SHAREHOLDERS

The Group attaches considerable importance to the effectiveness of its communication with its shareholders. The full report and accounts are sent to all shareholders and further copies are distributed to others with potential interest in the Group's performance.

Led by the Chief Executive, the Chief Operating Officer and the Finance Director, the Group seeks to build on a mutual understanding of objectives between the Company and its institutional shareholders by making general presentations after the interim and preliminary results; meeting shareholders and potential investors to discuss long-term issues and gathering feedback; and communicating regularly throughout the year via its investor relations programme. All shareholders have access to these presentations, as well as to the Annual Report and Accounts and to other information about the Company, through the investor relations website at www.tedbakerplc.com. Shareholders may also attend the Company's Annual General Meeting at which they have the opportunity to ask questions.

Non-Executive Directors are kept informed of the views of shareholders by the Executive Directors and are provided with independent feedback from investor meetings.'

Source: *Ted Baker Annual report and accounts 2017/2018*, http://www.tedbakerplc.com

Communications with shareholders thus take place on a regular basis to keep them informed of developments and other matters affecting them as shareholders. There is no attempt to keep matters hidden from the shareholders.

CORPORATE SOCIAL RESPONSIBILITY REPORTING

So far in this chapter, the main focus of corporate governance has been upon the directors of the company and their relationship with the shareholders. However, there are other stakeholders to consider together with a wider reporting and operational role for entities. Our discussions in Chapter 1 (The users of accounting information) reviewed the interests and information needs of other parties such as employees, customers, suppliers, the government and the general public. Should companies and businesses also be taking these other parties into account both in their operations and in their annual reports? Do companies have any reporting responsibilities beyond informing shareholders of profits generated and dividends paid?

The US economist, Milton Friedman, famously took a very strong line against businesses adopting any other approach than that of generating profit. Writing in *The New York Times Magazine* (September 13, 1970), Friedman quoted the following lines from his 1962 book Capitalism and Freedom:

> There is one and only one social responsibility of business—to use its resources and engage in activities designed to increase its profits so long as it stays within the rules of the game, which is to say, engages in open and free competition without deception or fraud.

On this view of a business, companies only exist to make a profit for shareholders and directors' sole responsibility is towards those shareholders. This view ignores entirely the effect that businesses and the products they produce have on the natural environment, on consumers, on communities and on other interested parties. As long as a profit is being made and made legally, nothing else is seen to matter. By extension, this argument proposes that directors should only report financial data and ignore any other performance measures and indicators.

By the 1960s, however, commentators and business people had begun to challenge the view that business had no other responsibilities beyond the mere generation of profit. Stakeholder theory presents the idea that directors and managers should balance the interests of all stakeholders (those with a stake or interest in a business) and not favour one group of interests over another. Employee welfare and development and a concern for the local environment and the people living within it were suggested as other measures that entities should consider when planning operations, designing new products and reporting on performance. This corporate social responsibility reporting approach is illustrated in Figure 9.7.

In the UK, this corporate social responsibility approach has also received attention in the Companies Act 2006. Section 172 of the Act sets out directors' duties in detail (emphasis added):

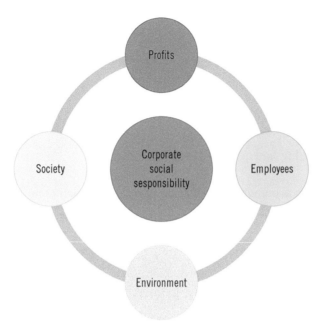

Figure 9.7 The corporate social responsibility reporting model for companies

Duty to promote the success of the company

Section 172 (1) A director of a company must act in the way he considers, in good faith, would be most likely to promote the success of the company for the benefit of its members as a whole, and in doing so have regard (amongst other matters) to—

(a) The likely consequences of any decision in the long term,

(b) The interests of the company's employees,

(c) The need to foster the company's business relationships with suppliers, customers and others,

(d) The impact of the company's operations on the community and the environment,

(e) The desirability of the company maintaining a reputation for high standards of business conduct, and

(f) The need to act fairly as between members of the company.

Notably, as indicated by the highlighted sections, directors are not just required to promote the success of the company for the benefit of shareholders (members) but for the benefit of other stakeholders and society as a whole as well. We saw in Chapter 1 (Users of accounting information) that there are various other user groups of financial accounting information besides shareholders, lenders and other creditors and it is the additional interests of these groups that the Companies Act 2006 requires directors to take into account.

This requirement to consider other interested parties as well as shareholders now extends to presenting information in the strategic report presented to shareholders. Section 414C of the Companies Act 2006 states that the following information should be presented by companies quoted on a stock exchange:

i.   environmental matters (including the impact of the company's business on the environment),

ii.   the company's employees, and

iii. social, community and human rights issues,

including information about any policies of the company in relation to those matters and the effectiveness of those policies.

WHY IS THIS RELEVANT TO ME?   Corporate social responsibility reporting

To enable you as an accounting professional to appreciate:

● That the current view is that annual reports should report information relevant to a wider range of stakeholders than just shareholders

● The directors' duties as set out in company legislation

● The wide ranging duties that directors must fulfil in promoting the success of the company

● That directors should consider a wider range of interests than just those of shareholders

---

9

SUMMARY OF KEY CONCEPTS   Can you recall all the requirements of the directors' duty to promote the success of the company? Go to the **online workbook** to revise these requirements with Summary of key concepts 9.6.

The rationale for corporate social responsibility reporting

Why have business organisations bought into the corporate social responsibility debate? Why have they chosen, voluntarily, to consider and report to a wider set of stakeholders on aspects of their operations which do not immediately generate additional profit for their shareholders?

Business organisations exist only to serve society, so society is the ultimate shareholder in every business. Therefore, society's concerns and interests should be awarded the same level of attention and importance as those of investors. Business does not operate independently of society and its expectations, therefore companies should be accountable not just to shareholders but also to society as a whole. This accountability would extend to the products produced and sold by a business and the resources entrusted to it. Employees should be treated with due consideration and enabled to fulfil their potential within the organisations they work for. Customers should not be harmed by the products they buy while suppliers should be treated fairly and not pressured to reduce their selling prices to enable buying organisations to profit at their expense. The public at large should expect organisations to avoid polluting the air, land and water sources and that all waste products from processes and operations are handled safely to protect individuals and the wider environment from harm.

Today's consumers want reassurance that the products they buy are sourced and produced ethically without causing harm either to the environment or to those individuals producing those products. Shareholders also want to be confident that the profits made by their companies are not generated from exploiting workers or the environment. Companies are eager to protect their reputations as reputational damage is difficult and time consuming to repair and can adversely affect sales and profits. Looking after the workforce, ensuring that suppliers are paid on time, looking into supply chains to check for unethical or environmentally unfriendly practices are all part of the risk management that organisations undertake to protect their reputation and shareholders' investment. Disclosing information on these aspects of company performance helps the public and other interested parties to assess the social responsibility of businesses and assists in enhancing each organisation's reputation for fair dealing and adherence to ethical principles. Customers like to buy goods and services from organisations which share their values, so considering other aspects of performance and reporting on these helps both to present entities in a positive light and to boost revenue and profits. Such actions also help to build the reputation of the business and show that it is caring for the long-term interests of all its stakeholders, not just the short-term interests of the directors and shareholders.

WHY IS THIS RELEVANT TO ME?   The rationale for corporate social responsibility

To enable you as an accounting professional to appreciate:

- That companies are accountable to society as a whole not just to investors
- That there are sound business advantages to adopting socially responsible policies
- That the reputation of a company is a valuable asset which requires protection from damage

9

GO BACK OVER THIS AGAIN!   Are you sure that you appreciate the reasons why companies adopt and report socially responsible attitudes and activities? Go to the **online workbook** and have a go at Exercises 9.9 to check your understanding.

SUSTAINABILITY AND ENVIRONMENTAL REPORTING

The ultimate long-term strategy for every business is to make its activities sustainable. What does this mean? *Our Common Future* (the Brundtland report) presented by the World Council on Environment and Development in 1987 defines sustainable development as that which 'meets the needs of the present without compromising the ability of future generations to meet their own needs'. This vision requires that all demands placed upon the natural environment by people and business organisations be met without reducing the capacity of the environment to provide for future generations. Businesses are therefore expected to concern themselves with issues such as climate change and energy use and to pay proper attention to the effects of their operations on the natural environment.

Unilever is one company that has been developing and reporting its sustainability strategy over many years. Give me an example 9.5 presents Unilever's strategy for sustainable business which forms part of the group's sustainable living plan.

GIVE ME AN EXAMPLE 9.5   Unilever's strategy for sustainable business

'We are living in a world where temperatures are rising, water shortages are more frequent, food supplies are increasingly scarce and the gap between rich and poor increasing. Populations are growing fast, making basic hygiene and sanitation even more of a challenge. At Unilever we can see how people the world over are already affected by these changes. And the changes will pose new challenges for us too, as commodity costs fluctuate, markets become unstable and raw materials harder to source.

We believe that business must be part of the solution. But to be so, business will have to change; there is not "business as usual anymore". Sustainable, equitable growth is the only acceptable business model. Our vision is to grow our business, whilst reducing our environmental footprint and increasing our positive social impact.

In 2010 we launched the Unilever Sustainable Living Plan, which is our blueprint for sustainable business. We will achieve our vision through our Plan, which is helping us to decouple our growth from our environmental impact while increasing our positive social impact, driving profitable growth for our brands, saving costs and fueling innovation.'

Source: https://www.unilever.com/sustainable-living/the-sustainable-living-plan/our-strategy/

Unilever is just one example of many businesses that have adopted sustainability and corporate social responsibility as part of their long-term strategy. Any annual report that you look at will provide details on these sustainability and CSR strategies together with statistics relating to what has been achieved over the past year and how improvements have been made. Have a look at Ted Baker's Sustainability report on pages 28–30 of the 2017/2018 Annual report and accounts, available at http://www.tedbakerplc.com/~/media/Files/T/Ted-Baker/results-and-reports/report/2018/ted-baker-annual-report-2017-2018.pdf

The rationale for adopting and reporting a sustainability strategy

As we have seen in this chapter, businesses must consider the long term not just the short term. A sustainability strategy represents the ultimate focus on the long term with the aim of ensuring the business's survival into the indefinite future. This approach accords well with shareholders' long-term investment horizon (this chapter, Long-term success v. short-term profits). However, there are many other benefits that a sustainability strategy brings. Give me an example 9.6 presents just four of the benefits generated by or expected from Unilever's adoption of its sustainable living plan.

GIVE ME AN EXAMPLE 9.6   Benefits of Unilever's sustainable living plan

Since the adoption of its sustainable living plan, Unilever has generated the following benefits:

- An annual return of 13 per cent on its shares over 10 years compared to an annual return of 5 per cent on the FTSE100 (Unilever is a constituent company of the FTSE100), a return over 10 years of 220 per cent v. a return of 66 per cent for the FTSE100 as a whole.
- A reduction in the water usage in its factories resulting in a saving of €50m in supply chain costs since 2008.

- A reduction of 40 per cent per tonne of production in CO_2 emissions from energy used in the group's factories by 2020, a figure at or below 2008 levels despite significantly higher production volumes.
- 60 per cent of raw materials were sourced from renewable sources by 2015.

Sources: https://www.unilever.com/sustainable-living/ and https://www.ft.com/content/1f2ea6dc-fe66-11e6-8d8e-a5e3738f9ae4

As is evident from Give me an example 9.6 Unilever's strategic focus on sustainability has also generated considerable benefits for shareholders in line with Friedman's insistence on profit generation as the only social responsibility of business. Positive news generates headlines for businesses together with favourable market reactions to both products and share prices. In these ways, adopting a sustainability strategy produces benefits for both shareholders and the environment and demonstrates that what is good for the environment also turns out to be good for shareholders and investors.

Companies are also recognising their wider duty of care to the public and the planet and their obligation to look after the natural resources entrusted to them. All stakeholders have an interest in the wellbeing of the planet. As a result of this interest, a stewardship report that focuses on the environment and on how natural resources have been managed and preserved is required by all these stakeholders alongside the financial results. Where damage has been caused to land, air or water, stakeholders will expect directors to report on the steps that have been taken to repair this damage and to prevent further damage in the future.

Environmental and sustainability reporting will assist companies in managing the risks that arise from any business activity. Actively seeking to avoid polluting natural resources will reduce the impact of economic penalties against organisations. The Deepwater Horizon oil spill in 2010 is estimated to have cost BP $61.6 billion (https://www.ft.com/content/ff2d8bcc-49e9-11e6-8d68-72e9211e86ab) and resulted in a fall in the share price which has not yet been recovered over the intervening seven years. Sound risk management policies are also applied by the capital markets: any potential investment which appears too risky will not attract funding or will be required to pay a higher rate of interest to compensate for the increased risk attached to the project (Chapter 8, The time value of money). Based on this principle, capital markets take into account not just ordinary business risks but also environmental risks and the environmental policies of companies seeking inward investment. Companies with more effective environmental risk management policies will attract funding at lower interest rates as the risks are lower. Ethical investment funds will withhold investment from companies which do not adopt a suitably responsible approach to the environment while socially responsible investors will avoid companies that fail to do the right thing. Again, this twin pronged approach benefits shareholders in reducing costs and increasing profits.

Sustainability information presented is relevant in that it assists consumers and investors in making rational economic decisions. The disclosure of such details indicates a fully transparent approach to reporting and shows the organisation as having nothing to hide. Such disclosure is also part of good corporate governance which dictates that all entities should report on all of their activities and their total impact. Competitive advantage may be another benefit of sustainability reporting as consumers favour organisations adopting a responsible approach to the use of natural resources and the environment over those with a less responsible approach.

WHY IS THIS RELEVANT TO ME?   Sustainability and environmental reporting

To enable you as an accounting professional to understand:

- How a sustainability approach enables businesses to promote their long-term success

- The commercial, finance, financial and reputational advantages gained by organisations promoting and reporting a sustainable and environmentally conscious approach in their businesses

---

GO BACK OVER THIS AGAIN!   Are you confident that you appreciate the reasons why companies adopt sustainability and environmentally responsible approaches in their businesses? Go to the **online workbook** and have a go at Exercises 9.10 to check your understanding.

9

CHAPTER SUMMARY

You should now have learnt that:

- Agency and information asymmetry problems arise when shareholders appoint directors to run companies on their behalf

- Shareholders need to be assured that directors are acting in the shareholders' best long-term interests and not in their own short-term interests

- Corporate governance is the system by which companies are directed and controlled

- Effective corporate governance involves executive directors, non-executive directors, external auditors, internal audit, the stock exchange listing rules and shareholders

- Executive directors run the company, non-executive directors run the board

- Non-executive directors make up the membership of the audit committee, the nominations committee and the remuneration committee

- External auditors report on the truth and fairness of the annual financial statements and their compliance with legislation and international financial reporting standards

- Internal audit undertakes investigations and reports on every aspect of a company's operations, internal control, strategy and corporate governance

- The Corporate Governance Code and the Companies Act 2006 require directors to promote the long-term success of their company

- Effective corporate governance requires that no one individual should have unfettered power and that all directors should run the business together as a body

- At least half of the directors on each board of directors should be independent non-executive directors

- Boards of directors and shareholders evaluate each director's performance

- The audit committee monitors the integrity of the annual report and accounts, receives reports from internal audit, monitors and evaluates internal control and oversees the external audit process and the external auditor

- Companies have a wider duty than just making profit for the shareholders

- Business organisations serve society and so are accountable to society as a whole

- Adopting socially responsible, environmentally friendly and sustainable business practices helps to generate long-term success for businesses through commercial, financing, reputational and risk minimisation advantages

QUICK REVISION Test your knowledge with the online flashcards in Summary of key concepts and attempt the Multiple choice questions, all in the **online workbook**.

9

END-OF-CHAPTER QUESTIONS

Solutions to these questions can be found in the **online workbook**

❯ DEVELOP YOUR UNDERSTANDING

❯ Question 9.1

Explain the rationale behind the requirements of the Corporate Governance Code.

❯ Question 9.2

Explain the rationale behind Corporate Social Responsibility reporting.

❯ Question 9.3

Why is sustainability such an important issue for businesses today?

>> TAKE IT FURTHER

>> Question 9.4

The aim of the Corporate Governance Code is control. Discuss.

>> Question 9.5

The only responsibility of business is to generate a profit. Discuss.

>> Question 9.6

The proper function of accounting is the measurement of profits and cash flows and the presentation of assets and liabilities. Discuss.

APPENDIX

Table 1 Present value of £1 at compound interest $(1 \div r) - n$

Periods of n	Discount rate as a percentage									
	1%	2%	3%	4%	5%	6%	7%	8%	9%	10%
1	0.9901	0.9804	0.9709	0.9615	0.9524	0.9434	0.9346	0.9259	0.9174	0.9091
2	0.9803	0.9612	0.9426	0.9246	0.9070	0.8900	0.8734	0.8573	0.8417	0.8264
3	0.9706	0.9423	0.9151	0.8890	0.8638	0.8396	0.8163	0.7938	0.7722	0.7513
4	0.9610	0.9238	0.8885	0.8548	0.8227	0.7921	0.7629	0.7350	0.7084	0.6830
5	0.9515	0.9057	0.8626	0.8219	0.7835	0.7473	0.7130	0.6806	0.6499	0.6209
6	0.9420	0.8880	0.8375	0.7903	0.7462	0.7050	0.6663	0.6302	0.5963	0.5645
7	0.9327	0.8706	0.8131	0.7599	0.7107	0.6651	0.6227	0.5835	0.5470	0.5132
8	0.9235	0.8535	0.7894	0.7307	0.6768	0.6274	0.5820	0.5403	0.5019	0.4665
9	0.9143	0.8368	0.7664	0.7026	0.6446	0.5919	0.5439	0.5002	0.4604	0.4241
10	0.9053	0.8203	0.7441	0.6756	0.6139	0.5584	0.5083	0.4632	0.4224	0.3855
11	0.8963	0.8043	0.7224	0.6496	0.5847	0.5268	0.4751	0.4289	0.3875	0.3505
12	0.8874	0.7885	0.7014	0.6246	0.5568	0.4970	0.4440	0.3971	0.3555	0.3186
13	0.8787	0.7730	0.6810	0.6006	0.5303	0.4688	0.4150	0.3677	0.3262	0.2897
14	0.8700	0.7579	0.6611	0.5775	0.5051	0.4423	0.3878	0.3405	0.2992	0.2633
15	0.8613	0.7430	0.6419	0.5553	0.4810	0.4173	0.3624	0.3152	0.2745	0.2394
16	0.8528	0.7284	0.6232	0.5339	0.4581	0.3936	0.3387	0.2919	0.2519	0.2176
17	0.8444	0.7142	0.6050	0.5134	0.4363	0.3714	0.3166	0.2703	0.2311	0.1978
18	0.8360	0.7002	0.5874	0.4936	0.4155	0.3503	0.2959	0.2502	0.2120	0.1799
19	0.8277	0.6864	0.5703	0.4746	0.3957	0.3305	0.2765	0.2317	0.1945	0.1635
20	0.8195	0.6730	0.5537	0.4564	0.3769	0.3118	0.2584	0.2145	0.1784	0.1486
21	0.8114	0.6598	0.5375	0.4388	0.3589	0.2942	0.2415	0.1987	0.1637	0.1351
22	0.8034	0.6468	0.5219	0.4220	0.3418	0.2775	0.2257	0.1839	0.1502	0.1228
23	0.7954	0.6342	0.5067	0.4057	0.3256	0.2618	0.2109	0.1703	0.1378	0.1117
24	0.7876	0.6217	0.4919	0.3901	0.3101	0.2470	0.1971	0.1577	0.1264	0.1015
25	0.7798	0.6095	0.4776	0.3751	0.2953	0.2330	0.1842	0.1460	0.1160	0.0923

				Discount rate as a percentage							
11%	12%	13%	14%	15%	16%	17%	18%	19%	20%	25%	30%
0.9009	0.8929	0.8850	0.8772	0.8696	0.8621	0.8547	0.8475	0.8403	0.8333	0.8000	0.7692
0.8116	0.7972	0.7831	0.7695	0.7561	0.7432	0.7305	0.7182	0.7062	0.6944	0.6400	0.5917
0.7312	0.7118	0.6931	0.6750	0.6575	0.6407	0.6244	0.6086	0.5934	0.5787	0.5120	0.4552
0.6587	0.6355	0.6133	0.5921	0.5718	0.5523	0.5337	0.5158	0.4987	0.4823	0.4096	0.3501
0.5935	0.5674	0.5428	0.5194	0.4972	0.4761	0.4561	0.4371	0.4190	0.4019	0.3277	0.2693
0.5346	0.5066	0.4803	0.4556	0.4323	0.4104	0.3898	0.3704	0.3521	0.3349	0.2621	0.2072
0.4817	0.4523	0.4251	0.3996	0.3759	0.3538	0.3332	0.3139	0.2959	0.2791	0.2097	0.1594
0.4339	0.4039	0.3762	0.3506	0.3269	0.3050	0.2848	0.2660	0.2487	0.2326	0.1678	0.1226
0.3909	0.3606	0.3329	0.3075	0.2843	0.2630	0.2434	0.2255	0.2090	0.1938	0.1342	0.0943
0.3522	0.3220	0.2946	0.2697	0.2472	0.2267	0.2080	0.1911	0.1756	0.1615	0.1074	0.0725
0.3173	0.2875	0.2607	0.2366	0.2149	0.1954	0.1778	0.1619	0.1476	0.1346	0.0859	0.0558
0.2858	0.2567	0.2307	0.2076	0.1869	0.1685	0.1520	0.1372	0.1240	0.1122	0.0687	0.0429
0.2575	0.2292	0.2042	0.1821	0.1625	0.1452	0.1299	0.1163	0.1042	0.0935	0.0550	0.0330
0.2320	0.2046	0.1807	0.1597	0.1413	0.1252	0.1110	0.0985	0.0876	0.0779	0.0440	0.0254
0.2090	0.1827	0.1599	0.1401	0.1229	0.1079	0.0949	0.0835	0.0736	0.0649	0.0352	0.0195
0.1883	0.1631	0.1415	0.1229	0.1069	0.0930	0.0811	0.0708	0.0618	0.0541	0.0281	0.0150
0.1696	0.1456	0.1252	0.1078	0.0929	0.0802	0.0693	0.0600	0.0520	0.0451	0.0225	0.0116
0.1528	0.1300	0.1108	0.0946	0.0808	0.0691	0.0592	0.0508	0.0437	0.0376	0.0180	0.0089
0.1377	0.1161	0.0981	0.0829	0.0703	0.0596	0.0506	0.0431	0.0367	0.0313	0.0144	0.0068
0.1240	0.1037	0.0868	0.0728	0.0611	0.0514	0.0433	0.0365	0.0308	0.0261	0.0115	0.0053
0.1117	0.0926	0.0768	0.0638	0.0531	0.0443	0.0370	0.0309	0.0259	0.0217	0.0092	0.0040
0.1007	0.0826	0.0680	0.0560	0.0462	0.0382	0.0316	0.0262	0.0218	0.0181	0.0074	0.0031
0.0907	0.0738	0.0601	0.0491	0.0402	0.0329	0.0270	0.0222	0.0183	0.0151	0.0059	0.0024
0.0817	0.0659	0.0532	0.0431	0.0349	0.0284	0.0231	0.0188	0.0154	0.0126	0.0047	0.0018
0.0736	0.0588	0.0471	0.0378	0.0304	0.0245	0.0197	0.0160	0.0129	0.0105	0.0038	0.0014

Table 2 Annuity table: the present value of £1 received or paid per year at a compound rate of interest $1/r - \{1/[r(1 + r)n]\}$

Periods of n	Discount rate as a percentage									
	1%	2%	3%	4%	5%	6%	7%	8%	9%	10%
1	0.990	0.980	0.971	0.962	0.952	0.943	0.935	0.926	0.917	0.909
2	1.970	1.942	1.913	1.886	1.859	1.833	1.808	1.783	1.759	1.736
3	2.941	2.884	2.829	2.775	2.723	2.673	2.624	2.577	2.531	2.487
4	3.902	3.808	3.717	3.630	3.546	3.465	3.387	3.312	3.240	3.170
5	4.853	4.713	4.580	4.452	4.329	4.212	4.100	3.993	3.890	3.791
6	5.795	5.601	5.417	5.242	5.076	4.917	4.767	4.623	4.486	4.355
7	6.728	6.472	6.230	6.002	5.786	5.582	5.389	5.206	5.033	4.868
8	7.652	7.325	7.020	6.733	6.463	6.210	5.971	5.747	5.535	5.335
9	8.566	8.162	7.786	7.435	7.108	6.802	6.515	6.247	5.995	5.759
10	9.471	8.983	8.530	8.111	7.722	7.360	7.024	6.710	6.418	6.145
11	10.368	9.787	9.253	8.760	8.306	7.887	7.499	7.139	6.805	6.495
12	11.255	10.575	9.954	9.385	8.863	8.384	7.943	7.536	7.161	6.814
13	12.134	11.348	10.635	9.986	9.394	8.853	8.358	7.904	7.487	7.103
14	13.004	12.106	11.296	10.563	9.899	9.295	8.745	8.244	7.786	7.367
15	13.865	12.849	11.938	11.118	10.380	9.712	9.108	8.559	8.061	7.606
16	14.718	13.578	12.561	11.652	10.838	10.106	9.447	8.851	8.313	7.824
17	15.562	14.292	13.166	12.166	11.274	10.477	9.763	9.122	8.544	8.022
18	16.398	14.992	13.754	12.659	11.690	10.828	10.059	9.372	8.756	8.201
19	17.226	15.678	14.324	13.134	12.085	11.158	10.336	9.604	8.950	8.365
20	18.046	16.351	14.877	13.590	12.462	11.470	10.594	9.818	9.129	8.514
21	18.857	17.011	15.415	14.029	12.821	11.764	10.836	10.017	9.292	8.649
22	19.660	17.658	15.937	14.451	13.163	12.042	11.061	10.201	9.442	8.772
23	20.456	18.292	16.444	14.857	13.489	12.303	11.272	10.371	9.580	8.883
24	21.243	18.914	16.936	15.247	13.799	12.550	11.469	10.529	9.707	8.985
25	22.023	19.523	17.413	15.622	14.094	12.783	11.654	10.675	9.823	9.077

				Discount rate as a percentage							
11%	12%	13%	14%	15%	16%	17%	18%	19%	20%	25%	30%
0.901	0.893	0.885	0.877	0.870	0.862	0.855	0.847	0.840	0.833	0.800	0.769
1.713	1.690	1.668	1.647	1.626	1.605	1.585	1.566	1.547	1.528	1.440	1.361
2.444	2.402	2.361	2.322	2.283	2.246	2.210	2.174	2.140	2.106	1.952	1.816
3.102	3.037	2.974	2.914	2.855	2.798	2.743	2.690	2.639	2.589	2.362	2.166
3.696	3.605	3.517	3.433	3.352	3.274	3.199	3.127	3.058	2.991	2.689	2.436
4.231	4.111	3.998	3.889	3.784	3.685	3.589	3.498	3.410	3.326	2.951	2.643
4.712	4.564	4.423	4.288	4.160	4.039	3.922	3.812	3.706	3.605	3.161	2.802
5.146	4.968	4.799	4.639	4.487	4.344	4.207	4.078	3.954	3.837	3.329	2.925
5.537	5.328	5.132	4.946	4.772	4.607	4.451	4.303	4.163	4.031	3.463	3.019
5.889	5.650	5.426	5.216	5.019	4.833	4.659	4.494	4.339	4.192	3.571	3.092
6.207	5.938	5.687	5.453	5.234	5.029	4.836	4.656	4.486	4.327	3.656	3.147
6.492	6.194	5.918	5.660	5.421	5.197	4.988	4.793	4.611	4.439	3.725	3.190
6.750	6.424	6.122	5.842	5.583	5.342	5.118	4.910	4.715	4.533	3.780	3.223
6.982	6.628	6.302	6.002	5.724	5.468	5.229	5.008	4.802	4.611	3.824	3.249
7.191	6.811	6.462	6.142	5.847	5.575	5.324	5.092	4.876	4.675	3.859	3.268
7.379	6.974	6.604	6.265	5.954	5.668	5.405	5.162	4.938	4.730	3.887	3.283
7.549	7.120	6.729	6.373	6.047	5.749	5.475	5.222	4.990	4.775	3.910	3.295
7.702	7.250	6.840	6.467	6.128	5.818	5.534	5.273	5.033	4.812	3.928	3.304
7.839	7.366	6.938	6.550	6.198	5.877	5.584	5.316	5.070	4.843	3.942	3.311
7.963	7.469	7.025	6.623	6.259	5.929	5.628	5.353	5.101	4.870	3.954	3.316
8.075	7.562	7.102	6.687	6.312	5.973	5.665	5.384	5.127	4.891	3.963	3.320
8.176	7.645	7.170	6.743	6.359	6.011	5.696	5.410	5.149	4.909	3.970	3.323
8.266	7.718	7.230	6.792	6.399	6.044	5.723	5.432	5.167	4.925	3.976	3.325
8.348	7.784	7.283	6.835	6.434	6.073	5.746	5.451	5.182	4.937	3.981	3.327
8.422	7.843	7.330	6.873	6.464	6.097	5.766	5.467	5.195	4.948	3.985	3.329

Table 3 Future value of £1 at compound interest $(1 + r)n$

Periods of n	Discount rate as a percentage									
	1%	2%	3%	4%	5%	6%	7%	8%	9%	10%
1	1.010	1.020	1.030	1.040	1.050	1.060	1.070	1.080	1.090	1.100
2	1.020	1.040	1.061	1.082	1.103	1.124	1.145	1.166	1.188	1.210
3	1.030	1.061	1.093	1.125	1.158	1.191	1.225	1.260	1.295	1.331
4	1.041	1.082	1.126	1.170	1.216	1.262	1.311	1.360	1.412	1.464
5	1.051	1.104	1.159	1.217	1.276	1.338	1.403	1.469	1.539	1.611
6	1.062	1.126	1.194	1.265	1.340	1.419	1.501	1.587	1.677	1.772
7	1.072	1.149	1.230	1.316	1.407	1.504	1.606	1.714	1.828	1.949
8	1.083	1.172	1.267	1.369	1.477	1.594	1.718	1.851	1.993	2.144
9	1.094	1.195	1.305	1.423	1.551	1.689	1.838	1.999	2.172	2.358
10	1.105	1.219	1.344	1.480	1.629	1.791	1.967	2.159	2.367	2.594
11	1.116	1.243	1.384	1.539	1.710	1.898	2.105	2.332	2.580	2.853
12	1.127	1.268	1.426	1.601	1.796	2.012	2.252	2.518	2.813	3.138
13	1.138	1.294	1.469	1.665	1.886	2.133	2.410	2.720	3.066	3.452
14	1.149	1.319	1.513	1.732	1.980	2.261	2.579	2.937	3.342	3.797
15	1.161	1.346	1.558	1.801	2.079	2.397	2.759	3.172	3.642	4.177
16	1.173	1.373	1.605	1.873	2.183	2.540	2.952	3.426	3.970	4.595
17	1.184	1.400	1.653	1.948	2.292	2.693	3.159	3.700	4.328	5.054
18	1.196	1.428	1.702	2.026	2.407	2.854	3.380	3.996	4.717	5.560
19	1.208	1.457	1.754	2.107	2.527	3.026	3.617	4.316	5.142	6.116
20	1.220	1.486	1.806	2.191	2.653	3.207	3.870	4.661	5.604	6.727
21	1.232	1.516	1.860	2.279	2.786	3.400	4.141	5.034	6.109	7.400
22	1.245	1.546	1.916	2.370	2.925	3.604	4.430	5.437	6.659	8.140
23	1.257	1.577	1.974	2.465	3.072	3.820	4.741	5.871	7.258	8.954
24	1.270	1.608	2.033	2.563	3.225	4.049	5.072	6.341	7.911	9.850
25	1.282	1.641	2.094	2.666	3.386	4.292	5.427	6.848	8.623	10.835

					Discount rate as a percentage						
11%	12%	13%	14%	15%	16%	17%	18%	19%	20%	25%	30%
1.110	1.120	1.130	1.140	1.150	1.160	1.170	1.180	1.190	1.200	1.250	1.300
1.232	1.254	1.277	1.300	1.323	1.346	1.369	1.392	1.416	1.440	1.563	1.690
1.368	1.405	1.443	1.482	1.521	1.561	1.602	1.643	1.685	1.728	1.953	2.197
1.518	1.574	1.630	1.689	1.749	1.811	1.874	1.939	2.005	2.074	2.441	2.856
1.685	1.762	1.842	1.925	2.011	2.100	2.192	2.288	2.386	2.488	3.052	3.713
1.870	1.974	2.082	2.195	2.313	2.436	2.565	2.700	2.840	2.986	3.815	4.827
2.076	2.211	2.353	2.502	2.660	2.826	3.001	3.185	3.379	3.583	4.768	6.275
2.305	2.476	2.658	2.853	3.059	3.278	3.511	3.759	4.021	4.300	5.960	8.157
2.558	2.773	3.004	3.252	3.518	3.803	4.108	4.435	4.785	5.160	7.451	10.604
2.839	3.106	3.395	3.707	4.046	4.411	4.807	5.234	5.695	6.192	9.313	13.786
3.152	3.479	3.836	4.226	4.652	5.117	5.624	6.176	6.777	7.430	11.642	17.922
3.498	3.896	4.335	4.818	5.350	5.936	6.580	7.288	8.064	8.916	14.552	23.298
3.883	4.363	4.898	5.492	6.153	6.886	7.699	8.599	9.596	10.699	18.190	30.288
4.310	4.887	5.535	6.261	7.076	7.988	9.007	10.147	11.420	12.839	22.737	39.374
4.785	5.474	6.254	7.138	8.137	9.266	10.539	11.974	13.590	15.407	28.422	51.186
5.311	6.130	7.067	8.137	9.358	10.748	12.330	14.129	16.172	18.488	35.527	66.542
5.895	6.866	7.986	9.276	10.761	12.468	14.426	16.672	19.244	22.186	44.409	86.504
6.544	7.690	9.024	10.575	12.375	14.463	16.879	19.673	22.901	26.623	55.511	112.455
7.263	8.613	10.197	12.056	14.232	16.777	19.748	23.214	27.252	31.948	69.389	146.192
8.062	9.646	11.523	13.743	16.367	19.461	23.106	27.393	32.429	38.338	86.736	190.050
8.949	10.804	13.021	15.668	18.822	22.574	27.034	32.324	38.591	46.005	108.420	247.065
9.934	12.100	14.714	17.861	21.645	26.186	31.629	38.142	45.923	55.206	135.525	321.184
11.026	13.552	16.627	20.362	24.891	30.376	37.006	45.008	54.649	66.247	169.407	417.539
12.239	15.179	18.788	23.212	28.625	35.236	43.297	53.109	65.032	79.497	211.758	542.801
13.585	17.000	21.231	26.462	32.919	40.874	50.658	62.669	77.388	95.396	264.698	705.641

TERMINOLOGY CONVERTER

Terms used in this book	Equivalent term or terms
Absorption costing	Full costing
Capital	Equity
Capital and reserves	Equity
Carrying amount	Net book value
Cost of capital	Hurdle rate of return
Equity	Capital, capital and reserves
Inventory	Stock
Revenue	Turnover, sales
Statement of financial position	Balance sheet
Statement of profit or loss	Income statement, statement of financial performance, profit and loss account

SEARCHING FOR THE ANSWERS?

You'll find complete, clearly-explained solutions to all the end-of-chapter questions in the student resources section of the online resources that accompany this book:

 www.oup.com/uk/scott_management-student-resources/

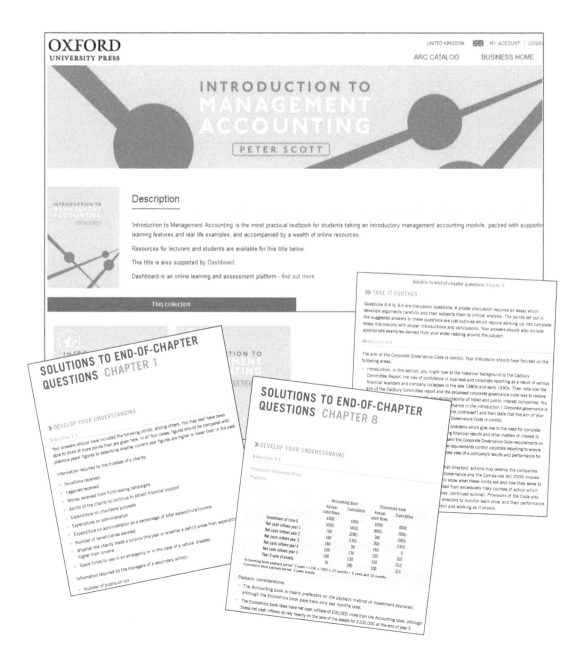

GLOSSARY

Abnormal gains This is a term used in process costing to describe and value the outputs from a process that are over and above the expected output from that process.

Abnormal losses This is a term used in process costing to describe and value outputs from a process that are below the expected output from that process.

Absorption costing The cost of products including all the direct costs of production and a proportion of the indirect costs of production based on normal levels of output.

Accountability Managers provide an account of how they have managed resources placed in their care. In this way, those appointing managers can assess how well their managers have looked after the resources entrusted to them.

Accounting The summarising of numerical data relating to past events and presenting this data as information to managers and other interested parties as a basis for both decision-making and control purposes.

Accounting rate of return An investment appraisal technique that averages the projections of accounting profit to calculate the expected rate of return on the average capital invested.

Accruals Expenses incurred during an accounting period but not paid for until after the accounting period end are still recognised as a liability in the statement of financial position and as an expense in the statement of profit or loss.

Accruals basis of accounting All income and expenditure are recognised in the accounting period in which they occurred rather than in the accounting period in which cash is received or paid.

Activity-based costing Overhead costs are allocated to products on the basis of activities consumed: the more activities that are associated with a particular product, the more overhead is allocated to that product and so the higher its cost and selling price will be.

Actual v. budget comparisons A comparison of forecast outcomes with actual outcomes on a monthly basis as a means of exercising control over operations.

Adverse variances Unfavourable variances.

Agency problem This problem arises in situations in which one person (the agent) is appointed to undertake a task by the principal. Agency theory says that the agent will always act in their own best interests, not in the best interests of the principal.

ARR See Accounting rate of return.

Attainable standard A standard that can be achieved with effort. This standard is neither too easy nor so difficult as to be unattainable.

Balance sheet Another term for the statement of financial position.

Break-even point The point at which sales revenue = fixed + variable costs. At the break-even point, an entity makes neither a profit nor a loss. Break-even point can be expressed in £s or units of sales. Break-even point cannot be used when more than one product or service is produced and sold. The break-even point is calculated by dividing total fixed costs by the contribution per unit of sales.

Budget The expression of a plan in money terms. That plan is a prediction or a forecast of future income, expenditure, cash inflows and cash outflows.

Budgetary control Comparisons between budgeted and actual outcomes to determine the causes of variances between forecast and actual results. The causes of differences are then identified to enable remedial action to be taken.

Budgeting The process of drawing up the budget.

Cadbury Report The name by which the report of the Committee on the Financial Aspects of Corporate Governance published in 1991 is most commonly known.

Capital account The equity part of the statement of financial position for sole traders. The capital account is the sum of the opening capital balance plus the profit for the year (minus a loss for the year) minus any drawings made by the sole trader during the year.

Capital investment The acquisition of new non-current assets with the aim of increasing sales, profits and cash flows to the long-term benefit of a business.

Capital investment appraisal An evaluation of the long-term cash generating capacity of capital investment projects to assist decision makers in allocating scarce investment capital resources to projects to maximise long run profits.

Carrying amount Cost or fair value of a non-current asset—the accumulated depreciation on that non-current asset. Net book value is an equivalent term that you might also come across to describe the result of deducting accumulated depreciation from the cost or fair value of a non-current asset.

Cash budget A detailed summary on a month-by-month basis of budgeted cash inflows and cash outflows.

Comparability An enhancing qualitative characteristic of financial information. Information should be comparable over time. The usefulness of information is enhanced if it can be compared with similar information about other entities for the same reporting period and with similar information about the same entity for other reporting periods. Comparability does not mean consistency, although consistency of presentation and measurement of the same items in the same way from year to year will help to achieve comparability. Similarly, comparability does not mean uniformity of presentation.

Consistency The presentation or measurement of the same piece of accounting information on the same basis each year.

Contribution Selling price less the variable costs of making that sale.

Conversion cost This term is used in process costing to indicate the labour and overhead incurred in a process to turn raw materials into the output from the process. Conversion cost is added to the cost of raw materials added to the process to calculate the cost of completed units.

Corporate governance The system by which companies are directed and controlled.

Corporate social responsibility Social and environmental considerations are integrated into the management of the operations of an organisation. May be abbreviated to CSR.

Cost accounting '[The] gathering of cost information and its attachment to cost objects (for example a product, service, centre, activity, customer or distribution channel in relation to which costs are ascertained), the establishment of budgets, standard costs and actual costs of operations, processes, activities or products; and the analysis of variances, profitability or the social use of funds' (*CIMA Official Terminology*).

Cost allocation The process of allocating costs, both direct and indirect, to products or services.

Cost centre A division of an entity to which attributable costs are allocated.

Cost drivers The level of activity associated with each cost pool used to allocate costs to products under activity-based costing.

Cost object 'A product, service centre, activity, customer or distribution channel in relation to which costs are ascertained' (*CIMA Official Terminology*).

Cost pools The allocation of indirect costs of production associated with particular activities in an activity-based costing system.

Cost of capital The level of return on an investment that is acceptable to a business given the level of risk involved. Also known as the hurdle rate of return.

Cost of sales The direct costs attributable to the sale of particular goods or services.

Cost-volume-profit analysis A management accounting technique used to determine the relationship between sales revenue, costs and profit. Abbreviated to CVP.

Costing The process of determining the cost of products or services.

Current assets Short-term assets that will be used up in the business within one year. Examples include inventory, trade receivables, prepayments and cash.

Current liabilities Short-term liabilities due for payment within one year of the year-end date. Examples include trade payables, taxation and accruals.

CVP See Cost-volume-profit analysis.

Depreciation The allocation of the cost of a non-current asset to the accounting periods benefiting from that non-current asset's use within a business. Depreciation is *not* a way of reflecting the market value of assets in financial statements and it does not represent a loss in value.

Direct cost The costs of a product or service that are directly attributable to the production of a product or the delivery of a service. Direct costs may be variable or fixed.

Direct labour efficiency variance The time taken to make the goods actually produced compared with the standard time that should have been taken to make those goods multiplied by the standard rate per hour.

Direct labour rate variance What labour hours actually cost compared with what the standard says the labour hours should have cost for the actual level of production achieved.

Direct material price variance What the materials for actual production cost compared with what the standard says they should have cost for that level of production.

Direct material usage variance The actual quantity of materials used to make the goods actually produced compared with the standard quantity that should have been used to make those goods multiplied by the standard cost per unit of material.

Directors Persons appointed by the shareholders at the annual general meeting to run a limited company on their behalf.

Discounting Future cash inflows and outflows are discounted to their present value using an entity's cost of capital.

Drawings Amounts taken out of a business by a sole trader for personal rather than business use. Drawings are in effect a repayment of the amounts owed by the business to the owner. Drawings are not an expense but a deduction from capital. Drawings are not permitted in limited liability companies.

Equity The capital of an entity on its statement of financial position. Equity is, in theory, the amount the owners of the business would receive if all the business assets and liabilities were sold and settled at the amounts stated in the statement of financial position.

Equivalent units Expressing partially completed units in a process at the end of an accounting period as the equivalent number of fully completed units.

Faithful representation A fundamental qualitative characteristic of financial information. Financial information must not only represent relevant economic phenomena (transactions and events), but it must also faithfully represent the phenomena that it purports to represent. Perfectly faithful representation of economic phenomena in words and numbers requires that the information presented must have three characteristics: it must be complete, neutral and free from error.

Favourable variances Differences between actual and forecast results arising from higher income or lower expenditure.

Financial accounting The reporting of past information to parties external to the organisation.

First in first out A method of stock valuation. The units of product that were acquired at the earliest date are those that are sold first. In process costing, an assumption is made that the work in progress units at the start of the accounting period are the units that were completed first before any production of new units commenced.

Fixed cost A cost that does not vary in line with production or sales over a given period of time.

Fixed overhead expenditure variance The difference between the actual fixed overhead expenditure incurred and the forecast level of fixed overhead expenditure.

Gross profit Sales less the direct costs of making those sales.

IAASB International Auditing and Assurance Standards Board.

IAS International Accounting Standard.

IASB International Accounting Standards Board.

Ideal standard The best that can be achieved. Ideal standards tend to be unrealistic and unachievable as they would only ever be attained in a perfect world.

IFRS International Financial Reporting Standard.

Income statement An equivalent term for the statement of profit or loss.

Indirect cost Costs that cannot be attributed directly to units of production. Also known as overheads.

Information asymmetry This arises in situations in which one party knows much more about a subject than another as a result of a principal delegating a task to an agent.

Internal rate of return The discount rate applied to the cash flows of a capital investment project to produce a net present value for the project of £Nil.

Inventory A stock of goods held by a business.

IRR See Internal rate of return.

ISA International Standard on Auditing.

Key factor = Limiting factor.

Limiting factor A scarcity of input resources, such as materials or labour, is referred to as a limiting factor in the production of goods or services. When input resources are scarce, entities calculate the contribution per unit of limiting factor to maximise their profits in the short term.

Management accounting Cost and management accounting is concerned with reporting accounting and cost information to users within an organisation to assist those internal users in making decisions and managing the business.

Margin of safety The difference between the current level of sales in units and the break-even point in units of sales.

Marginal cost The additional cost incurred in producing one more unit of product or delivering one more unit of service. Also known as the variable cost of production.

Materiality The IASB Framework defines materiality thus: 'Information is material if omitting it or misstating it could influence decisions that … users … make on the basis of financial information about a specific reporting entity. In other words, materiality is an entity-specific aspect of relevance based on the nature or magnitude, or both, of the items to which the information relates in the context of an individual entity's financial report.'

Net present value The total of the discounted future cash inflows and outflows from a project. Projects with a positive net present value are accepted, while projects with a negative net present value are rejected.

Non-current assets Assets held within the business long term for use in the production of goods and services. Non-current assets are retained within the business for periods of more than one year and are not acquired with the intention of reselling them immediately or in the near future.

Normal losses The expected losses from a process. Normal losses are never given a monetary value.

Normal standard What a business usually achieves.

NPV See Net present value.

Opportunity cost Opportunity cost is the loss that is incurred by choosing one alternative course of action over another, the benefits given up to use a resource in one application rather than taking the next best alternative course of action. Opportunity cost is only a relevant consideration when resources are limited: when resources are unlimited there is no opportunity cost.

Payback The number of years it will take for the cash inflows from a capital investment project to pay back the original cost of the investment.

Period costs Fixed costs incurred in the administration, marketing and financing of an entity relating to the period in which they are incurred.

Present value The discounting of future cash inflows and outflows to express all cash flows in the common currency of today, thereby facilitating a fair comparison of projected cash inflows and outflows for evaluating different capital investment proposals.

Prime cost The total direct cost of producing one product or one unit of service.

Process costing The collection and assignment of costs to products or outputs produced in a process. Process costing is used to value products or outputs that are indistinguishable from one another.

Production cost The total direct costs of producing one product or one unit of service plus the proportion of fixed production overheads allocated to products and services on the basis of the normal level of production.

Profit The surplus remaining after all expenses are deducted from sales revenue.

Profit and loss account Another term for the statement of profit or loss.

Relevance A fundamental qualitative characteristic of financial information. To be relevant, information must be capable of making a difference in the decisions made by users.

Relevant information may be predictive and assist users in making predictions about the future or it may be confirmatory by assisting users to assess the accuracy of past predictions. Relevant information can be both predictive and confirmatory.

Relevant costs The costs that will be incurred if a certain course of action is followed. Relevant costs are the costs that influence decision making.

Revenue Sales of goods and services made by an entity in the ordinary (everyday) course of business.

Sales price variance The difference between the standard selling price and the actual selling price multiplied by the actual quantity sold.

Sales returns The cancellation of a sale by a customer.

Sales volume variance The actual sales – budgeted sales in units multiplied by the standard contribution per sale.

Sensitivity analysis Changing the assumptions on which forecasts are based to determine the effect of those changes on expected outcomes.

Stakeholder theory The theory that a business's moral and ethical values should be applied in the management of organisations for the benefit of all stakeholders rather than just for the benefit of shareholders.

Standard costing The costs and selling prices of products are estimated with a reasonable degree of accuracy. Comparisons of actual and standard outcomes are then undertaken to determine the variances between expected and actual outcomes with a view to revising standards where necessary.

Statement of financial position A summary of the assets, liabilities and equity of an entity at a particular point in time.

Statement of profit or loss A summary of income and expenditure for a given period of time.

Stewardship The process of looking after resources entrusted to a person.

Stock A different term for inventory.

Sunk costs Sunk costs are past costs which have no influence over future decision making. Sunk costs represent expenditure that has already been incurred which no future action will change or alter.

Sustainability The long-term objective of business entities, aiming to remain in operational existence for the indefinite future.

Timeliness An enhancing qualitative characteristic of financial information. The decision usefulness of information is enhanced if it is available to users in time for it to be capable of influencing their decisions. While the decision usefulness of information generally declines with time, information that can still be used in identifying trends continues to be timely in the future.

Time value of money Money received today is worth more than money received tomorrow due to the impact of inflation and the uncertainty surrounding the receipt of money in future time periods.

Turnover The term used in financial statements in the UK to represent sales or revenue.

Understandability An enhancing qualitative characteristic of financial information. Understandability should not be confused with simplicity. Financial statements that excluded complex information just because it was difficult to understand would not result in relevant information that was faithfully presented. Reports that excluded such information would be incomplete and would thus mislead users. Readers of financial reports are assumed to have a reasonable knowledge of business and economic activities in order to make sense of what they are presented with but when they are unable to understand the information presented, then the IASB recommends using an adviser. To help users understand information presented, that information should be classified, characterised and presented clearly.

Unfavourable variances Differences between actual and forecast results arising from lower income or higher expenditure.

Variable cost The costs of a product or service that vary directly in line with the production of a product or delivery of a service. Also known as the marginal cost of a product or service.

Variable overhead efficiency variance The time taken to make the goods actually produced compared with the standard time that should have been taken to make those goods multiplied by the standard variable overhead rate per hour.

Variable overhead expenditure variance The variable overhead actually incurred in the production of goods compared with the standard expenditure that should have been incurred for the level of actual production.

Variances Differences between expected, forecast or budgeted and actual financial results.

Verifiability An enhancing qualitative characteristic of financial information that enhances the usefulness of information that is relevant and faithfully represented. Verifiability provides users with assurance that information is faithfully presented and reports the economic phenomena it purports to represent. To ensure verifiability, it should be possible to prove the information presented is accurate in all major respects. The accuracy of information should be capable of verification by observation or recalculation.

Weighted average cost A method of valuing closing inventory. The weighted average cost valuation divides the total costs incurred in an accounting period by the number of units produced during the same period to calculate the average cost of each unit of production. This average cost is then used to calculate the costs of finished goods and work in progress produced during the period.

Work in progress Units of production which are partially complete at the end of an accounting period. Units of work in progress are completed in the next accounting period.

INDEX

Note: Tables and figures are indicated by an italic *t* and *f* following the page number.